CAMBRIDGE
BEFORE DARWIN

THE IDEAL OF
A LIBERAL EDUCATION,
1800–1860

CAMBRIDGE
BEFORE DARWIN

THE IDEAL OF
A LIBERAL EDUCATION,
1800–1860

MARTHA McMACKIN GARLAND

The Ohio State University

CAMBRIDGE UNIVERSITY PRESS

Cambridge

London   New York   New Rochelle

Melbourne   Sydney

Published by the Press Syndicate of the University of Cambridge
The Pitt Building, Trumpington Street, Cambridge CB2 1RP
32 East 57th Street, New York, NY 10022, USA
296 Beaconsfield Parade, Middle Park, Melbourne 3206, Australia

First published 1980

Printed in Great Britain by The Anchor Press Ltd
and bound by Wm Brendon & Son Ltd
both of Tiptree, Essex

British Library Cataloguing in Publication Data
Garland, Martha McMackin
Cambridge before Darwin.
1. University of Cambridge – History
I. Title
378.426'59   LF119   80–40327
ISBN 0 521 23319 4

CONTENTS

PREFACE

During the first part of the nineteenth century Britain experienced sweeping changes in the very fabric of its society. Urbanization and industrialization greatly modified English economic and social life. Political changes followed, symbolized by the great reform bills, portents of a coming spirit of democracy. The intellectual climate also was transformed. Spurred by industry, the sciences made tremendous strides and their successful methods began to be used on new problems – the history of the earth, the authenticity of Scripture, man and his mind. There was a flourish of popular piety: the High Church Oxford Movement, Low Church Simeonite 'enthusiasm', a vigorous growth of nonconformity, and even – crudely – puritanical and prudish 'Victorian morality'. Ironically, at the same time that virtue and religion seemed to be at their zenith, a new skepticism began to appear in intellectual circles. Faith and reason no longer could be expected to reveal One Truth, as geology, criticism, and psychology began pushing back and limiting the domain of revealed religion. It is in the context of this evolving and – some might say – disintegrating society that I have examined some of the ideas underlying changes at one of England's most characteristic institutions, the University of Cambridge.

It was possible for university scholars to take a hard reactionary attitude toward the changes in nineteenth-century England, and there were a few members of the University who greeted every new suggestion with alarm and active opposition. And there were a small number of quite radical dons who were prepared to accept almost any innovation – intellectual, governmental, or religious. Far more typical, however, were scholars who saw some changes as inevitable and necessary, but who wanted reform to come cautiously and gradually. Such conservative reformers felt that the University must improve itself to prevent its being revolutionized from outside; they wanted better instruction and harder-working scholars, and they wanted to rid Cambridge of various inequities which they recognized. But they saw much that was good in the 'old ways', they were fearful of very rapid change, and they seemed to see – more clearly than more liberal reformers – that some of the new ideas carried to their natural conclusions would spell the collapse of their working synthesis between faith and reason and the disintegration of the prevailing intellectual world view.

The reforms these conservatives undertook were in a way 'typically English'. For their inspiration they turned to old ideas and long-standing traditions – for example, to the notion that classics and mathematics should form the basis of an undergraduate education. Then they reworked the traditional concepts into something quite new, in fact reinventing from the outworn curriculum of the eighteenth century the very idea of a Liberal Education. This reformed program mirrored the larger intellectual world in many ways – it implied a view of man's mind and of epistemology, it assumed an integration of the various scholarly disciplines, it reflected an intellectual climate in which science and religion each revealed part of a single, unified Truth.

Such a synthesis did not long survive its authors or the shock of Darwin's publication. After 1860 the more radical position triumphed: education was broken up into small compartments, intensive specialized scholarship replaced any idea of a general education, bars against dissenters were dropped and the colleges ceased to be (or to pretend to be) surrogate family units providing 'sound knowledge and religious education'. With the old methods went the old world-view – no longer at all certain that all understanding leads to God, scholars began moving away from the grand, eternal questions and to be satisfied with little specialized areas of knowledge which they tried to grasp fully without any hope of integrating them into a larger whole. While it had been in the ascendency, however, the Cambridge ideal of a Liberal Education had provided an intellectual framework which was very attractive. And even after it ceased to exist in practice at Cambridge, it remained a theoretical goal – perhaps unattainable – towards which many educational institutions (especially small colleges in the United States) continued to strive. It is perhaps one of History's rejected ideas which nevertheless retains a lot of its appeal.

The research which has led to this book was begun in Cambridge in 1969. My family and I were living in Clare Hall; the hospitality shown me by the Hall – and especially by the President and Mrs Brian Pippard – was extremely generous and much appreciated. I am also grateful for having been allowed to use the resources of the University Library and later of the Library of Trinity College.

At Ohio State University I have profited from many discussions with Professors June Fullmer and Franklin Pegues. I am especially grateful to R. Clayton Roberts who helped me to improve the footnotes and to the Department of History for a travel grant which enabled me to return to England to complete my research. I am also much indebted to my parents and to my husband Jim.

Philip Poirier was my supervising professor at Ohio State. His fine mind, solid scholarship, dry wit, and gentle criticism made him for me an ideal mentor. His untimely death in March 1979 was a sad loss to his family, his colleagues, and his students. It is to his memory that I dedicate this book.

Martha McMackin Garland

1980

CHAPTER I

AN ACADEMIC ANCIEN REGIME

In 1800 the University of Cambridge was to some extent a center of teaching and of learning, an institution dedicated both to the education of the young and to the advancement of thought. But any analysis of Cambridge is bound to be misleading unless it emphasizes another aspect of the University's character: it was a branch of the Church of England. Nearly all Anglican clerics studied at Cambridge or at Oxford. Degrees were granted only to members of the Established Church. University regulations included compulsory chapel and required courses in theology. And the colleges controlled vast networks of ecclesiastical patronage with which to help young graduates launch their clerical careers. Thus when a man went up to Cambridge he was doing much more (and in some ways much less) than enrolling himself in an educational program. He was joining a religious society – a college – in which he could have life-long membership and from which, if he chose to exert himself, he could expect permanent financial and emotional support.

Such an institution was a remarkably pleasant, tranquil place in which to live. For the permanent members of the colleges, the fellows, life could be very attractive indeed. Fellowships for life were awarded not on the basis of a candidate's academic promise but as a reward for his achievements as an undergraduate; in consequence, while fellows generally were bright, at least insofar as intelligence could be measured by a rigorous mathematical examination, there was no guarantee or even expectation that they would lead a life of real scholarship while serving as Cambridge dons. Furthermore, since teaching obligations were minimal and residence in many cases not even required, a college fellowship could become – often in combination with one or more other ecclesiastical livings – a nearly perfect sinecure. If a fellow chose to remain in residence, he was provided with comfortable rooms and elegant meals; his responsibility to a handful of students was little more than formal; and he was free to indulge his taste for fine port, whist, gardening, or reading, as he liked. A single restriction marred this otherwise ideal situation: dons were required to remain celibate. Only a comparatively small number chose therefore to make of their college positions a lifetime career. Most held their fellowships only until a living became available to them, and then they married. Those who remained at Cambridge satisfied their ambitions (and augmented their incomes) by assuming college offices or university professorships. But it is clear that a life lived entirely in college could become a rather lonely affair, often ending in marked eccentricity.[1]

For the junior members of the colleges, the students, Cambridge life was also generally pleasant. They, of course, did not experience the financial security guaranteed the fellows; but their families usually provided them with lavish amounts of spending money, and, except for the few students who aspired to honours and fellowships, the academic demands were slight. Young and energetic, with plenty of free time, in comfortable surroundings and freed for the first time from parental controls, students designed for themselves a convivial life of wine-parties, breakfasts, late night discussions, gambling, boating, and occasional study. Although in principle the collegiate relationship was supposed to provide a warm and friendly substitute for family life, in practice the junior and senior members of a college saw very little of each other, usually formally. However, isolation of the students from the fellows was not generally regarded as a weakness. Indeed, it was often explicitly assumed that the primary benefit to be derived from the collegiate experience lay not in the influence of the senior members but in the close and long-lasting friendships formed between a student and his peers.[2] As a German observer wrote:

Our universities produce learned men in the several sciences, or men for practical life . . . The English Universities on the contrary, content themselves with producing the first and most distinctive flower of the national life, *a well educated 'Gentleman'* . . . We scarcely need add that even during the University residence the studies are by no means the only thing that brings about this result. A complicated machinery of reciprocal influences lies in the manners, habits and other relations peculiar to the English College life, bearing upon the education of the youth and the development of their feelings and characters . . . a glance at the University Calendars may convince us that in all the world one cannot be in better company than 'on the books' of the larger Oxford or Cambridge colleges.[3]

Many Englishmen of the eighteenth century would have agreed with this positive assessment.[4] But the various reform currents of the early nineteenth century would sweep through the old universities as well as through other British institutions, and shortly after 1800 Cambridge was to find itself criticized both by outsiders and from within. Almost all aspects of the University – collegiate government, the connection with the Church, teaching methods, entrance and graduation standards – were suddenly subjected to searching, sometimes hostile reevaluations. Central to such reassessment was concern about the university curriculum. Interestingly Cambridge had long been quite proud of its course of studies, and indeed, in comparison with Oxford (the only comparison frequently made), it had every right to be. The study of classical literature had long been at the core of the academic programs of both of the older universities, and at Oxford classics (together with a smattering of theological reading) continued to be the main object of undergraduate attention. At Cambridge, however, the program had been broadened by the addition of a mathematical course, required since the seventeenth century when Newton had been a member of Trinity College. The 'pass' standard in neither classics nor mathematics was very high, but Cambridge had at least made a gesture at including both the sciences and the arts, at cultivating 'the Reason as well as the Literary Taste'[5] of the student. Furthermore, about mid-way through the eighteenth century the examination system had been reformed so that although pass or 'poll' (from *hoi polloi*) men could get by with 'two books of Euclid's Geometry, Simple and Quadratic Equations, the early parts of Paley's Moral Philosophy'[6] and some simple translation from Latin, better students could follow a more elevated route to graduation in the form of the 'tripos' or honours degree. Separated from the 'passmen' by an early oral examination ('disputatione'), honours candidates sat for a five-day series of rigorous written mathematical examinations, at the end of which they were individually ranked on the basis of comparative merit. The position in the honours list – the first twelve students were called wranglers, and the 'senior wrangler' was widely regarded as semi-divine – was very important, for it was the basis for the awarding of college fellowships. Because

3

of the difficulty of the honours or tripos examination, as well as the scrupulous fairness with which it was administered and the supposed objectivity of the methods of ranking, most late-eighteenth-century Cantabrigians had been blinded to the obvious weaknesses of their system. In the first place, because the study of the classics was not encouraged within the context of the tripos examination system but rather by a series of prizes and medals for which only honours students were privileged to compete, literature was studied seriously only by a very few. A dedicated classicist had first to show himself to be an accomplished mathematician, a requirement which undoubtedly forced many potential scholars to be satisfied with a poll degree. The other traditional component of the curriculum – theology – had been similarly pushed into the background: in the face of eighteenth-century rationalism, strictly religious education had given way to a vague kind of 'moral philosophy', drawn almost entirely from the works of John Locke and William Paley. Neither author was studied with much intensity; the part of the exam in which they were covered was generally regarded by the undergraduates as an 'easy day'.[7] And Paley's work seemed to some to be inherently unsuitable, being mainly a popularization of utilitarian political thought. Furthermore, even the much respected mathematical examination itself was very narrow in scope, taking no cognizance of new 'continental' methods of analysis, nor indeed ranging much beyond the limits of traditional Newtonian geometry. Critics of the Cambridge curriculum, therefore, would in the first part of the nineteenth century stress the need for a broader, more modern, mathematical course, a renewed emphasis on classical excellence, and a more sophisticated approach to theology and philosophy. There would be an increasingly strident outcry about the disgracefully low standard demanded from the majority of students. And some critics would go so far as to assert that even the best imaginable combination of classics, mathematics, and religion was too narrow a basis for a university curriculum, especially in an age in which literary criticism, political and economic thought, and the biological and physical sciences were making enormous strides.

Criticisms of Cambridge's curricular shortcomings thus focused attention on a related weakness of the University: its failure to provide systematic support for scientific research or encouragement for advanced scholarship. England at the turn of the century was not without her great thinkers; but it is easy to demonstrate the

4

comparative isolation of scientists like John Dalton, Thomas Young, and Michael Faraday,[8] and to show that having the support of a community of scholars would probably have been beneficial to their work. The French had the lavishly endowed Academy of Science, while in Germany and Scotland the universities served as organized centers of research. English scientists, in contrast, depended on a series of privately (and therefore inadequately) funded societies and institutes, most of which were to become important only during the course of the nineteenth century. The Royal Society predated the Paris Academy of Sciences but without the support of public funds had not flourished in a way comparable to its French rival. The Royal Institution was established by Count Rumford only at the beginning of the nineteenth century, and the British Association was not founded until 1830.

Furthermore, the situation was even worse in the humanistic fields. The universities had a monopoly on English literary or philosophical studies, but they were organized mainly to help undergraduates pass examinations: Oxford and Cambridge continued to use the most conservative texts and methods, apparently ignorant of the new 'scientific' philological and linguistic techniques being developed in Germany. In 1809 and 1810, the *Edinburgh Review* published a series of scathing articles contrasting English classical scholarship with that of the continent and even of the Scottish universities;[9] and the defense mounted by the old universities did little to dispel the doubts raised by these criticisms.[10] This failure of the universities to become involved in research was a double liability: on the one hand, English scholars had to struggle with their work in isolation and without support; on the other, the new knowledge which modern scholarship was revealing was kept from the young thinkers at the universities, so that Cambridge mathematicians knew nothing of LaPlace's *Mécanique Céleste* and classicists read Greek and Latin totally without benefit of the discoveries of comparative philology.

It was possible to argue that not learning but the diffusion of learning was the University's main role and that the endowments of the various colleges had been given to support undergraduate teaching, not to advance research. In some cases this was patently true – various prizes in classics, for example, were supported precisely to encourage undergraduate excellence, while many of the grants to the colleges had been earmarked for instructional purposes.

This was not a wholly adequate answer, however. In the first place, whatever the intentions of the original founders, the value of Cambridge endowments had increased so dramatically that the colleges were hard pressed to find enough educational projects on which to spend them.[11] In practice most of the funds were distributed as prizes – in the case of fellowships, lavish, life-long prizes – for undergraduate accomplishments. The colleges were usually too small to justify investment in equipment for specialized subjects like science; collegiate instruction was mostly conducted on a tutorial basis and only in the core subjects of classics and mathematics. The central University, in contrast, was comparatively poor; and while it should logically have provided lecture rooms, laboratories, and museums for general use of all the students, funds for such purposes were not available. Nor would the individual colleges agree to pool their resources; jealous of their independence they clung to the letter, while grossly perverting the spirit, of their benefactors' wills.

The central University did have some resources in the form of various professorial endowments, and in principle these funds should have been used to support a more generalized curriculum as well as advanced research. The purpose of a professor's endowment was to provide a salary to a mature scholar so that he might have the leisure to pursue his researches; he would then lecture on his findings to Cambridge students, thus both advancing his discipline and enriching the intellectual quality of university life. In practice the endowments were usually too small to provide an adequate salary unless the holder had an additional source of income. A professorship could be effectively combined with a fellowship; but since the holders were frequently older men who had left college and married, the more usual combination was a professorial chair with an ecclesiastical living, with the living often some distance from Cambridge. In such circumstances residence was not usually required, and in the early part of the century it was not unusual for a professor to fail to deliver any lectures whatsoever.[12] Even those scholars who remained in Cambridge and faithfully lectured to undergraduates, however, found that they were fighting an uphill battle. Honours students could not waste time with professorial lectures, since their content would not be tested at the tripos; and pollmen – sometimes required to show a certificate of attendance from at least one professor – often filled the lecture rooms only to read their newspapers or to sleep. Thus since the University systematically failed to support the professoriate either through the examination system or with adequate financial resources, it is hardly surprising that Cambridge at the turn of the century was something less than a thriving center of research.

By 1800 another aspect of Cambridge's undergraduate program had also begun to come under public scrutiny: it was increasingly argued that the University was failing at its main task, the training of members of the Anglican clergy. Perhaps not surprisingly many potential clerics were less than enthusiastic mathematicians; it was thus usual for future ecclesiastics to 'go out in the poll', bearing with them comparatively little education. Furthermore the occasional cleric who graduated with honours was almost inevitably offered a college fellowship and thereby kept out of contact with any parishioners. Letters testimonial for graduates going out to clerical livings were granted automatically with the degree; a critic in 1809 suggested, among other things, that dons should 'be more circumspect in granting testimonials for orders . . . and that the University should try to increase the necessity of religious study among the undergraduates, by granting no degrees to those who are void of ecclesiastical information'.[13] There were three theology professors at Cambridge, and some reformers argued that attendance at their lectures should be required and that their subject matter should be tested in the examinations. Others argued that theology and practical ecclesiastical subjects could be better taught after the baccalaureate and away from the hurly burly of Cambridge. Several reforms would include proposals for honours examinations in theology, for a more serious theological program before the M.A. and even for separate theological colleges designed to complete the work which undergraduate training left undone. The nineteenth century would be much concerned with improving the University's approach to clerical education.

By 1800 several factors had combined to call into question the older views of the universities as tax-exempt religious centers established to educate clergymen for service in the national Church. The extraordinary wealth accumulated by the colleges – even in comparison with other ecclesiastical institutions – made Oxford and Cambridge seem like latter-day successors to the monasteries dissolved by Henry VIII. This was a new *mortmain* with its grasp tightened around an ever-increasing share of English capital. For example, even a small and comparatively poor college, St

7

Catharine's, was able to support fourteen fellowships and thirty-one scholarships, as well as to provide four permanent ecclesiastical positions to the recipients of its patronage. And Trinity College, the wealthiest of the foundations, supported the master, sixty fellows, seventy-two scholars, sixteen sizars, and six minor scholars. In addition the College controlled three headmasterships, forty-eight vicarages, ten rectories, and nine perpetual curacies.[14] While this system was developing the proportion of non-Anglicans in the English population had increased, particularly with the successes of the Methodists during the eighteenth century. The new dissenters, often drawn from the middle class, were more articulate and more determined to win equality than had been their Stuart and Georgian predecessors. It was becoming ever more difficult to argue that the Established Church was the genuine expression of the national religious will. Besides, the Church itself was increasingly under attack because of internal abuses. Its failure to serve the poor in the expanding cities, its inadequate missionary effort in the colonies, its tolerance of pluralism and absenteeism among the clergy – all roused the righteous indignation of serious dissenters and of 'evangelical' members of the Church itself.

As the nineteenth century wore on, not surprisingly, resentment towards the Established Church would spill over to its academic branches. Concern about the inadequacies in clerical training have been mentioned. Even more worrisome were the increasingly rancorous public protests against the inordinate wealth of the colleges, including several demands for parliamentary investigation and even threats of confiscation.[15] The supposed low moral tone of the University, particularly with respect to undergraduate life, was contrasted with its avowed religious purposes. 'Anachronistic ritualisms', like the enforced celibacy of fellows, were sharply questioned. But the single issue which was undoubtedly the most intensely and hostilely debated was the question of the universities' religious exclusiveness, the refusal of Oxford or Cambridge to allow non-Anglicans to take degrees. If ecclesiastical education had remained the chief task of the universities or if the institutions had remained comparatively modestly endowed or if the Church of England had maintained a firm grasp on the affection of most articulate Englishmen, it is possible that the old universities could have remained Anglican preserves. But the various social changes of the nineteenth century made such an arrangement increasingly unsatisfactory; and ironically university reform itself, making Oxbridge degrees at once more highly respected and less traditionally theological, would contribute to the increasing demand for the admission of dissenters. The battle was a long and heated one, begun at the turn of the century and not really ended until 1871. In the process the nature of the relationship between the Church and the University would be transformed.

As critics both inside and outside the University considered the various curricular and ecclesiastical problems already mentioned, they began to perceive Cambridge as an institution in need of general, structural reorganization. Each suggested improvement seemed to raise a new series of problems; and time and again reformers found their efforts frustrated by the fundamental conservatism of the university constitution itself. By the 1830s some critics would come to believe that sweeping governmental reform would have to precede any genuine academic improvements, and to see the disproportionate power of the colleges as the fundamental problem facing Cambridge. It has already been noted that the finances of the University were controlled by the collegiate bodies; it was also true that, whether intentionally or not,[16] the colleges had come to possess the lion's share of political power. The central university government itself was run by a group made up of Masters of some of the colleges, with the chief executive officer, the Vice-Chancellor, chosen from among their number. Only this central body – the 'Caput' or the 'Heads' – could initiate legislation, and any one of them had veto power in any matter. Subsequent approval by the Senate (the rest of the university fellows) was not automatic, but in practice the Senate usually followed the lead of the Caput. Such a government might have been a workable if somewhat top heavy form of representative democracy if the Heads had been subject to any kind of periodic electoral review. But Masters were selected for life; the highly hierocratic nature of Cambridge society usually prevented their being effectively criticized by those beneath them in the collegiate structure; and the fact that Masters could (and did) marry while fellows remained single, led to a sharp social demarcation between the closed circle of the Heads and all the other fellows at the University. The Caput thus tended to be an isolated, elderly, conservative body, one with the power to frustrate any democratically initiated efforts at change. The social unity of the Heads, and their isolation from the rest of the university community, unfortunately did not mean that they were politically unified in efforts to support the central University. For despite their social ties with the other members of the Caput, Masters were foremost and fundamentally members of their own colleges. And there was a strong tendency for each Head to see as his primary responsibility the preservation of the wealth, the privileges, and the independence of his individual society. Thus socially cliquish yet fiercely jealous for their separate colleges, the Heads were a body preeminently unsuited to the task of centralized university reform.

To some extent these constitutional difficulties were not simply a consequence of the social and psychological backgrounds of the individual college leaders; part of the problem lay with the central legal foundation of the colleges and the University. Each society had a collection of statutes which its officers swore on oath to uphold; in many cases these primitive statutes and bequests severely limited the possibility of any change or reform. Frustrated by such legal problems as well as by the conservative attitude of the university government, some of even the most loyal Cambridge dons gradually began to conclude that an external body, probably Parliament, would need to take the initiative.

The pressure for external action would be intensified by growing and increasingly hostile attacks on Cambridge in the popular press. Liberal journals like the *Edinburgh Review* frequently lambasted the old English universities for faults ranging from the narrowness of their subject matter to failure to provide adequate religious leadership. But even more inflammatory of public opinion were the occasional pamphlets published by individuals and directed against the moral turpitude believed to be prevalent at Oxford and Cambridge. One such extremely popular work was *The Melancholy and Awful Death of Lawrence Dundas, Esq., with an Address to the Younger Members of the University, on the Evil Nature, Tendency, and Effects of Drunkenness and Fornication, followed by an Appeal to the University on the Laxity of its Discipline and Licentiousness*. It was written in 1818 by a country parson, F. H. Maberley. Mr Dundas had fallen drunk into a ditch on his way to Barnwell, Cambridge's red-light district, and had died of exposure. Maberley made this undoubtedly melancholy event the occasion for a general attack on the morals of undergraduates, extrapolating from an extreme case to present a general picture which was almost certainly exaggerated.[17] Maberley's standards were themselves rather extreme – he advocated total abstinence from wine,[18] and he was even offended by the university museum's possession of paintings of nudes[19] – but there was no question that many of the abuses he exposed were in fact real ones. Undergraduates were notorious for their profligate expenditure of money, and the problem of controlling student debts was one which troubled even the most conservative and uncritical of the dons. Samuel Taylor Coleridge's flight into the Light Dragoons to avoid his Cambridge creditors is well known;[20] less well-remembered are the constant collegiate efforts to control student expenditure through supervision by college tutors.

Attempts would also be made to control student 'debauchery'. While the University resisted the frequent suggestion that a censor of public morals be appointed,[21] Cambridge did have 'proctors' who roamed the city streets empowered to arrest noisy students as well as town rowdies and prostitutes. Each college had its own parietal rules, and failure to be 'within the walls' by closing time could result in serious punishment. Undergraduates were required to wear their gowns when in the town of Cambridge, thus making them more easily observable. Ceilings were placed on the debts which townsmen, particularly wine-sellers, were allowed to let students incur. Despite these efforts, however, it is clear that the typical Cambridge undergraduate led anything but a monastic existence and indeed that his physical pleasures often interfered seriously with his intellectual and spiritual development.

A partial explanation for the lavishness of Cambridge life lay in exaggerated class-consciousness. Social delineations were sharp and taken seriously. Members of the upper classes could enter college as noblemen or 'Fellow Commoners'. Distinguished by special caps and robes, they were granted many privileges, including eating at high table, sharing the fellows' Common Room, and – in the case of the nobility – graduating without taking any examinations. At the other end of the scale were scholarship students, 'sizars' who had to serve table to pay their college fees and who were generally looked down upon by the ordinary students.[22] The stress laid on these social distinctions without doubt explains a great deal of the 'display' in which undergraduates felt it necessary to indulge. If the contacts made in college were to be useful in later life – if, indeed, such friendships were the main benefit to be gained from the collegiate experience – it is easy to understand why undergraduates felt it important to prove themselves to be convivial fellows.

The evil effects of adolescent peer-group pressure should have been somewhat mitigated by the sobering influences of the senior fellows, and contemporary collegiate propaganda did emphasize the many benefits of the 'familial' side of college life. However, even discounting the fact that many of the fellows shared the tastes and social attitudes of the undergraduates and were thus hardly models of rectitude,[23] the practical impact of the seniors on the juniors was normally quite insignificant. On entering college each student was assigned a tutor whose nominal role was to oversee the student's intellectual and moral growth. In fact each tutor had a large number of nearly anonymous students with whom he usually had only a formal, bureaucratic relationship. (For example, one of William Whewell's pupils had been dead for some months before it came to Whewell's attention; and Whewell – generally later regarded as a 'reforming don' – felt not guilty at his own laxness, but annoyed at his servants for not having informed him.)[24] Most of the teaching was done in small college lectures, and ambitious students unfailingly hired private coaches. The official tutor thus was mainly only a disciplinarian, whose most typical responsibility was to serve as a collector of debts. The relationship between a 'reading man' (a serious student) and his private coach, on the other hand, could be quite warm and cordial,[25] but since it lay entirely outside the domain of collegiate regulation (coaches were often Cambridge graduates, who had refused fellowships to marry; most of them lived comparatively impoverished lives on the fringes of academia) this tie could not be counted on to reinforce any standards other than purely academic ones.

The religious bond was also supposed to contribute to the familial nature of collegiate life, but, at the beginning of the century, religion seems in practice to have mattered little to most undergraduates. Therefore official efforts, such as the requirement of undergraduate attendance at chapel, served more as irritants than as inspiration. The role of compulsory chapel, indeed the right of the University to influence at all the religious lives of its students, would become vexed questions, especially with the mounting pressure to admit dissenters. But even before this the harsh disparity between the ideal and the actual in undergraduate behavior – as in almost all aspects of university life – had begun to be apparent and painful to even the most loyal of Cambridge's sons. Reform was clearly inevitable.

CHAPTER 2

REFORM FROM WITHIN

Although our major concern is with scholars who reformed Cambridge from within, it is important to begin by saying something about the groups and individuals outside the University who did so much to make reform seem necessary; for without external pressure it is not clear that Cantabrigians would have moved so soon, nor gone so far. Outsiders attacked the old universities for a variety of reasons. Whig politicians and others who espoused liberal political principles tended to be critical of many aspects of 'privilege' in English society. Thus from very early in the century the *Edinburgh Review*, in the hands of Sydney Smith,[1] provided a platform for liberal criticism of the Established Church and the universities, often using the Scottish or German universities as a standard of comparison. This Scottish/Whig attack continued throughout the first part of the century. In the 1830s there was another series of critical articles in the *Review*, this time written by an Edinburgh philosophy professor, William Hamilton.[2] Hamilton's theme, like Smith's earlier, was that the English universities offered too narrow a curriculum, were bastions of privilege and conservatism, and were unaware of international intellectual developments. Probably because of the close ties between England and Scotland – Hamilton and Smith, for example, were both graduates of Oxford – such criticisms were taken seriously,[3] and ultimately many of the Scottish suggestions for improvement were put into effect.

Other 'Whiggish outsiders' included Sir Charles Lyell, the geologist, another Oxford graduate. His many travels, particularly in America, and his scientific interests made him critical of the English educational system.[4] There was the great schoolman Thomas Arnold, who in reforming Rugby gave impetus to a general movement to improve English schools and universities.[5] At 'the other University' itself there were – particularly later in the century –

reformers like Benjamin Jowett[6] of Balliol or Mark Pattison[7] of Lincoln who would contribute to a general progressive movement. In Parliament, liberal politics often included a concern for university reform. As the century wore on members of the Whig party more and more frequently objected to what they viewed as the excessive privilege and unnecessary exclusiveness of Oxford and Cambridge. In the early thirties public petitions were presented to the House of Commons calling for university reform; there seemed to be considerable support for government action.[8] By 1850 Lord John Russell's liberal government was finally ready to appoint an investigative body, a royal commission to 'Inquire into the State, Discipline, Studies, and Revenues of Oxford and Cambridge'.[9]

Religion could also serve to stir critics of the Cambridge system. Dissenters who suffered directly from the exclusiveness of the universities could be particularly bitter, as was R. M. Beverley in his 1833 'Letter . . . on the Present Corrupt State of the University of Cambridge'.[10] Dissenters were continually active politically in an effort to secure the removal of religious entrance tests and other 'disabilities'. And alumni like Augustus DeMorgan who came to unorthodox religious opinions in later life also advocated the removal of rigid religious restrictions. Within the Established Church various types of religious enthusiasm could inspire criticism of the universities: the Maberley pamphlet mentioned in the first chapter grew out of the puritanical zeal of a country parson, while 'high Church' reformers of the Oxford Movement concerned themselves with improving the universities[11] as did latitudinarians like Frederick Maurice[12] and Charles Kingsley.[13] In particular the presence in Cambridge of the great evangelical leader Charles Simeon naturally contributed to a religious seriousness within the community. Although he was unpopular with some ecclesiastical authorities, many undergraduates and some senior members of the University took Simeon's views very seriously. As an officer of King's from 1788 until 1830 he exerted a powerful influence on his own college, and through his very effective preaching as the minister of Holy Trinity Church he was able to reach people throughout the University. He was especially concerned in both a theoretical and a practical way with improving the theological training which young clerics underwent.[14] At the other extreme, even complete unbelievers, a group which became more visible later in the century, had reason to criticize the establishment-bound universities; T. H. Huxley was

notable but not alone as an agnostic reformer of English education.[15]

Besides Whig politics and religious concerns a third force external
to the old universities also contributed to a general atmosphere of
criticism and educational reform: the developing spirit of social
improvement. Naturally this overlapped with the other two forces,
especially liberal politics, but in some ways a distinct movement –
one tinged with radical or socialist tendencies – can be perceived.
Such a political philosophy took cognizance of the increasingly
technological nature of English society; it opposed undue stress on
artificial class distinctions; and it favored the development of a
much broader-based system of public education. Here too Frederick
Maurice[16] was an active proponent of reform, as were John Stuart
Mill,[17] Henry Brougham, Thomas Campbell,[18] and William Ewart.[19]
In general such 'advanced liberals' were not interested in attacking
the old universities directly, but in establishing alternative or parallel
educational systems to benefit the wider public. Their efforts during
the century resulted in the foundation of the University of London
and of various 'redbrick' provincial universities; they also set up
many 'Workingmen's Institutes' as well as libraries and museums
available to the working classes. Such institutions did not directly
threaten Oxford or Cambridge; at the same time their existence
raised a number of issues about democratized education and broadened curricula which would gradually come to pervade English
educational thought, even at the most conservative levels.

This ferment for educational reform within British society at
large was met within Cambridge by three separate attitudes: there
was a moderate-sized but not very active group of extreme reaction-
aries who resisted all change; a much smaller collection of 'radicals'
who pressed for immediate and drastic reform; and a very large,
very influential body of moderate 'conservative reformers' who saw
the need to improve the *status quo* but did not want to sever their
connection with the best of the University's past.

The extreme conservatives were driven by a variety of motives.
Some, especially among the older fellows, seemed incapable of
considering the possibility of any changes in the system with which
they were familiar; even in the midst of controversy they produced
tracts evidencing a surprising amount of confidence and self-
satisfaction. J. M. F. Wright, for example, published in 1827 a
completely uncritical book of reminiscences in which he described

a pleasant life at Trinity, in his view the best of all possible colleges.[20] And the defenses of the established courses of studies – e.g. by L. Wainewright at Cambridge, Edward Copleston at Oxford[21] – indicated that at least some university residents regarded contemporary external criticisms as totally irrelevant.

Other dons were conservative – even reactionary – not because they refused to listen to external criticism but because they were frightened by it. Early nineteenth-century Englishmen, especially Tories, were keenly aware of the excesses to which the French had recently been led, and dire warnings about political extremism had the effect of making any kind of change seem very dangerous. Burke's careful analysis of the interrelated, slowly developing nature of society represented the thoughtful side of British conservatism; but there were members of the upper classes who found the French example so horrifying that only complete rigidity seemed a safe political stance. This tendency was exaggerated among Cambridge conservatives by the relationship between the University and the Established Church. It was common to identify the fortunes of the two institutions with one another and to assert that an attack on one would inevitably spell the decline of the other. Thomas Turton, the Regius Professor of Divinity, for example, strenuously resisted any efforts to open the University to non-Anglicans; he felt that the resultant religious turmoil would be damaging to the spiritual development of the undergraduates and ultimately to the Church.[22] Christopher Wordsworth, brother of the poet and between 1820 and 1841 the Master of Trinity, also opposed the admission of dissenters or any modification in university regulations which would weaken the tie with established religion.[23] George Corrie, after 1838 the Norrisian Professor of Divinity and later Master of Jesus College, took a consistently conservative line in university affairs, usually tying his position to concern for the welfare of the Church.[24] And it was common, even among dons prepared to tolerate reform in some areas of university life, to see a close link between education and religion and to grow alarmed when that link seemed in any way threatened. As W. Dalby, a conservative don, wrote in an 1834 pamphlet: 'Let us tell our representatives, respectfully, but firmly, that it is our conviction, that they who propose to unChurch the universities mean to un-Christianize the nation.'[25]

In addition a strongly conservative attitude was taken by some dons simply in defense of their personal privileges. Occasionally this

position was taken on the comparatively elevated grounds of preserving the sanctity of ancient oaths, as when various college officers
agreed to testify before the University Commission only 'so far as
such action was consistent with the wishes of [their] founders'.[26]
But others, simply determined to resist change at any cost, took a
more down-to-earth, even cynical line: an early attempt by Lord
Radnor to impose external reform elicited this remark in Corrie's
diary: 'I trust he will find himself grievously mistaken if he supposes
we shall concede to him any *principle* in alterations . . .'[27] And in an
1834 controversy at Trinity College over compulsory chapel the
conservative dons expressed as much dismay over the openness of the
debate and the 'break in the ranks' of the fellows as they seemed to
feel over the basic issue.[28] Whatever their motives, however, such
reactionary conservatives were comparatively few in number (fewer,
in fact, all the time as the century wore on), so that their position
was relatively unimportant within the university political scene.

Even less significant were the handful of Cambridge 'radicals'.
Religious constraints tended to keep the Cambridge population
politically and philosophically moderate. In the first place, since
dissenters could not be granted degrees, very few of them bothered
to attend the University at all; and secondly, dons who became
skeptics later in life almost inevitably felt uncomfortable in college
and resigned their fellowships. There were a few orthodox members
of the Church of England who felt that justice required the 'opening'
of the University; but the 1834 forced resignation of Connop
Thirlwall as tutor at Trinity showed that such arguments could not
be pressed too strenuously, nor too publicly. And while intellectual
curiosity led some scholars into untraditional fields, the reaction of
the university community to the 'Germanizing' philology of Julius
Hare and F. D. Maurice made it clear that religious orthodoxy
prescribed strict boundaries in curricular matters as well as with
respect to personal behavior and belief.[29] After the middle of the
century such religious bonds would begin to weaken, and by the
1860s and 70s skeptics and educational radicals like Henry Sidgwick,
John Seeley, and Henry Jackson would be in clear control of the
reform movement at Cambridge. During the early 1800s, however,
to understand the changes at the University one must look neither
to the right nor to the left but to the solid body of moderate opinion.

Moderate reformers could be found throughout the University,
but it was at the two largest colleges, St John's and Trinity, that the

strongest pressure for improvement was exerted. The small colleges produced an occasional man of real talent and flexible mind – Charles Babbage[30] or William Hopkins[31] of Peterhouse, James Hildyard[32] of Christ's or J. H. Crowfoot[33] of Caius and King's, for example – but by and large their emoluments, limited teaching staffs and small endowments tended to attract only mediocre students and to make teaching and constitutional innovations difficult if not impossible. Others of the small colleges – e.g. Clare – were not poor, but were heavily dominated by the aristocracy. This also tended to exert a conservative influence. At St John's and Trinity on the other hand, there were large numbers of excellent students and capable fellows. The diversity of talents among the senior members made flexible, specialized teaching arrangements possible. Their huge endowments meant that the colleges could afford to improve their educational arrangements, paying tutors and fellows enough to guarantee their presence within college walls. A history of successes in the university degree competitions gave Trinity and St John's a sense of confidence, so that they felt able to experiment with their teaching methods without fear of destroying their reputations for excellence.[34] And Trinity at least had a long-standing association with the British liberal political world, going back to the college's reorganization as a bastion of the new order at the time of Henry VIII.

'Johnian' reformers included a number of significant scientists: John Herschel, the mathematician and astronomer, was an undergraduate and fellow at St John's; and although he did not reside at the University after his graduation, through his various Cambridge friendships he had a significant influence on later curricular developments.[35] John Henslow, the botanist, entered St John's in 1816. From 1827 until his death in 1861 he held the university professorship of botany, and although after 1839 he only resided in Cambridge intermittently, Henslow was a continual force in the university reform movement. John Haviland, professor of medicine between 1817 and 1851, was another reformer who had attended St John's. Furthermore, the College itself was early and active in pushing academic reform: by 1765 St John's had established a twice-yearly system of public examinations; one of the results was that Johnians were almost always placed creditably and often triumphantly in the wrangler lists of the early nineteenth century.

Pride of place for university reform, however, must really go to

Trinity College, for it was there that the vast majority of the 'moderate reformers' were located. The early years of the nineteenth century saw arriving at Trinity a group of extremely capable undergraduates. These young men befriended each other, in time became fellows of their college, and together eventually had a powerful impact on the University. George Pryme came first, arriving in 1799. Pryme was an exceptional scholar, especially in classics; by the time he was elected a fellow of Trinity in 1805 he had earned the nickname 'Prize Pryme' because of all the awards he had accumulated. He studied for the bar in London, then returned to Cambridge in 1808 to practice law. After 1816, despite some resistance to innovation from the university government, he offered a series of 'unofficial' lectures in political economy; the course was so clearly a success that in 1828 the Senate established a chair in political economy, which Pryme held until 1863. Politically a Whig, he was active in borough government and even sat in the House of Commons for a brief period; throughout his life he consistently advocated university reform.[36]

In 1800 arrived James Henry Monk, afterwards the Bishop of Gloucester and Bristol. He received his B.A., as seventh wrangler, second Chancellor's medalist, in 1804 and was elected to a fellowship the following year. As an assistant classical tutor at Trinity (where 'his pupils carried off the greater part of the high classical honours in Cambridge')[37] and then as the Regius Professor of Greek (after 1809) Monk was largely responsible for the establishment of the classics tripos examination in 1822. Though he left the University quite early in the century in order to pursue his ecclesiastical career, his influence was very important as part of the beginning push for reform.

Adam Sedgwick, the first of the brilliant young men later known as the 'Northern Lights', entered Trinity in 1804. An extraordinarily likeable, charming man, Sedgwick was plagued throughout his life by ill health and a tendency to procrastinate. Nevertheless as a thoughtful liberal both in politics and within the University he did a great deal to move Cambridge along the lines of moderate reform. He received his B.A. in 1808 (as fifth wrangler) and was elected to a fellowship in 1810. Unlike many of his contemporaries, he was never away from Cambridge for any period of time, his only church preferment being the canonry at Norwich, where he resided during the summer vacation. Sedgwick was an assistant tutor (1815) and

Vice-Master (late 1840s) of Trinity, and within the larger University held the offices of Senior Proctor (1827), Secretary to the Chancellor (1849) and – most important – Woodwardian Professor of Geology (after 1818). When elected to the latter position Sedgwick had no real knowledge of geology, but he quickly trained himself in it and was very soon recognized to be both an outstanding teacher and a respected scholar. Throughout his life he was active in improving the University, helping to establish several learned societies, advocating the admission of dissenters, pressing for a broadened curriculum, and serving as a Royal Commissioner in the reform movement of the 1850s.[38] Adam Sedgwick is necessarily one of the most important characters in any story of nineteenth-century Cambridge.

Also in 1804 Trinity saw the arrival of William Clark, who would, after taking a medical degree in London, become the University Professor of Anatomy. He graduated as seventh wrangler in 1808 and was elected a fellow in 1809. Together with John Haviland, the Johnian mentioned above, Clark did a great deal to lay the foundations for the study of the biological sciences at Cambridge. He collected and arranged for the housing of a wide variety of specimens and displays, and he was influential in the establishment of the natural science tripos in 1848. His son, John Willis Clark, was also a reforming fellow of Trinity and an anatomist, as well as being Adam Sedgwick's biographer.

In 1809 Joseph Romilly arrived at Cambridge. A very close friend of Sedgwick's, Romilly was another ardent university reformer and political liberal, supporting such left-wing political stances as the Greek fight for independence and Catholic emancipation. A fellow of Trinity after 1815 Romilly was elected Registary of the University in 1832; while never a real leader he could be counted upon to lend his support to the reform movement.[39]

Much more powerful and influential than Romilly, and entering Trinity in the same year, was George Peacock. A private pupil of Sedgwick's, with whom he maintained a life-long friendship, Peacock graduated in 1813 as second wrangler and second Smith's Prizeman[40] and was elected to a fellowship the following year. Even as an undergraduate he had been interested in improving the education at Cambridge: in 1812 he had joined with Herschel and Babbage to found the Analytical Society, dedicated to introducing continental mathematics to the University. He held several offices both within Trinity and in the University, and from his earliest days advocated a wide variety of reforms. In 1839 he left Cambridge to become the Dean of Ely Cathedral, but his interest in his Alma Mater by no means declined. In 1841 he published a very important survey entitled *Observations on the Statutes of the University of Cambridge* in which he concluded that governmental overhaul, not mere tinkering, would be a necessary part of any genuine educational improvement. In 1850 and again in 1855 Peacock served on the Royal Commissions appointed to investigate and reform Cambridge; by this point many of his old friends had become less interested in real change and Peacock became rather unpopular because of his continuing 'extremism'.

For Trinity 1812 was a good year, for it was then that Julius Hare, the philologist and historian, and two more of the 'Northern Lights', Richard Sheepshanks and William Whewell, entered their names on the college books. Hare was in some ways unusual among this group of young scholars: for one thing his lack of mathematical interest and ability kept him completely off the wrangler list and made him ineligible for any prizes or honors whatever. On the other hand, his early education had been remarkable and, in addition to an excellent classical background absorbed at Charterhouse, Hare had developed an extraordinary ability in modern languages, particularly German. Graduating in 1816, he was elected a fellow two years later, after which he went on an extensive scholarly tour of the Continent. He returned to Trinity as a classical lecturer in 1822. In that post he had a great influence on his colleagues and students for ten years, until he retired to his family parish and a permanent life of scholarship. Even from Hurstmonceux he maintained a lively interest in the University, and through his friends still at Cambridge he continued to make suggestions for university improvement.[41]

Richard Sheepshanks, on the other hand, was a talented mathematician and scientist, graduating in 1816 as tenth wrangler. He was elected to a fellowship the following year but moved almost immediately to London and never again resided at the University. Sheepshanks was not a liberal in university affairs and did not approve of many of the administrative changes which the next thirty years brought. When in 1842 Whewell asked him to return to Cambridge, therefore, Sheepshanks refused, saying he would not want to be in conflict with his old friends.[42] But he did press for a few reforms, actively promoting, for example, the establishment in

1828 of an observatory at Cambridge. And he maintained a warm and positive interest in his Alma Mater, offering conservative suggestions for reform at several points throughout the century.[43]

The third important freshman of the Trinity entering class of 1812, William Whewell, was destined to be the central figure in the development of early nineteenth-century Cambridge. The son of a master carpenter from Lancashire, Whewell was an enormous, physically powerful man of a rather brusque, almost rude manner. He had phenomenal energy[44] and engaged in a huge range of activities, scientific, administrative, literary, and social. Whewell never developed a narrow scholarly specialty, attacking instead topics as varied as international law, moral philosophy, the regulation of the tides, and advanced mathematics. His contemporaries sometimes felt that this diversity weakened him by diffusing his energies too broadly – common wisdom had it that 'science was his forte and omniscience was his foible'[45] – but in the long run many of them concluded that his breadth of vision provided an extremely valuable unifying force in the scholarly world. As the geologist Sir Charles Lyell wrote to Whewell in 1836:

> There was a time when I used to regret that you had not concentrated your powers on some one of the physical sciences and been a giant in that, or at least that you had been satisfied with some two or three of the Arts and Sciences but I have for some years come round to the belief that you have been exercising the calling for which Nature intends you and for which she gave you the strength and genius and that you have given a greater impulse to the advancement of science among us by being a universalist and by mastering so much of chemistry, mineralogy, astronomy, geology and other branches than you would have done if restricted to the perfecting of one alone.[46]

Whether a particular science might have benefited from a more specialized attack from Whewell is a moot point; what is clear is that his universalism was very useful to the University through which he channeled almost all of his efforts.

Whewell had shown a great deal of promise as a boy, and as a Trinity undergraduate he distinguished himself immediately. Herschel, the senior wrangler of 1813, was his good friend, as was the brilliant mathematician Charles Babbage. Within Trinity his closest companions were Sheepshanks and Hare, with both of whom he maintained life-long contact. In his second year Whewell won the Chancellor's medal for a prize poem, but when he graduated in 1816 he was – to his friends' chagrined surprise – only second wrangler and second Smith's Prizeman. (Whewell had supposedly been lulled into a false sense of security by his chief competitor's apparent failure to study hard.)[47] The following year he was made a fellow of Trinity.

Even as a very young man Whewell was interested in improving the intellectual life of Cambridge; active in the newly formed Cambridge Union, a political debating club, in 1818 he joined with Peacock and Sedgwick to found the Cambridge Philosophical Society. Whewell supported Herschel, Babbage, and Peacock in their efforts to introduce modern mathematics to Cambridge; in teaching mathematics at his college and as a moderator of the university examinations (1820, 1828) he insisted that students learn and apply the 'continental' notation and concepts. In 1818 he became an assistant tutor at Trinity, and in 1823 he was made tutor. The latter position was mainly administrative, but he surrounded himself with very capable assistants like Hare and Connop Thirlwall, so that undergraduate instruction prospered under Whewell's guidance.

Between 1828 and 1832 he served as the Cambridge professor of mineralogy, in which capacity he wrote several works on mineralogical classification and one of the Bridgewater Treatises, on the relationship between astronomy and natural theology. During this period he became highly respected as a man of science, serving as an officer in a variety of national scientific organizations. He held his college tutorship until 1838, when he was elected to the professorship of moral philosophy. From that point forward he directed his attention to philosophical, ethical, and legal questions as well as to scientific ones. In 1841 when he was on the point of leaving Cambridge for a more concentrated life of scholarship – perhaps in a country parish – Whewell was appointed by Sir Robert Peel to the mastership of Trinity College. This position was an ideal one: it made it possible for him to marry and still remain at Cambridge. It gave him a comfortable, influential position within the College. And it made him, as one of the 'Heads', one of the natural leaders of the whole university community. As Master of Trinity he spent the last twenty-four years of his life making significant contributions to critical scholarship and to moderate university reform.

One of Whewell's closest friends during his early years at Cambridge was another Trinity man, two years his junior, Connop

Thirlwall. Thirlwall had been at Charterhouse with Julius Hare and, like Hare, was much more interested in literature and the arts than in mathematics. He did manage to gain a high enough rank in the mathematical tripos to qualify for honours, however, and he graduated in 1818 as First Chancellor's Medalist. He was made a fellow in the same year. Thirlwell then joined Hare, whose close personal friend and longtime scholarly collaborator he was, on a continental tour, strengthening his familiarity with the German language and with German theology and philosophy. He also studied for the bar for a time, but found the law to be thoroughly unsatisfying; more rewarding were his scholarly pursuits which resulted in the 1825 translation of Schleiermacher's *Critical Essay on the Gospel of St Luke* and the 1828 translation of Neibuhr's *History of Rome*. In 1827 he returned to Trinity (at Whewell's invitation) to become assistant tutor and for the next seven years served his college and the University in a variety of positions.[48] Thirlwall was a political and university liberal, and in 1834 his rather radical and public position with respect to compulsory chapel caused a rift with the Master of Trinity and led to Thirlwall's resignation. Appointed to a country living he continued to engage in serious scholarship while pursuing an ecclesiastical career; he was eventually appointed to the Bishopric of St David's. Like Hare, Herschel, and others who left Cambridge, however, he continued to be concerned about university affairs and through his friends to exert an influence for reform.

The last of this first generation of Trinity reformers was the mathematician and Astronomer Royal, George Biddle Airy. Airy arrived at Trinity in 1819, graduated as senior wrangler and first Smith's Prizeman in 1823, and was made a fellow and assistant tutor of the College in 1824. His mathematical ability and scientific interests made him a natural protégé of Sedgwick, Whewell, Sheepshanks, Herschel, Babbage, and Peacock, all of whom supported him in his various academic pursuits. Airy was Lucasian Professor of mathematics after 1826, Plumnian Professor of astronomy after 1828, and Astronomer Royal after 1835. He had very strong opinions about the proper methods of teaching mathematics, especially with reference to the importance of physical experimentation, and even after his national duties called him away from Cambridge he continued to work actively for reform of the mathematics and science curricula.[49]

What general observations can be made about these young scholars? First, almost without exception they shared a commitment to the Church of England. To have graduated from Cambridge in the first place, of course, they had to have been willing to sign an oath of loyalty to the Church. Then those who wanted to retain their fellowships were all required within a brief space of time to take holy orders – thus Hildyard, Crowfoot, Monk, Sedgwick, Romilly, Peacock, Hare, Whewell, Henslow and Thirlwall were all actually ordained ministers. Some of these even went on to active ecclesiastical careers, with Monk and Thirlwall rising all the way to the episcopacy and Peacock and Hare serving in parishes. Others who abandoned their fellowships but became professors or other officers of the University – Hopkins, Haviland, Pryme, Clark, Airy – were also tied to the Church through their various oaths and through the powerful traditional connection between the University and the Church. Even among those 'pure scientists' who left Cambridge and pursued their studies in the larger world – Babbage, Sheepshanks, Herschel – there was no apostasy or even apparent disaffection from the Established Church; these men saw no conflict between scientific inquiry and theological truth. In his 1831 *Preliminary Discourse on the Study of Natural Philosophy* Herschel expressed his confidence in this 'grand and indeed only character of Truth . . . its capability of enduring the test of universal experience, and coming unchanged out of every possible form of fair discussion'.[50]

At the same time that they were loyal to the Church, however, these scholars were by no means given over to religious 'enthusiasm'. There was no Cambridge corollary to the Oxford Movement.[51] Even those who became professional ecclesiastics were usually known more for their scholarship than for their inspirational qualities: Thirlwall's biographer describes him as a man 'not devoid of true faith. His sermons exhibit a sound, practical religious spirit – lacking in fervour, perhaps; like his History, cold and lucid. They might have been delivered in exposition of an ethical ideal rather than of an inspired faith.'[52] And Hare was conscientious but hardly warm or personally effective as a pastor.[53] It was common to postpone the actual taking of religious orders until very near the deadline imposed by college statutes,[54] and then to view the Church more as a system of financial support than as a true vocation. Sedgwick, for example, was appointed by Melbourne's government to a canonry at Norwich; this is the description of the job which he sent to a friend:

Our Residence is severe while it lasts. [The six prebends rotated in service, Sedgwick residing during two months of university vacation.] We are not permitted to be away from our house for a single night. Attending service regularly, and preaching generally once each Sunday, are duties which are looked for. We have also to give certain dinners of ceremony to the officers of the Cathedral. Giving and receiving dinners constitutes a formidable service in a city like this.

What my stall may do for me in the end I cannot say, but I am quite sure that for the first year it will make me poorer than I have been since I knew how to spell my own name. My fees and furniture will run me into debt to the tune of six hundred pounds at the very least. . . . If my life be spared the stall will I doubt not turn out a very comfortable thing. I hope I may count upon its producing me nearly £600 a year. This, together with my Senior Fellowship and Professorship, must surely enable me soon to lift my head above water. My clerical employment here is a good thing, and I mean not to flinch from it. The preaching I spoke of is not compulsory; but has been commenced of late years by some of the new comers.[55]

If they were less enthusiastic than Simeonites and lower church than their contemporaries at Oxford, the leaders of Cambridge were nevertheless conscientious in their commitment to the Church. The pluralism which was so common in the eighteenth century began dying out during the nineteenth; Peacock, Sedgwick, Thirlwall and the others made a genuine effort to reside in their parishes and to accept their clerical responsibilities. And they continued to feel very strongly that the well-being of the Established Church and that of the nation were inextricably intertwined.[56]

Commitment to the Church was the first quality which these scholars shared. Secondly, they were all devoted in a new way to academic work of high quality. Many of them were scientists; together they provided a community which lent support to some of the greatest scientific geniuses of the age – Maxwell, Faraday, Darwin. Particularly in geology/biology, but also in mechanics and mathematics, they were open to new methods and determined to examine specific and detailed evidence. As the modern scholar Walter Cannon points out:

the dedication of men working in the physical as well as in the biological sciences to the quest for factual complexity is demonstrable, and this should dispose of any idea that a simple, arid, so-called 'Newtonianism' characterized science in England in the first half of the nineteenth century.[57]

They were prepared to examine new materials – German theology, geological sub-strata – and to look at old materials in new ways (as with the critical examination of Scripture exemplified in Thirl-wall's work). They were prodigiously productive, maintaining constant scholarly contact with each other through their books and in the journals of the learned societies which they founded and supported. Although most of them specialized in one or two fields of study, they were flexible and interested in many things; Whewell, for example, published a series of elegaic poems at the death of his first wife and Sir John Herschel took time from his astronomy to compose an English hexameter translation of Homer. They believed in a 'liberal' education, one integrating a familiarity with scientific thought and a knowledge of classical literature. And they tried to guarantee that successive generations of Cambridge undergraduates would be exposed to the best of the traditions in which they had been molded.

These early-nineteenth-century Cambridge dons, then, were by no means revolutionaries. They respected the institutions – religious, political and educational – in which they had been nurtured, and they wanted to preserve the best of the past. At the same time they were earnest, conscientious, 'Victorian' men who were determined to live up to the spirit as well as the letter of their various obligations. And their intellectual energy made them chafe at anachronistic restrictions which limited the growth of scholarship.

Sir Robert Peel had appointed Whewell to the mastership of Trinity College, and in a broad sense Whewell and his friends were all 'Peelites' – that is, while they were essentially conservative about institutions, they were in favor of 'improvement'. And if they were shown that improvement could be achieved only through dramatic reform, most of the dons were prepared to take the measures necessary. Within the structure of old forms, they changed Cambridge almost beyond recognition.

CHAPTER 3

MATHEMATICS – THE CORE OF 'PERMANENT STUDIES'

Would you study Surgery? The Differential Calculus treats of the peculiar affections of the *groin*, and will facilitate the treatment of consumption, and all other diseases of the liver, by making you fully acquainted with the structure of the *latus rectum*. The Accoucheur may arrive at skill and eminence in his art, by investigating the *generation of solids*. The Natural Philosopher should study *eccentricities;* and the Moral Philosopher the theory of *rational functions*. The Botanist may learn easy methods of discovering *roots;* the Antiquarian may examine the *Arc* . . . Ergo, Mathematics ought to be the especial study of every member of the human family.[1]

This undergraduate lampoon of an introductory lecture in mathematics articulated a fundamental truth about early nineteenth-century Cambridge attitudes: the discipline of mathematics was at the very heart of the University. It formed the basic subject matter for all the undergraduates; until 1822 it was the only, and, until the fifties the most highly regarded, route to academic honor; it was generally viewed as the only really effective means of strengthening a man's intellectual capacities and academic self-discipline. At least in part out of respect for Newton and his memory the subject was endowed with a mystique which made it an object of near religious veneration. It is not surprising that many of the improvements and reforms which the University undertook during the first half of the century were related to mathematics.

Change began as early as the second decade of the century with the arrival at the University of a group of very talented undergraduate mathematicians. They included Charles Babbage, John Herschel, William Whewell, George Peacock, and – slightly later – George Biddle Airy and Augustus DeMorgan. The first four, particularly Herschel, Babbage and Peacock, had been interested in mathematics at a rather sophisticated level before they ever came up

28

to Cambridge and had read widely and intensively in a number of contemporary mathematical works. Cambridge, indeed England in general, found itself in a rather peculiar situation with respect to modern mathematics, in large part stemming from an exaggerated adulation of Sir Isaac Newton. Newton and Leibniz, as is well known, had almost simultaneously invented the calculus at the end of the seventeenth century, but each had developed his own system of notation, Newton using a 'dot' ($\dot{d}$) to indicate differentials, while Leibniz used the dy/dx notation. The two representations meant the same thing. But the Leibnizian notation contained explicitly the concept of a quotient, making it more effective for certain kinds of mathematics which developed later, particularly under the influence of the French. Since, independent of its essential usefulness, the Leibnizian notation was the language employed by continental mathematicians, Englishmen, in order to be able to read such work, needed to be able to convert from the dy/dx to the dot formulation with which they were familiar. This technique was simply not taught to young students, either at school or at university.[2] Babbage, Peacock, and Herschel as undergraduates banded together to try to introduce to the University of Cambridge, in its reading program and eventually at the examination level, the concepts of the continental notation. To accomplish this aim they organized themselves into what they called the Analytical Society. Babbage described their purpose – imitating the language of contemporary religious societies – as the conversion of the English mathematics to 'The Principles of pure D-ism, in opposition to the Dot-age of the University'.[3]

As very young men these undergraduates wrote papers for the journal of the Analytical Society, which they published periodically; most of the articles were in fact contributed by Herschel and Peacock, but Babbage and Whewell also wrote occasional tracts. More important than their undergraduate efforts was their impact on the university examination system after they became adult members of their colleges. Whewell, an early member of the Society although not one of its founders, in 1819 published *An Elementary Treatise on Mechanics*, using the continental notation. The work contained problems suitable for instruction at the undergraduate level and helped to bring into prominence and popularity the new mathematical language.[4] Very soon after his graduation Peacock became a fellow and tutor at Trinity, and in those capacities served for several successive years as an examiner in the university mathematical tripos. In this role he introduced into the examinations a series of questions using the new notation, so that at the highest official level of the University – the tripos – a transformation had taken effect by the 1820s.[5]

It is difficult to exaggerate the significance of this change in notation, for it opened to English mathematicians whole new fields of thought. Up until this time the material which undergraduates prepared was limited almost entirely to examinations of and parses on Euclid – very complex, detailed, systematically taught geometry. But algebra was at a comparatively primitive level, and the calculus in any kind of sophisticated way was really not available to undergraduates. This meant, among other things, that the work of Frenchmen like LaPlace and Lagrange was entirely inaccessible. Troublingly, England had as one of its prize possessions a university ostensibly committed to mathematics but in fact at least a hundred years behind the contemporary mathematics of other nations. The introduction of the continental notation was very like the introduction of a foreign language; it made available to English scholars a wide range of mathematical thought previously beyond their reach.

Having begun their scholarly association as undergraduates and having succeeded in reorganizing the 'language' of British mathematics, these young scientists continued to maintain close contact with one another. They became very influential in British scientific circles, both in their early days as creative scientists and later as precursors of or influences on more innovative thinkers like Boole, Hamilton, Stokes, and Clerk Maxwell. Furthermore, they shared certain mathematical concerns and tendencies, so that to assess their joint scholarly contributions is to a considerable extent to understand the direction of early-nineteenth-century British mathematics.

The first characteristics these scholars shared can be discussed in terms of a dichotomy described by J. T. Merz in his *History of European Scientific Thought in the Nineteenth Century*:

To some, mathematics is only a measuring and calculating instrument, and their interest ceases as soon as discussions arise which cannot benefit those who use the instrument for the purposes of application in mechanics, astronomy, physics, statistics, and other sciences. At the other extreme we have those who are animated exclusively by the love of pure science. To them pure mathematics, with the theory of numbers at the head, is the one real and genuine science, and the applications have only an interest in so far as they contain or suggest problems in pure mathematics.

Newton would serve as an excellent example of the first class; Gauss would tend to fall into the latter category.[6] Whether because they venerated Newton and his example, or because excessive isolation had kept them unfamiliar with the more theoretical works of the continent,[7] or because of their essentially concrete, geometric orientation, or simply because they were Englishmen and liked to see results, most of these Cambridge mathematicians ended up in Merz's first category, as very practical scientists. They understood mathematical theory, but most of them were more interested in the concrete extensional world than in research into pure mathematical ideas. Herschel and Airy, though extremely clever mathematicians, became first and foremost astronomers, putting their theoretical understandings to work in such direct ways as organizing and analyzing catalogues of stars. Herschel mapped the Southern skies, discovered and recorded the locations of a number of double stars, and developed a method of scanning the heavens using the parallax of fixed stars. Only a small percentage of his published papers were on pure mathematical topics;[8] his main strength was as an experimental scientist.[9] Furthermore he had great faith in the practical usefulness of science: the scientist should derive great comfort from the fact that

speculations apparently the most unprofitable have almost invariably been those from which the greatest practical applications have emanated . . . The speculations of the natural philosopher, however remote they may for a time lead him from beaten tracks and everyday uses, being grounded in the realities of nature, have all, of necessity, a practical application, – nay more, such applications form the very criterions of their truth; they afford the readiest and completest verifications of his theories.[10]

Airy, who became Astronomer Royal in 1835, was even more of an experimentalist than Herschel, delivering university lectures on such 'applied' topics as mechanics, hydrostatics, pneumatics, and optics.[11] As a very young man he published a series of *Tracts* in which the newly introduced analytical methods were 'applied with great success to various physical problems',[12] and at the Royal Observatory he was noted for his practicality and inventiveness, both with respect to equipment and to observatory recordkeeping. His biographer characterizes Airy thus:

His nature was eminently practical, and any subject which had a distinctly practical object, and could be advanced by mathematical investigation, possessed interest for him. And his dislike of mere theoretical problems and investigations was proportionately great . . . His great mathematical powers and his command of mathematics are sufficiently evidenced by the numerous mathematical treatises of the highest order which he published . . . But a very important feature of his investigations was the thoroughness of them. He was never satisfied with leaving a result as a barren mathematical expression. He would reduce it, if possible, to a practical and numerical form, at any cost of labour . . .[13]

Babbage, who did so much to introduce French analytical methods to Cambridge and England, on leaving college abandoned pure mathematics almost entirely[14] and spent the remainder of his life inventing various mechanical contrivances, most notably his famous 'calculating engine'. Even Whewell, who continued to teach mathematics and to write textbooks for some time after his graduation and who probably did more than any other single individual to reorganize the mathematical part of the Cambridge undergraduate curriculum, failed to pursue the study of pure mathematics in later life. Whewell's scientific attention was concentrated in the main on philosophic and historical questions,[15] and even his own basic scientific research was of a practical, not theoretical, nature.[16]

Only Peacock and DeMorgan remained true to pure mathematics, Peacock dedicating his efforts to establishing algebra on a firm theoretical base[17] and DeMorgan extending Peacock's work and generalizing algebraical rules to apply to all of formal logic.[18] Despite the theoretical nature of their scientific interests, however, even DeMorgan and Peacock were extremely practical men in their professional and academic lives, the former helping to found the University of London, the latter contributing to a number of significant organizational reforms at Cambridge.

A second characteristic of these scholars was their concern with popularizing mathematical wisdom. They all published articles in learned journals and communicated their more sophisticated ideas to their scholarly colleagues,[19] but they also spent a surprising amount of energy explaining mathematical concepts to the general public. To the encyclopedic works of the Victorian period these scholars contributed many articles of varying levels of sophistication.

The *Edinburgh Encyclopaedia*, published during the 1820s under the editorship of David Brewster, printed articles by Herschel on 'Mathematics' and 'Isoperimetrical Problems' and by Babbage on 'Notation' and 'Porisms'. The *Encyclopaedia Metropolitana*, a serious, nearly scholarly work which assumed that its readers were possessed of a solid traditional mathematical education, contained articles by Airy on 'The Figure of the Earth' and 'Tides and Waves', by Babbage on 'The Diving Bell' and 'Principles of Machinery', by Herschel on light, heat, sound, and physical astronomy, by De-Morgan on the calculus of functions and the theory of probability, by Whewell on Archimedes and electricity, and by Peacock on arithmetic.

In a different category were the *Penny Cyclopaedia* and the *Cabinet Cyclopaedia*, directed very much to the general reading public. For the former DeMorgan wrote well over six hundred articles, while Airy contributed papers on gravitation and on the Greenwich Observatory. Herschel wrote 'A Treatise on Astronomy' for the *Cabinet Cyclopaedia*. He was careful in his introduction to make it clear that his book would require only an elementary knowledge of mathematical principles, while at the same time warning that a work so limited could of necessity only hope to place the student

on the threshhold of this particular wing of the temple of Science, or rather on an eminence exterior to it, whence we may obtain something like a general notion of its structure . . . Admission to its sanctuary is only to be gained by one means, – *a sound and sufficient knowledge of mathematics* . . .[20]

Despite the limitations imposed, Herschel – and his colleagues, through their participation in similar projects – explicitly believed in the value of such popular works:

although it is something new to abandon the road of mathematical demonstration in the treatment of subjects susceptible of it . . . it is always of advantage to present any given body of knowledge to the mind in as great a variety of different lights as possible . . . [This book's aim is] to present in each case the mere ultimate *rationale* of facts, arguments, and processes.

and thus to make clear both to the public and to serious scientists some of the astronomical truths often obscured in complex mathematics.[21]

Even within the mathematical community their efforts could be viewed as largely a public relations campaign. The Analytical Society itself was not so much concerned with discovering new truth as with making accessible to England older ideas which had long been available on the continent, and the later activities of the Society's members were often directed at the production of text-books and problem books which would make the new methods readily comprehensible to undergraduates.[22] Even DeMorgan, who was one of the most productive members of the group, especially in pure mathematics, received much of his renown not for his original work but for explaining and popularizing the work done by LaPlace and his successors on probability theory.[23]

Furthermore it was in large part through the efforts of these men that vital organizations were formed through which mathematical scientific discoveries could be shared. The Analytical Society and the Philosophical Society of Cambridge were both entirely of their creation, while the British Association itself could hardly have gotten started without their initial push.[24]

A third characteristic of these Cambridge mathematicians grew directly out of their involvement with undergraduate teaching: they felt very strongly that the logical processes employed to solve problems should be explicit, so that students would acquire a habit of clear thinking as much as – or more than – a system for getting answers. English mathematicians had always been strongly enamored of Euclid and the precise way in which his thought progressed from one clearly understood axiom to another well-defined and (once understood) apparently undeniable truth, with no vague, steps or complex formalism to becloud the simplicity of his logic.[25] A man disciplined in Euclidean mathematics would inevitably, according to Whewell, acquire an ability to reason with precision and clarity:

He knows that all depends upon his first principles, and flows inevitably from them; that however far he may have travelled, he can at will go over any portion of his path, and satisfy himself that it is legitimate; and thus he acquires a just persuasion of the importance of principles, on the one hand, and, on the other, of the necessary and constant identity of the conclusions legitimately deduced from them.[26]

Students should understand not only results but the processes by which they arrived at them. In 1845, for example, a member of the

Senate complained that candidates for the ordinary degree were not receiving a satisfactory background in fundamental mathematical reasoning:

The manner of answering the Arithmetical questions shews that the attention is directed merely to obtaining results: the nature of, and the reasons for, the processes being employed by almost all entirely disregarded . . . When the processes of Arithmetic are gone through in connexion with the theory of those processes, the subject is one which admits of being highly serviceable as an educational discipline; and it would seem therefore very desirable, that the science should be cultivated here in such a manner as to ensure, in some degree, this result.[27]

Because of their determination to keep the logical processes clearly before the student, many Cambridge mathematicians felt a kind of uneasiness with the increasing curricular dependence on algebra and calculus, where too-mechanical manipulations sometimes seemed to obscure underlying logic. Various regulations of the university examination system attempted to maintain an emphasis on the more straightforward Euclidean approach, so that as the more 'modern' analysis became part of the examination subject matter it was always accompanied by several preliminary days of testing in very basic mathematics. Whewell certainly recognized the efficiency and significance of analytical methods, but he was concerned lest they assume too important a role in the examination structure. In 1845 he wrote:

the recommendations of analytical forms of mathematics are such as these; – their supplying easier solutions of the problems with which the mathematician has to deal; – the symmetry and generality of their processes; – and their having, in consequence of these qualities, superseded geometrical methods in the mathematical literature of modern times . . . Mathematics, in the shape of Geometry, holds its place as an element of great and incomparable value among the permanent studies of a Liberal Education [because] it offers to us examples of solid and certain reasoning, by which the reasoning powers, and the apprehension of demonstrative proof, may be exercised, unfolded, and confirmed. This is eminently true of the Geometrical Forms of Elementary Geometry, Trigonometry, Conic Sections, Statics, and Dynamics. It is not true to the same extent, and hardly at all, of the Analytical Methods of treating the same subjects. For, in the Geometrical Form of these sciences, we reason concerning subjects in virtue of the manner in which the subjects are conceived in the mind. In the Analytical Methods, on the other hand, we reason by means of symbols, by which symbols, quantities and the relation of quantity are represented; and by means of the general rules of combining and operating upon such symbols; without thinking of anything but these rules. When the supposed fundamental conditions are once translated into the language of Analysis, we dismiss from our minds altogether the conceptions of things which the symbols represent; whether lines, angles, velocities, forces or whatever else they may be. The mode of proceeding is the same, whichever of these be the matter in question; and the steps of the process are not acts of thought, in any other way than as the application of an assumed general rule to a particular case is an act of thought. We arrive at our conclusion, not by a necessary progress, in which we see the necessity at every step, but by a compulsory process, in which we accept the conclusion as necessary in virtue of the necessary truth of our rules of procedure, previously proved or supposed to be proved. In the one case, that of geometrical reasoning, we tread the ground ourselves, at every step feeling ourselves firm, and directing our steps to the end aimed at. In the other case, that of analytical calculation, we are carried along as in a railroad carriage, entering it at one station, and coming out of it at another, without having any choice in our progress in the intermediate space . . . It is plain that the latter is not a mode of exercising our own locomotive powers; and in the same manner analytical processes are not a mode of exercising our reasoning powers . . . It may be the best way for men of business to travel, but it cannot fitly be made a part of the gymnastics of education.[28]

Airy's objections to an extreme dependence on the 'new' mathematics arose from a slightly different source; he was not comfortable with concepts which had no correlation to the physical world:

I do not know that one branch of Pure Mathematics can be considered higher than another, except in the utility of power which it gives. Measured thus, the Partial Difference Equations are very useful and therefore stand very high, as far as the Second Order. They apply, to that point, in the most important way, to the great problems of nature concerning *time,* and *infinite division of matters,* and *space:* and are worthy of the most careful study. Beyond that Order they apply to nothing.[29]

Or again:

I have not the smallest confidence in any result which is essentially obtained by the use of imaginary symbols. I am very glad to use them as conveniently indicating a conclusion which it may afterwards be possible to obtain by strictly logical methods; but until these logical methods shall have been discovered, I regard the result as requiring further demonstration.[30]

36

The desire, then, to keep Cambridge mathematics essentially Euclidean was strong, both because of the explicitness of the logical processes in geometry and because of its applicability to the extensional world.

Some, however, of this Cambridge group stood the problem on its head: if algebra and analysis were not rigorous, rather than being rejected, these branches of thought should be reformed. It was precisely to the task of putting algebra on a rigorous base that George Peacock turned most of his scholarly attentions. His *Treatise on Algebra*, published in 1830,

sought to give the subject a logical structure comparable to that of Euclid's Elements . . .; he attempted . . . to formulate the fundamental laws of arithmetic – the commutative and associative laws for addition and multiplication and the distributive law for multiplication over addition. This approach, amplified later in a two-volume work of 1842–1845, marks the beginnings of postulational thinking in arithmetic and algebra.[31]

His work was really only a beginning, in part because he was the first English pioneer in the field and in part because in 1830 communication between British and continental mathematicians was still rudimentary.[32] But Peacock unquestionably broke important ground, and Augustus DeMorgan and Sir William Rowan Hamilton (of Dublin) followed up on his work during the next twenty years in a very productive way. In an 1865 letter to John Stuart Mill, DeMorgan assessed Peacock's achievements thus:

You are perhaps aware that Peacock published two works on algebra. The first, in one volume, is that which treats the subject most generally. He is in full possession of all except what relates to the exponent . . . Peacock had very nearly attained the idea of algebra as a *formal science*, in which every result of the form is to have meaning. His *permanence of equivalent forms* would have developed itself into formal algebra capable of any number of material applications, if he had been a logician – I mean a student of logic.[33]

DeMorgan himself was concerned with extending and revising the groundwork on which much of the new mathematics was built.[34] MacFarlane says of his work that

[Peacock's] new theory of algebra as a science of symbols and of their laws of combination was carried to its logical issue by DeMorgan; and

37

his doctrine on the subject is still [1901] followed by English algebraists in general.[35]

DeMorgan explained algebra as an entirely symbolic system, in which internal consistency was a prerequisite but from which no necessary connection with the external world could be demanded. He formulated an inventory of algebraic relationships, but viewed them not as necessary rules but as 'formal laws, that is arbitrarily chosen relations to which the algebraic symbols must be subject'.[36] In the relevant chapter of his book, *Trigonometry and Double Algebra*, DeMorgan wrote:

It is most important that the student should bear in mind that, *with one exception*, no word or sign of arithmetic or algebra has one atom of meaning throughout this chapter, the object of which is symbols, and their laws of combination, giving a symbolic algebra which may hereafter become the grammar of a hundred distinct significant algebras. If any one were to assert that + and − might mean reward and punishment, and A, B, C, etc. might stand for virtues and vices, the reader might believe him, or contradict him, as he pleases, but not out of this chapter. The one exception above noted, which has some share of meaning, is the sign = placed between two symbols as in A=B. It indicates that the two symbols have the same resulting meaning, by whatever steps attained.[37]

DeMorgan went on to apply his mathematical understandings to the discipline of formal logic, making important contributions particularly with respect to the concept of the quantification of terms.[38] Mill had high regard for DeMorgan's logical work: describing how the doctrine of limits freed differential calculus from apparent paradoxes and objections raised by Berkeley (among others), Mill wrote:

so deeply did those objections go into the heart of the subject, that even after the false theory had been given up, the true one was not (so far as we are aware) worked out completely in language open to no philosophical objection by anyone who preceded the late Professor DeMorgan, who combined with the attainments of a mathematician those of a philosopher, logician, and psychologist . . . the puzzle arising from the conception of different orders of differentials – quantities infinitely small, yet infinitely greater than other infinitely small quantities – had not (to our knowledge) been thoroughly cleared up . . . by any one before Mr. DeMorgan.[39]

And in a letter to DeMorgan's widow, C. J. Munro – a former pupil – assessed his mentor's logical work thus:

The fact is known that, having very thoroughly worked at the generalizations of Mathematics in theory and practice, Mr. DeMorgan was enabled to establish with perfect precision the most highly generalized conception of Logic, perhaps, which it is possible to entertain. It is no new doctrine that Logic deals with the necessary *law of action* of thought, and that Mathematics apply these laws to necessary *matter* of thought; but by showing that these laws can and must be applied with equal precision and equal necessity to all kinds of relations, and not only to those which the Aristotelian theory takes account of, he so enlarged the scope and intensified the power of Logic as an instrument, that we may hope for coming generations, as he must have hoped, another instalment of the kind of benefit which history shows we ourselves owe to the Aristotelian theory, not merely in the analysis of our mental operations, but in the everyday practice of them.[40]

Their sustained scientific and personal contact with one another, and their shared mathematical rigor, interest in geometry, concern for publicizing their mathematical understandings, and practical or 'applied' bias, made these scholars into what can legitimately be viewed as a Cambridge group or 'network'.[41] This is true even though Herschel, Babbage, Peacock, DeMorgan, and Airy all left Cambridge as comparatively young men, to conduct their professional lives elsewhere. However it was up to those scholars who remained in residence at their Alma Mater, particularly William Whewell, to put into effect within the University those principles which the group had come to view as sound.

Whewell wrote three important practical tracts about university education. In 1835 he published a short pamphlet entitled *Thoughts on the Study of Mathematics as a Part of a Liberal Education*, devoted – in the words of his biographer Todhunter – 'to upholding the educational superiority of mathematics over logic, and . . . to the discussion of some faults in the manner of teaching mathematics, by which benefit of these studies may be seriously diminished'.[42] The pamphlet, by no means meant to be a definitive study, was the object of a very hostile attack from Sir William Hamilton, the Edinburgh philosophy professor, in the next issue of the *Edinburgh Review*.[43] Despite this criticism Whewell remained convinced of the correctness of his views, which he reprinted as an appendix to a later educational work and which he inserted in essence into his *Philosophy of the Inductive Sciences*.

In 1837 he published a longer book entitled *On the Principles of*

English University Education. To some extent this work represented a response to the *Edinburgh* criticisms and a justification of the basic educational program which Cambridge had established. At the same time it was not merely a rationalizing defense of the status quo. Whewell offered what he regarded as a philosophically sound explanation for the pattern of the curriculum; furthermore he was critical of some existing practices and at several points in the book called for curricular reform.[44]

In 1845 he published *Of a Liberal Education in General; and with Particular Reference to the Leading Studies of the University of Cambridge.* In the intervening decade the English universities had been much attacked from within and without for their inflexibility and the narrowness of their curricula; in particular Whewell's earlier justifications of the University had been criticized by no less a thinker than the geologist, Sir Charles Lyell, in his 1845 book *Travels in North America.*[45] In response Whewell's book was rather defensive, essentially reiterating and supporting the position he had outlined in the earlier works. In addition approximately half the new book was dedicated to describing the improvements which Cambridge had carried out in the recent past and to asserting the advantages of the collegiate (as opposed to a university-wide) system of instruction.[46] *Of a Liberal Education in General,* then, is a more conservative book than its predecessors, one which shows clearly Whewell's educational philosophy in the somewhat ossified form which it assumed during his later years.

The three works taken together presented Whewell's basic epistemological ideas as well as his practical attitudes toward mathematical instruction. Underlying his whole approach was the belief that the mind was composed of separate, discretely functioning 'faculties' – distinct collections of skills and abilities which enabled a person to order and make reasonable his world. Education, therefore,

consists, not in accumulating knowledge, but in educing the faculties of man. It does not consist of *information*, in the modern sense of the term, but in the formation of the mind. It requires, not merely occasional performances, but permanent habits . . .[47]

In particular, a liberal education should concentrate on developing man's most important intellectual capacities; the most useful academic disciplines would be those such as are fitted to educe two principal Faculties of man, considered as an intellectual being; namely, Language and Reason.

Language and Reason are attributes of Humanity intimately connected with each other. Without the use of Language, we could not express general propositions, or derive them from each other, in virtue of their forms of expression, in the manner which also we call Reasoning. Without the use of Reason, we could not conceive objects and their connexions in a general and abstract manner, and therefore could not apply to them names, and use Language. The Reason cannot express itself without Language; Language cannot be employed without the Reason . . . while the classical literature of Greece and Rome thus supplies us with studies by means of which the powers and properties belonging to one of our principal human faculties, Language, may be exhibited in their influence in his education; we have, in other writings . . . works by the study of which as a part of education, the other principal human faculty mentioned, the Reason, may also be exemplified in its most complete form, and educed in each person's mind. I speak now of mathematical works, in which truths respecting measurable quantities are demonstrated by chains of the most rigorous reasoning, proceeding from Principles self-evident, or at least certain.[48]

One can hardly avoid the conclusion that Whewell's epistemology was a kind of 'reading backward' from the Cambridge curriculum; that is, since mathematics and classics were the core of the University's studies, the faculties which they trained were assumed to be the most basic of man's intellectual abilities. In other words Whewell seemed to be rationalizing (both in the sense of 'making reasonable' and in the sense of 'justifying and vindicating') the Cambridge program through his philosophy. Whatever the genesis of the basic premises, however, the rest of Whewell's argument followed coherently and consistently from them. These faculties, which existed almost like separate organs, needed to be exercised in order to be developed. Mathematics was perceived to be a mental discipline, a system of intellectual callisthenics which should strengthen the mind much as physical exercise would strengthen the body.

In *Thoughts on Mathematics* . . . Whewell considered the two subjects which had traditionally been used for developing and educing the 'reasoning faculty' – mathematics and logic. He concluded:

These may be considered respectively as the teaching of reasoning by practice [mathematics] and by rule [logic]. In the former study, the student is rendered familiar with the most perfect examples of strict inference; compelled habitually to fix his attention on those conditions on which the cogency of the demonstration depends; and in the mistaken and imperfect attempts at demonstration made by himself or others, he is presented with examples of the most natural fallacies, which he sees exposed and corrected. In studying logic, on the other hand, a person finds the conditions formally stated under which an inference is legitimate; he is enjoined to see that in any given case these conditions are satisfied; and if a fallacy exists, he is provided with rules by which it may be condemned and made more glaringly wrong.

Now I venture to say that the former kind of teaching is, in my opinion, likely to be the more efficacious of the two. For reasoning – a practical process – must, I think, be taught by practice better than by precept, in the same manner as fencing or riding, or any other practical art would be.[49]

And it should be stressed that Whewell by no means felt that mathematical training would draw out only narrow mathematical reasoning; the clarity and precision of thought thus taught would establish habits of wide applicability:

we know that, in fact, the employments of the youth have a great share in forming the character of the man; and that pursuits leave traces of their indirect effect on the habits, long after they themselves have ceased to exist. But in this case we are not left to reasoning and conjecture. No one who knows the recent history of this University can doubt that the mathematical studies of its members have produced a very powerful effect on the general character of their mental habits. Anyone who is acquainted with the lawyers, of men of business, or statesmen, whom the University has produced in our own and the preceding generation, knows, from observation of them and from their own declarations, that their mathematical pursuits here have in no small degree regulated their mode of dealing with other subjects.[50]

Whewell, of course, realized that, good as it was, mathematics was subject to some limitations as an educational tool. It was impossible, for example, to endow men with the ability to reason inductively:

a practical instruction in Inductive Reasoning is not possible, except so far as it depends on the cultivation of the Deductive Faculty. We may lead men to feel the force of demonstration, but we cannot teach them to discover new truths.[51]

The distinction between induction and deduction Whewell defined succinctly ('To obtain consequences from principles is Deduction;

to obtain general truths from particular facts is Induction'[52]), and there is no doubt that he viewed inductive reasoning as the higher process, indeed the basis of all scientific discovery.[53] But he was persuaded that the kind of inspired spark of intuition which was the mark of induction could not of itself be drawn out of an individual through any kind of training; rather by teaching deduction (through mathematics) the University could ensure that its students would be able to evaluate their intuitive perceptions rigorously and to organize their ideas by testing them systematically against empirical data. Furthermore, even if mathematics could not give men the specific skills which would enable them to make scientific discoveries, by means of it they would be

brought into an acquaintance with the most recent and profound researches, and thus feel themselves called upon to sympathize with the struggles and successes, the hopes and anticipations of the great men of their times, whose names and discoveries would be an inheritance to later generations.[54]

Indeed Whewell assumed that the Cambridge undergraduate should learn about the 'modern sciences' and that many would go on to pursue research in them. But he was convinced that they could not provide a substitute for the fundamental truths and skills which were conveyed by mathematical discipline.[55]

If in his assumption that the mind is made up of various faculties and in his belief that, like a muscle, it needed to be exercised in order to be developed, Whewell showed himself to be influenced by Lockean concepts, his concerns about the difficulty of educing the inductive faculty and his views on the development of scientific ideas through time connected him at least to some extent to the philosophy of Kant.[56] A modern student of Whewell, Robert E. Butts, summarizes his position thus:

Fundamental Ideas are what the activity of mind contributes to knowing. Whewell likens some of them . . . to Kant's forms of intuition. Others . . . play for Whewell something akin to the role of Kant's categories . . . Furthermore, in its treatment of some of the Fundamental Ideas, especially space and time, Whewell's account of their epistemological status deviates little from Kantian theory . . . What is significant for our purposes is not this evident similarity of his doctrine to Kant's (which Whewell readily admits), but rather the novel features of Whewell's position, which his subsequent discussion brings forth. For Whewell's central (and largely novel) contention is this:

'The Progress of Science consists in a perpetual reduction of Facts to Ideas . . . Necessary Truths belong to the Subjective, Observed Facts, to the Objective side of our knowledge. Now in the progress of that exact speculative knowledge which we call Science, Facts which were at a previous period merely Observed Facts, come to be known as Necessary Truths; and the attempts at new advances in science generally introduce the representation of known truths of fact, as included in higher and wider truths, and therefore, so far necessary . . . Such steps in science are made, whenever empirical facts are discerned to be necessary laws; or, if I may be allowed to use a briefer expression, whenever facts are idealized.'[57]

This belief of Whewell's in the progressive accumulation of necessary truth through historical time helps to explain his apparently conservative insistence on the primacy of the traditional disciplines. He was constantly concerned that students should not try to understand modern concepts (either scientific or literary) until they had completely absorbed the basic ideas contained in the writings of the scholars of the past. The University should provide the student access to modern or 'Progressive' studies.

But in order to [achieve] present and future progress, an acquaintance with the past is requisite. In order that we may share in what men are doing in the world of intellect, we must share in what they have done. In order that we may walk onwards, we must feel the ground solid under our feet. Considered with reference to mental progress, a large portion of education is preparatory only; but it is an indispensable preparation. Any attempt to put aside this permanent preparatory portion of education, would make our education worthless. It would make real progress impossible. The past alone can make the present and the future intelligible.[58]

Whewell's insistence on students beginning their university work with the traditional subjects[59] grew out of more than just his perception of Ideas as something historically progressive, however. He was also influenced by a deep concern, which many of his Cambridge contemporaries shared, that individual students should develop their ideas with rigor and clarity, always able to trace each concept back to its fundamental axioms. He was thus, as mentioned above, particularly suspicious of analysis as a subject for use in educating the young. It made possible very elevated and sophisticated mathematical manipulations without requiring students to understand the

44

groundwork which made such techniques valid. Or in Whewell's words:

Let [the student] be certain that he knows the path up to this summit and down from it; and let him shun the common fault of taking indistinctness as evidence of generalization, for this is to suppose ourselves on a mountain because we are in a mist.[60]

Whewell was also committed to the 'permanent' studies out of a desire to maintain the stability of the university curriculum. Students, and a society in general, should be able to depend on the universities to preserve and teach a solid, only slowly changing collection of the best of human knowledge:

Universities, so far as they are schools of *general* cultivation, represent the permanent, not the fluctuating elements of human knowledge. They should be progressive, for otherwise, they cannot be permanent; but the progress in which they ought to share, is not one which can be estimated from year to year, but rather is reckoned by centuries. They have to transmit the civilization of past generations to future ones, not to share and show forth all the changing fashions of intellectual caprice and subtlety. They ought not, therefore, rapidly or easily to introduce changes into the subjects of their study. They ought to wait till novelties have been well discussed and firmly established, before they adopt them into their elementary course. I am here, of course, not speaking of *professional* education . . . But in that fundamental education, of which I have principally treated, the old ways are not lightly to be abandoned. As I have already said, I should be sorry to see Euclid lose his ancient place, or even his ancient form, in our system.[61]

This desire for a stable curriculum led Whewell to be hesitant about changing requirements or adopting new textbooks. For example when in 1839 Airy inquired about revising his *Tracts*, Whewell decidedly replied that they should be left unchanged.[62] And he also felt that a constantly changing board of examiners led to an unhealthy degree of 'perpetual innovation' on the examinations, so that candidates became excessively dependent on private tutors.[63]

In addition to his epistemological belief in the logical 'priority' of the traditional subjects, to his insistence on logical rigor in the training of students, and to his concern for curricular stability, Whewell added a fourth, more authoritarian reason for his commitment to the 'Permanent Studies': student discipline. It was imperative, he believed, that students should respect their teachers as the purveyors of permanent truths and that young men should not set themselves up as the equals of older scholars in some kind of 'critical' academic process. In a section of *Principles of English University Education* entitled 'On the Moral Effect of Practical and Speculative Teaching' he contrasted the stability of mathematics with the constant change of opinion in a discipline like philosophy. The latter kind of subject

places [students] in the position of critics instead of pupils. In mathematical and other practical teaching, the teacher is usually, and almost necessarily, much the superior of his scholar in the knowledge which they cultivate together; and the scholar cannot but feel this, and must consequently be led to entertain a docile and confiding disposition towards his instructor. On the other hand, when a system is proposed which offers its claims to him, and asks his assent, which he may give or refuse, he feels himself placed in the situation of an equal and a judge, with respect to his professor. And if . . . he goes through several phases of philosophical opinion, and gives his allegiance to a succession of teachers, he can hardly fail to look upon them with a self-complacent levity, which involves little of respect . . . Now this want of docility, confidence, and respect when it prevails in the student towards his teacher, cannot I think, be looked upon otherwise than as a highly prejudicial feeling, and one which must destroy much of the value and usefulness of the education thus communicated.[64]

Whewell's various philosophical and theoretical views on education had very practical implications. From his belief that the mind needed to be exercised in order to develop came a commitment to the active tutorial instruction carried on in the Cambridge collegiate system. Whewell called this kind of teaching 'practical' – the student would be required to recite and respond to questions, to participate actively in his own educational process.[65] He contrasted this approach, used in college instruction, with the larger university lectures, on more advanced topics, in which the students were expected only to listen passively:

it has been the practice, in recent discussions on this subject, to distinguish between College Lectures and Professional Lectures: and the distinction is an important one, if it be understood as implying that, in Professorial Lectures, the student is a listener only, and is not called upon to shew, by taking any part in the lecture, that he is a prepared listener. The distinction being thus understood, if we inquire whether College Lectures should be superseded by Professorial Lectures in our University, we cannot hesitate to reply, that such a change would be a grievous damage to English Education . . . Professorial Lectures are especially suited to those [disciplines] which we have called Progressive Studies, in which the student is to be instructed in the views at which his most active-minded contemporaries have arrived. But with regard to Permanent Studies, the impression which, in a Liberal Education, they ought to produce upon the mind, is eminently promoted by College Lectures fuch as we have described; and can by no means, be derived from Prosessorial Lectures alone.[66]

Whewell's assertion of confidence in the college system of instruction was partly based on pedagogical theory as outlined in his various educational treatises, but it was also at least in part a defensive response to critics of the University like Lyell[67] and Hamilton who argued that the colleges had usurped the educational function, the power, and the endowments of the University, and that educational goals would be well served by a revival of the authority of the university professors.[68] In any case, Whewell's defense of the status quo, whether theoretically or practically inspired, had a significant impact on the future political structure of the University and did a great deal toward preserving the prerogatives and the teaching functions, especially in the 'permanent' subjects, of the collegiate foundations. Especially as he grew older, and no doubt largely because of his role as Master of Trinity College, Whewell became an increasingly ardent defender of college privileges, so much so that he really ceased to be a reformer and took an almost reactionary stance with respect to university politics. But during his middle years, Whewell's desire to preserve continuity and order in the mathematical curriculum, led to his determination to carry out several practical reforms. First he wanted, as mentioned above, to establish a Board of Mathematical Studies, an ongoing supervisory committee which would guarantee that mathematical examination procedures, personnel, and subject matter remained stable from year to year. Such a board, composed of the three university mathematics professors and the moderators and examiners of the current and two preceding years, was proposed in 1843 but rejected by the Senate. Its purpose would have been to make the subjects of the mathematical tripos 'more steady, and their nature and extent better known'.[69] Such a board was eventually established by a grace of the Senate in 1848; Whewell was a member of the syndicate which made the proposal.[70]

Whewell also felt that it was imperative for a strong relationship to exist between the material taught in lectures, either collegiate or professorial, and that demanded in examinations,

inasmuch as, however ingenious and profound may be the lectures delivered to the students, the attention given to them, in a system in which the Examinations are the door to distinction, will be very feeble and scanty, if they do not in great degree prepare students for the Examinations.[71]

To deal with this problem[72] the University established a committee in 1843

To consider whether it [was] desirable to take any measures and if so what, to secure a correspondence between the Mathematical and Classical Examinations of the University, and the Mathematical and Classical Lectures of the University Professors.[73]

The committee recommended that sharply defined lists of examination topics, both for the tripos and for the Smith's Prize, should be published annually and that examiners should take such statements 'as guides' in their proposing of questions.

His conviction that mathematical subjects should be 'rigorously' taught, with an emphasis on elementary principles and basic logical processes, led Whewell to have definite ideas about suitable subject matter. As mentioned above, he preferred elementary mathematics to the more advanced, formal calculus and analysis. And he had a strong bias in favor of concrete topics, with which students could really come to grips, instead of abstract subjects which they would only imperfectly understand. With respect to the poll or ordinary degree he went so far as to say that he would

let a knowledge of some portion of Mechanics and Hydrostatics be introduced among the requisites for a degree; and if necessary, let the knowledge of Algebra be required no longer, for I can hardly believe that this part of our mathematical teaching is of much value in any point of view. Very plain and easy systems of Mechanics and Hydrostatics would answer the purpose which I recommend, but they must be of an appropriate character. They must not, for instance, be of what is called a *popular* nature, consisting of assertions without reasoning, and propositions of the most different kind and evidence wanted, must contain none but the most rigorous demonstrations, although none but the most simple calculations.[74]

Whewell's emphasis on elementary subjects thoroughly taught was clearly shared by other members of the University, for various reforms of the mathematics examination scheme moved in the directions he outlined. Senate Grace Books make continual reference to syndicate reports recommending basic, fixed, elementary topics for the examinations, both tripos and ordinary.[75]

Whewell's commitment to the concept of a 'liberal education' – one in which both the reasoning faculty and the literary taste would be developed – led him to an almost rigid insistence on the importance of mathematics. He felt it would be a dereliction of duty to neglect either aspect of his two-part educational program, and even when other scholars were moving towards lightening the mathematics requirement for classicists, Whewell dogmatically refused to change his position. An undergraduate at Trinity between 1840 and 1845 wrote in his memoirs of 'imperious Whewell . . . doing his worst to make mathematics' the 'sine qua non' of the Trinity program,[76] and complained vociferously of the heavy mathematical burden under which Trinity classicists were forced, mainly by Whewell, to labor.[77] When the classical tripos was first established in 1822 it was required that any candidate for classical honours first should have received honours in the mathematical tripos;[78] this requirement was only very slowly relaxed, Whewell in opposition all the way. When in 1849 it was recommended that students be allowed to sit for classical honours after having achieved only a first class in the ordinary degree examination, Whewell refused to sign the syndicate report.[79] The lower requirement was, nevertheless, instituted.

Whewell's pedagogical theories are the most visible of those of contemporary Cambridge dons, both because he wrote explicit educational treatises and because his position as Master of Trinity made him important in university politics. But he was by no means isolated or unique in his attitudes. Adam Sedgwick agreed with Whewell on most important points, feeling very strongly, for example, that good science must depend on experience-based induction.[80] He also supported Whewell's argument that through the hard work and discipline of mathematics[81] a student's mind would gain 'a habit of abstraction, most difficult to acquire by ordinary means, and a power of concentration of inestimable value in the business of life'.[82] J. F. W. Herschel also agreed with Whewell about the necessity for practical but not overly radical reforms. In an October 5, 1845, letter Herschel wrote:

I perfectly agree with you in thinking that young men taking their degree cannot possibly have had time, and cannot except in a few almost miraculous cases of precocity have maturity of thought and enlargement of view enough to grasp the whole of mathematics and that it is infinitely better to ensure by the practice of teaching and examinations a full possession of certain considerable and fundamental portions of them wide enough to afford a basis of any subsequent study.

Still, I think the examinations should be so framed as to allow every reasonable opportunity for excessive reading to shew itself, but that specialties such as the fancies of particular men may lead them to set an undue value on should be practically repressed by never allowing their acquisition to excuse deficiency in the more essential and fundamental course.[83]

Although there was much public pressure to open up the curriculum and make the mathematics requirement more flexible for those not really dedicated to the discipline, conservatism on this point was also widespread. In 1848 F. Whaley Harper, a classical lecturer at Sidney Sussex College, wrote that to lower the mathematical requirement for classics honours candidates would be pandering to the multitudes and would constitute a direct violation of the University's public responsibility:

I have experienced in myself the benefit of even the present minimum of requisition for mathematical honours and I feel truly grateful for the salutary compulsion of the University which forced it upon me.[84]

And J. R. Crowfoot, a fellow of Caius and a reformer on most issues, wrote a letter to the local newspaper in 1849 arguing that any new tripos must follow after an adequate training in the traditional subjects:

if our Classics and Mathematics are of use as a good training for more delicate, and, in truth, severer studies, as well as for practical life, we ought to be cautious lest we set aside what we have so long appreciated. The unsoundness in theology of our German neighbours I believe . . . to have arisen mainly from their not being familiar with the rules of strict demonstration.[85]

By mid-century, then, mathematical instruction at Cambridge was not so much revolutionized as it was renovated – no major upheaval in subject matter or teaching techniques or examinations had taken place, nor had mathematics ceased to be an important subject at Newton's Alma Mater. What the conservative reformers had done was to make practice conform to principle. The ideal of rigorous mathematics rigorously taught had become a reality. Modern, continental, mathematics was readily available to Cambridge undergraduates by 1850; on the other hand the solid traditional material contained in Euclid was still a preeminent part of the course. Efforts had been made to increase the effectiveness of the university professors, but the colleges were still viewed as the primary and proper centers of undergraduate instruction. If the examination system was too much emphasized, so that students were driven to private tutors in their zeal to compete effectively, still the exams were of a high standard, scrupulously administered, and constantly supervised by the University so as to extract maximum productive effort from the undergraduate. The rationale for curricular dependence on mathematics had been articulated – the discipline was an essential part of a liberal education, training man's faculties toward good mental habits which would be useful to him in whatever later endeavors he undertook. New subjects might come to be taught at the University, and more advanced sciences certainly were already pursued systematically by senior scholars; but mathematics as a central part of an undergraduate education seemed by 1850 to have been defended as an unassailable part of the Cambridge program.

CHAPTER 4

REACTION AGAINST PALEY
AND THE BENTHAMITES

Reforms of the mathematical curriculum, admirable as they were, only touched the small number of students who were pursuing honours. Far more central to the typical undergraduate experience were the courses which made up the ordinary or 'poll' degree, and after about 1820 the material in this curriculum too began to come under scrutiny. Particularly carefully examined were the works that stood at the heart of the general program: the collected writings of the philosopher and natural theologian, William Paley.

Paley had been a Cambridge man himself. In some ways he was the very epitome of an eighteenth-century Cambridge scholar. Practical, unemotional, down-to-earth, he was certainly a good man and an honest divine, but by no means filled with any sort of religious enthusiasm. On the other hand he did evidence a certain political awareness and was sympathetic to the various liberal philosophies developing in England and France during the last part of the eighteenth century. He was even somewhat critical of the established forces operating within the English Church,[1] and as a result was denied the preferment which many people thought his due. If Paley's life reflected the style of the eighteenth century, his works very nearly provided a synopsis of eighteenth-century thought. He made no pretense to be a great creative thinker, but he had a remarkable synthesizing ability. Generous in acknowledging his sources,[2] he summed up the works of others with a style at once so attractive and so clear that his writings captured the imagination of men of his own and successive generations. His works, covering a range of subjects, had an impact on education, particularly at Cambridge, seemingly out of proportion to their inherent worth. After his death, it has been noted,[3] Paley had the distinction of being viewed – like Euclid or Cicero – as a subject rather than as a man.

His three main works were *Natural Theology*, *Principles of Moral and Political Philosophy*, and perhaps best known, *The Evidences of Christianity*. The books are related, although their purposes and subject matter are, of course, not identical. In *The Evidences of Christianity* and *Natural Theology* he examined the external world, in one case through historical analysis, in the other through the study of nature, biology and geology. In both books his aim was to show that 'natural' religion was in harmony with revealed religion, to show that it was believable and indeed probable that the religion revealed to man through the Christian tradition was supported and vindicated in terms of what one could understand from other sources. Almost immediately both of these works achieved great popularity, both because of their appealing and persuasive style and also because they dealt with issues which had been disturbing the public mind for some time. In the late 1700s the whole corpus of Biblical literature had begun to be subjected to rigorous literary analysis. Ultimately this trend would lead to a general skepticism growing out of a humanized and de-mythologized view of the Bible. In Paley's era – much affected by the rationalism of Newton and the skepticism of the French *philosophes* – the historicity of Scripture, particularly in its miraculous aspect, was subjected to logical examination by a number of scholars. The questions raised were puzzling and regarded as threats to traditional religious beliefs. Paley laid such fears to rest. His argument in *The Evidences of Christianity* was based essentially on the believability of the Christian miracles. If Christ healed the sick, fed the multitudes, and – most importantly – rose from the dead, his teachings and his assertions of divinity would have to be accepted. To Paley the fervor and enthusiasm of the early Christians, who 'passed their lives in labours, dangers, and sufferings . . . solely in consequence of their belief in the truth of Christian history',[4] were utterly convincing. No other miraculous tradition had ever been supported so earnestly by contemporary witnesses.[5] Thus, Paley concluded, the supernatural narrative of Christianity was uniquely true. He went on to examine several types of secondary evidence – to compare, for example, Christian stories with those appearing in contemporary, non-Christian sources[6] – and to consider and resolve various problems raised by skeptics.[7] Altogether Paley's book provided a clear, logical, and convincing compendium of the arguments for the truth of the Christian tradition.

Even more troubling questions were raised in 'natural theology', a subject of very great popular interest in the late eighteenth century. The biological sciences and geology had made great strides during the past hundred years, and as the nineteenth century opened, scholars were involved in very heated debates about the evidence uncovered. Geologists in particular had realized that the Mosaic version of creation was very hard to understand literally, since it seemed quite clear that the earth was much older than the four or five thousand years contemplated by Bishop Ussher. An active debate raged about the historicity of the Mosaic deluge, about the method by which the earth had been created, and about the significance and meaning of fossils, particularly those of species now extinct. There was concern about how the crust of the earth had evolved – whether through a series of floods and other catastrophic acts of the Creator or by the gradual process of forces still in operation. To answer these questions Paley wrote his *Natural Theology*.

Teleological from start to finish, the work tried to prove the existence of a beneficent creator through an examination of the evidence available in his acts of creation. Filled with remarkable optimism, Paley managed to explain every item of the natural world in such a way as to reinforce the view of God with which eighteenth-century Englishmen were comfortable. He asserted in essence that the whole of the natural world evidenced design and hence a Designer; that the fitness of organs to their purposes, the organization and symmetry apparent in nature, the suitability of certain environments to the creatures which inhabit them testified to the existence of a divine plan and a divine Planner:

In crossing a heath, suppose I pitched my foot against a *stone* and were asked how the stone came to be there, I might possibly answer that for anything I know to the contrary it had lain there forever; nor would it, perhaps, be very easy to show the absurdity of this answer. But suppose I had found a *watch* upon the ground, and it should be inquired how the watch happened to be in that place, I should hardly think of the answer which I had before given . . . Yet why should not this answer serve for the watch as well as for the stone; why is it not as admissible in the second case as in the first? . . . This mechanism being observed – it requires indeed an examination of the instrument, and perhaps some previous knowledge of the subject, to perceive and understand it; but being once, as we have said, observed and understood – the inference we think is inevitable, that the watch must have had a maker – that there must have existed at some time and at some place or other, an artificer or artificers who formed it for the purpose which we find it actually to answer, who completely comprehended its construction and designed its use.[8]

Furthermore, the essential characteristics of the Creator were also revealed. For to have contrived such a complex watch as the universe and to have kept it running, the Creator would necessarily and logically have the attributes of omnipotence, omniscience, omnipresence, eternity, self-existence, necessary existence, and spirituality.[9] And it could further be shown conclusively that the Deity was one and that he was beneficent.

To deal with the difficult problem of the existence of evil, Paley turned to two basic principles: first, although there are undoubtedly evil effects in the world of nature 'in a vast plurality of instances, in which contrivance is perceived, the *design* of the contrivance is *beneficial*'.[10] Snakes, for example, are venomous not to kill other animals but to provide for their own safety and food.[11] Infants delighting in the pleasure of learning to speak, old cats dozing in the sun, civilized man enjoying a sophisticated meal or young shrimps leaping exuberantly out of the sea all exhibit clearly the overwhelming benevolence of the Creator, and occasional pain or suffering is an accidental, unintended by-product in a complex and essentially joyful creation. Secondly, Paley felt that the Deity, whenever possible, preferred to use pleasure rather than pain to accomplish his purposes; that indeed nature is full of 'excessively' pleasant experiences. Even the apparently painful arrangement whereby animals devour one another is on balance productive of happiness, for it prevents old and weak animals from dying of gradual deterioration, it provides the carnivores with exhilarations of the hunt as well as the palate, and it allows all of nature to indulge itself in the joys of 'superfecundity'.[12]

The beauty of Paley's argument lay in its inclusiveness. All aspects of nature, instead of posing problems as they would later, illustrated characteristics of the Creator: the abilities of animals to function in their particular environments proved God's beneficence; similarities from one species to another, even when maladaptive, illustrated God's orderliness. Evil and suffering were explained away as part of a greater good. Since the emphasis was on the adaptiveness of the world to the needs of God's creatures, and not the other way around, it was unlikely that any new scientific discoveries would shake the synthesis. For God's purposes could always be assumed large enough to encompass even the most anomalous of fossils or vestigal organs.

It seems hard now to believe that Paley's other work, *The Principles of Moral and Political Philosophy*, was ever so popular or influential as were the *Evidences* or the *Natural Theology*, because while the latter two provided somewhat creative solutions to questions troubling the popular imagination, the *Principles* was really little more than a textbook on utilitarianism. Furthermore it was written at about the same time that Bentham was handling the same subject with a great deal of fanfare and shortly after Hume's very intelligent and perceptive treatment; again apparently the charm and clarity of Paley's writing style had a great deal to do with his work's popularity. The *Principles of Moral and Political Philosophy* described a system of morality based on the principle of 'the greatest number', or 'the greatest happiness principle'. Paley did not develop, like Bentham, a calculus of pleasure and pain, but he did assert repeatedly that the morality of an act could be tested in terms of its production of utility or happiness.[13] The only real difference between him and Bentham[14] was that Paley, in calculating human happiness, included pleasure and pain in the hereafter. Thus he included the sanctions of religion – the possibility of eternal punishments or rewards – in his system of morality, so that an act was good not only if it was productive of happiness here on earth but also if it was likely to get its actor into heaven. God was thus brought into the equation: the Good and the Useful could be defined as the Will of God, certified in terms of eternal rewards. There were problems with Paley's formulation: one was that he almost seemed to bring God within the compass of moral rules, rather than viewing Him as the author of them. God, too, seemed to be constrained by the greatest happiness principle. The other difficulty, which did not seem to be very important in the eighteenth century but which began to trouble people more and more throughout the nineteenth, was that Paley's approach seemed intensely selfish, in a peculiar way more so because it included divine sanctions. The Paleyan individual, because he was concerned with his own afterlife, would think much more in terms of his own personal good than of benefits for the community. Paley's philosophy contained little organic, societal emphasis. Nevertheless he brought together the thought of earlier utilitarians like John Gay and Abraham Tucker.[15] And he stated the case for the utilitarian principle clearly and in a way which was attractive to the pragmatic and rather unromantic minds of the late-eighteenth-century Englishmen, particularly those at Cambridge.

That such synthetic and rather prosaic works should have had a very great impact on a university of the stature of Cambridge might at first seem surprising, but on reflection it is not hard to understand. Paley's books were important not as 'research' – an aspect of Cambridge almost completely ignored around 1800 – but as part of the undergraduate curriculum; there, as in any society, one would expect to find not the most modern or advanced but the most basic, elemental, widely believed thought of the age.

As early as 1787 Paley's works formed a central part of the curriculum; in his first year at Cambridge William Wordsworth was required to read *The Principles of Moral Philosophy*.[16] In 1821 and 1822 the examination system was reorganized so as to provide for an honours degree in classics, and at that point the required readings for various programs were explicitly set out: all students during their second year would sit for an examination (the 'Previous') covering either the four Gospels or the Acts of the Apostles, one Greek and one Latin classic, and Paley's *Evidences of Christianity*.[17] Based on their performance, students were designated honours candidates or 'pollmen'; the latter then had to prepare for their degree examination by working up some Euclid, Homer, Cicero and scriptural history as well as Paley's *Principles of Moral Philosophy*.[18] Candidates for mathematical honours were not required to prepare the Homer or Cicero, but – in addition to complicated papers on mathematics – they continued to answer questions on scriptural history and on Paley.[19] Students who, having gotten honours in mathematics, proceeded to the classics honours examination, wrote extensive papers of Greek and Latin translation, composition, and interpretation as well as answering questions on divinity (covering the Bible, Butler's *Analogy*, and Paley's *Natural Theology* and *Evidences*) and logic and moral philosophy (Locke's *Essay on Human Understanding*, Butler's *Preface and Three Sermons* and Paley's *Principles of Moral Philosophy*).[20] Thus, while not providing the most important or most rigorous part of the curriculum, Paley touched everybody, so that later scholars, even those who came to reject his ideas, often spelled out their early debt to his works.[21]

Furthermore Paley's preponderance in the curriculum was not limited to the early part of the nineteenth century. The examination system was not reformed in any radical way until the late forties and fifties, but throughout the intervening years various graces were presented to the Senate to improve it – for example, to raise the standards of the 'Previous', or to strengthen the ordinary degree examination – and in each of these early improved examination systems Paley was still very much in evidence. In 1836 for example, the poll degree continued to require an examination on the *Principles of Political and Moral Philosophy*, and *The Evidences* continued to be an important part of the 'Previous'. In 1843 a committee pointed out with satisfaction that Paley's *Evidences* and his *Moral and Political Philosophy* still formed an important base of the theological curriculum.[22]

However, despite the frequency with which Paley's books were cited, dons at Cambridge – especially the 'moderate reformers' with whom we are most concerned – were not wholly pleased with his influence. Because actual legislative reform was long in coming it would be easy to overlook their growing misgivings, but opposition to Paley certainly existed by the thirties and probably even before. The earliest important public attack came in a sermon delivered by Adam Sedgwick in Trinity College Chapel on Commemoration Sunday in 1832. Sedgwick was very popular with the students, and his sermon – which was down-to-earth and delivered with friendly warmth – had a great impact. A number of undergraduates asked Sedgwick to have his talk published, which he did; indeed, the sermon had gone through five editions by 1850 and came to serve through Sedgwick's middle years as a kind of continuing platform from which he presented his views on various public subjects. The new editions added voluminous introductions and a series of appendices, so that he eventually came to refer to the work as a 'grain of wheat between two millstones'.[23] The grain of wheat, the sermon itself, is what concerns us here, because in it Sedgwick conveyed his attitudes towards the Cambridge curriculum in general.

Sedgwick divided his sermon into three sections, each one dealing with one of the main bodies of material handled in the undergraduate program of study: 'Natural Philosophy' (what we would call 'science'), the classics, and finally – by far the biggest section – 'Moral Philosophy' (in modern terms, the social sciences). Sedgwick expressed general satisfaction with the way science and classical literature were treated. Science or 'natural philosophy' to Cambridge of course, meant almost entirely mathematics – Newtonian physics as conveyed through the use of Euclidean geometry. But in his observations on even so limited a discipline Sedgwick illustrates that in their attitudes to the natural sciences even the reformers of the University were at this point certainly not critical of the Paleyan approach. Paley, of course, was not a scientist; and even his work *Natural Theology* was by no means a science text. Nevertheless, his attitude towards natural phenomena permeated the entire undergraduate curriculum. It is important to see that Sedgwick, though a professional geologist, was just as teleological as Paley. On the issue of nature's purposefulness there was no disagreement whatsoever. Sedgwick could and did advocate understanding nature as fully as possible; but like Paley he assumed that through examining the mechanism one would come to a greater appreciation of the virtues of the mechanic, that the existence of a contrivance would convince the students of the existence and the beneficence of the contriver.

Every being possessing life may first be considered apart from the rest of nature. Its bodily organs are produced by powers of vast complexity and understood only in their effects – confirmed in their operation to the individual being, and entirely separate from the ordinary modes of atomic action. Yet these organs thus elaborated, exhibit throughout a perfect mechanism, in all its parts . . . exactly fitted to the vital functions of the being. Contrivance proves design: in every organic being we survey . . . we see a new instance of contrivance and a new manifestation of an intelligent superintending power.

This proof is so strong that it never has been and never can be gainsaid. It is in vain that we attempt to shut out the belief in an intelligent Creator by referring all phenomena to a connected succession of material causes, not one of which is fully comprehended . . . We do not understand that complicated material action by which the God of nature builds up the organic structure of a sentient being: but we do, in part at least comprehend the adaptation of its mechanism to various ends, and we see those ends, and we see those ends accomplished: and this is enough to **warrant** our conclusion.[24]

Thus, while from the vantage point of the twentieth century it is easy to assume that it was Paley's teleological approach and his rather naive theological attitudes which would make him quickly outdated, it is important to note that in the pre-Darwinian middle part of the nineteenth century this aspect of his work was still commanding acceptance.

On the teaching of the classics, Sedgwick had very little to say. Assuming without question that the classics should form a necessary part of undergraduate study, he examined mainly those aspects of classical study which could have moral benefit. Through reading about ancient man and his social and political problems, students, he observed, would enrich their understanding of moral behavior. The classics could even have religious impact:

It is . . . certain that the study of an ethical system, grounded on the moral and social feelings, and exemplified by that course of action which in all ages has been honoured by the virtuous and the wise, is not only a good practical training for the mind . . . but prepares it for the acceptance of religious truth.[25]

Indeed, despite the fact that they did not have the benefits of the Christian revelation 'many of the writers of antiquity had correct notions on the subject of natural religion. The argument for the being of a God, derived from final causes, is as well stated in the conversations of Socrates, as in the *Natural Theology* of Paley.'[26] Sedgwick did feel that perhaps the University neglected the meaning in classical literature in favor of an emphasis on formalism and pedantic criticism.[27] But in general he was well pleased with the important role the classics played in the undergraduate experience.

It was not until Sedgwick examined the moral philosophy curriculum that he found much amiss. This third section of the *Discourse* really raised the central issues of Sedgwick's sermon, though moral philosophy was certainly not the most important part of the curriculum. There were at least two reasons for this apparently misplaced emphasis: first Sedgwick said little about the sciences or the arts because he was essentially satisfied with the way they were taught, whereas he was very critical of the structure of this third section of the curriculum. Secondly, although moral philosophy was not the basis of an honours tripos, honours graduates were in a very small minority; most of the students in attendance at the Trinity Chapel would have been pollmen who had found moral philosophy a significant part of their program.

Sedgwick criticized in turn each of the two basic Cambridge textbooks in moral philosophy, Locke's *Essay on the Human Understanding*, and Paley's *Principles of Moral and Political Philosophy*. Sedgwick's attack on Locke was rather poorly thought out and quite clearly unphilosophical. Although he was no doubt familiar with Locke, he merely tried, in an openly subjective way, to show those aspects of Locke's *Essay* with which he felt himself out of sympathy. Locke had, in Sedgwick's view, presented a 'degraded' picture of human personality by treating as insignificant those features of character like imagination or conscience which made it possible for man to function as a moral creature. Sedgwick found the *Essay* and its impact on later thought to be mechanistic, amoral, and cold.

In fact, of course, the problem was not that Locke had denied the existence of moral qualities in man, but that they had simply not been part of his subject. The *Essay* had not tried to present a total 'system' of personality but had dealt with only one aspect of man, the way he learns. Sedgwick demanded more from the *Essay* than it had ever pretended to give.

Defenders of Locke – and the sermon received critical attention far beyond the bounds of the University – made Sedgwick's essay look foolish, attacking it rather unfairly as a philosophical work. In those terms there was undoubtedly much to criticize.[28] Nevertheless there was something perceptive in Sedgwick's emotional response to Locke:

With all its faults, the 'Essay on the Human Understanding' is a work of great power . . . Its greatest fault is the contracted view it takes of the capacities of man – allowing him, indeed, the faculty of reflecting and following out trains of thought according to the rules of abstract reasoning; but depriving him both of his powers of imagination and of his moral sense. Hence it produced, I think, a chilling effect on the philosophic writings of the last century: and many a cold and beggarly system of psychology was sent into the world by the authors of the school of Locke; pretending at least, to start from his principles, and to build on his foundations.[29]

Turning to Paley, Sedgwick began by saying how deeply moved and convinced he had been by his earliest reading of the *Principles of Moral and Political Philosophy*.

Truth after truth seemed to flash on the mind with all the force of demonstration – on questions too which, in other hands, seemed only involved in mystery and doubt. On this account, if there be a defective principle in his system, it ought the more boldly to be combated lest the influence of his name and the charm of his philosophic manner, lead us only the farther from the truth.[30]

Sedgwick objected to the *Moral Philosophy* on several levels: Paley was too systematic, reducing very complex and subtle principles which are not really scientific to syllogisms and single rules. For example, it is impossible to know the attributes of God in any kind of logical way, since God is so much larger than anything man's understanding could encompass. Similarly efforts to understand politics or political thought in terms of logical propositions are clearly doomed to failure.[31]

More essentially, perhaps, Sedgwick objected not only to Paley's reductionism but to the particular simple rule which Paley had selected as his base. The principle of utility, the greatest happiness principle, Sedgwick found worldly, selfish, and debased, and unconnected with any serious attempt to understand the will of God.

The utilitarian scheme starts . . . with an abrogation of the authority of conscience – a rejection of the moral feelings as the test of right and wrong. From first to last, it is in bondage to the world, measuring every act by a worldly standard, and estimating its value by worldly consequences. Virtue becomes a question of calculation – a matter of profit and loss; and if man gain heaven at all on such a system, it must be by arithmetical details . . . A conclusion such as this offends against the spirit breathing in every page of the book of life . . .[32]

It may well be that Sedgwick misunderstood Paley, who was neither absolutely secular nor exclusively individualistic. Paley would not have tied man's behavior entirely to a worldly standard. He saw God and God's sanctions as playing an important part in any 'calculation' of virtue, and he certainly felt that it would often be useful for a man to reject his own selfish needs in exchange for a great good.[33] Sedgwick almost willfully ignored any softening moderation in the *Moral Philosophy*; and beyond that – even if he had been correct in his evaluation – he was unfair in lumping together the whole utilitarian school, especially since it was precisely during this period that utilitarianism – as modified by Godwin and then later by John Stuart Mill – was becoming increasingly socially conscious and less centered on the individual. Sedgwick ignored this later movement and in fact seems to have been unaware of it.[34]

Finally, although Sedgwick was a political liberal – at least within the context of Cambridge University – and hardly so paranoid about continental social developments as were many of his contemporaries, there is evidence that a significant part of his concern about utilitarianism grew precisely from the use to which it had been put by political radicals since the late eighteenth century.[35] He objected, without naming him, to Bentham and his universalized, over-simple notion of society; Sedgwick held a more organic Burkean view of social structure, stressing the particular historical experiences which formed any individual social unit.[36] He rejected the idea that utilitarian principles universally applied could explain or improve political behavior; in his own words: 'Universal systems, like universal nostrums, savour more of political quackery than political philosophy.'[37]

In discussing the French *philosophes* Sedgwick objected not only to the excesses to which their ideas had led, but also to what he thought to be the basic underlying assumption: that man is, within the context of a human society, perfectible. He asserted, in keeping with the teachings of orthodox Christianity, that 'no external change of government whatsoever can make [man] approach toward a state of moral perfection – an idle dream of false philosophy, contradicted by all the records of mankind and directly opposed to the word of God'.[38] If the French writers had 'accepted, even in the humblest degree, the doctrines of the religion of Christ, they would never have made such portentous errors in estimating the moral character of man'.[39] In summary, Sedgwick viewed Paleyanism, and utilitarianism in general, as selfish, secular, anti-Christian, and impracticable. The philosophy had had a pernicious influence; Cambridge would be wise to reduce Paley's place in the university curriculum.

Sedgwick's rather practical criticisms received widespread acceptance within the Cambridge community. But there were also more abstract, philosophical forces at work to undermine Paley's influence. Coleridge, a severe critic of utilitarianism and of atomistic views of society was specifically concerned with the University's dependence on Paleyan thought. In his *Aids to Reflection* in 1825 he wrote:

I more than fear the prevailing taste for books of natural theology, physico-theology, demonstrations of God from Nature, and the like. Evidences of Christianity! I am weary of the word. Make a man feel the want of it; rouse him . . . to the self knowledge of his need of it, and you may safely trust to its own evidence – [40]

The poet had a significant influence on some of the brightest young men at Cambridge, particularly the translators of Neibuhr,

Julius Hare[41] and Connop Thirlwall. Undergraduates together during the second decade of the nineteenth century and then teaching fellows at Trinity in the late twenties, Hare and Thirlwall were unusual for their time in being interested in the works of German theological and philosophical writers. Thirlwall translated Schleiermacher's rather skeptical *Essay on St. Luke,* and together they translated the heterodox *History of Rome* by Neibuhr. Familiar with Hegel[42] and with the sophisticated, critical currents of contemporary German theological philosophy, these young men were, not surprisingly, offended by the naive blend of Bible and Paley which passed for theology at Cambridge.

Hare and Thirlwall in turn influenced a number of younger undergraduates, especially a group who came up to Cambridge in the thirties and formed a social club-cum-discussion-group called the Apostles.[43] Included were several young men who would eventually be very influential in what came to be called the Broad Church movement: J. M. Kemble, Frederick Denison Maurice, John Sterling, R. C. Trench, Alfred Tennyson, Richard Monckton Milnes. For the Apostles, opposition to the over-simple Paleyan theology and to Bentham's utilitarian philosophy was an article of faith. Maurice was very strongly opposed to Bentham and to the use of Paley as a text for undergraduates. Within the club he served as a defender of Coleridge's metaphysics and Wordsworth's poetry against the utilitarian teaching.[44] Other members of the group were John Kemble, who almost lost his degree because of his impudently strong criticism of Paley in an examination paper,[45] and Monckton Milnes who later was a liberal member of parliament. On Milnes' election Hare wrote that it would be good to have another M.P. who rejected the 'dregs of utilitarianism' and was prepared to operate on some higher principles.[46]

While these philosophical and poetic influences were at work on the thinking of some of the younger, more literary members of the University, critical attitudes toward Paley continued to spread among the older, practical, scientific scholars. Probably the most influential of such pragmatic reformers was William Whewell. Like Sedgwick – and unlike the Coleridgean school – Whewell found nothing objectionable in Paley's exercises in natural theology. To prove the existence and to demonstrate the beneficent attributes of the Creator through an examination of his works seemed a very reasonable exercise to Whewell; and both as a young man and as a mature scholar he published his own teleological views.[47] But with, respect to Paley's influence on the moral philosophy curriculum Whewell was early and open in his hostility. In 1834 he had dedicated a collection of sermons to Hare, and in thanking him Hare wrote:

What you say . . . about the pernicious influence of our teaching Paley on the morals of the country, I have long thought. May you prosper in substituting something better for him.[48]

Whewell's most substantial expressions of dissatisfaction with Paley were contained in two semi-philosophical works, *Elements of Morality* (1845) and *Lectures on the History of Moral Philosophy in England* (1852).

Like Sedgwick, Whewell was disturbed by Paley's dependence on 'utility' or 'expedience' as the ultimate standard of human behavior. An action ought not merely to be judged as 'useful' – one must know 'useful for what?' Ends, not means, should be important to the moralist; and Paley, Whewell felt, had substituted methods for purposes, thus presenting a debased view of man's nature.

Expedient implies, according to its entymology, a way out of difficulties. But Morality places before us a higher object than merely to escape from difficulties. She teaches us to aim at what is right.[49]

Utilitarianism was based on a desire to substitute relative, earthly standards for absolute, divine ones.[50] Thus, according to Whewell:

[Paley] tears the notion of obligation loose from the idea of duty. We are obliged when we are impelled by the will of another: not, as hitherto, when we are commanded by Him whose commands we know to be right; – but by the will of *another* – *any* other . . . Such was the consequence of Paley's disposition to represent everything in a practical form. And thus obligation ceases to have any connexion with what we *ought* to do; and indeed to have any moral aspect whatever. In previous ways of treating the subject, the circle of our duties and obligations, or any part of it, was not deformed, because it was referred to its natural centre, the central idea of God. But the centre of the line which represents Paley's obligation is arbitrary and variable; and thus would tend to disfigure and confound the form of duty.[51]

Furthermore, even had 'expediency' or the greatest happiness principle provided an adequately elevated standard for human behavior, utilitarianism would still not have been, in Whewell's view, a practical way of arriving at moral judgments. It would be impossible, he thought, to estimate accurately the effects of any particular action; calculations of 'expediency' would be so complex as to be useless, especially, he insisted, since pleasures differed qualitatively as well as quantitively.[52] Utilitarians admitted, of course, that minute-to-minute decisions about expediency would be impossibly difficult, and laid down general rules for human behavior; but the rules themselves were based on general interpretations of utility. Even this principle Whewell rejected, feeling that it was impossible to prove that human happiness would be increased by the general acceptance of particular rules. For example, 'The Rules, *to be temperate* and *to be truthful*, are not established by showing that they lead to the greatest amount of Human Happiness; for we have no means of estimating the amount of Human Happiness which results from any given hypothesis.'[53]

Of course, the fact that it is difficult to estimate all the effects of an individual act never keeps us, under any system of morality, from making decisions and attempting to evaluate our own behavior, as Whewell's critics, particularly John Stuart Mill,[54] were quick to point out. Furthermore, Whewell's own attempts to define an absolute moral standard were certainly no more rational than those of the utilitarians. He tended to italicize words and to capitalize abstract terms in a seeming effort to impart meaning to his sentences, but his rolling periods circled back on themselves without really solving the problems he saw in the work of Bentham and Paley.[55] Nevertheless it is obvious that there was some validity in Whewell's criticisms of utilitarian method. Almost no one today would regard seriously a moral system which, like Bentham's 'calculus', tried to assign quantitative values to the pleasant or painful experiences of life, especially if such a system failed to consider the qualitative differences among various types of feelings and motives. And in a complex industrial society the difficulty of estimating the long-range effects of any individual action is not so trivial or unimportant as Whewell's critics would have made it appear.[56] Without providing really satisfactory answers, the Master of Trinity at least asked several of the right questions.

There was another side to Whewell's distress with Paley and the utilitarians: he felt that their philosophy was potentially subversive of established society, of the State. Whewell was by no means a reactionary, as can be seen from his attitudes toward university reform. But he did want reform and improvement to come gradually and peaceably, and he was very much opposed to any efforts to change the established order through the use of force.

Every Christian [in a constitutional state] may and ought to exert his constitutional Rights, so far as they extend, both to preserve the State and the Laws from all needless and hasty innovation, and to effect such improvements as both time and circumstances require; using the light of Religion as well as of Morality and Polity, to determine what really is improvement.[57]

The laws of [no] State allow the citizens to have recourse to arms for the sake of bettering the Constitution; . . . Not that we allow that despotic Governments are never to be improved; but they are not, as a general Rule, to be improved by armed insurrections, but by improving the condition of the people; by promoting the moral and intellectual culture of the Governed and of the Governors.[58]

Whewell liked the world more or less the way it was and he viewed with alarm the cavalier way in which the utilitarians seemed to treat the safeguards of the established order. In reality Paley was hardly more radical than Whewell, a fact which the latter philosopher recognized.[59] But Paley's tone was much more cynical and potentially disruptive to society than was Whewell's.[60] And the don was offended and troubled by Paley's lack of reverence for the constitution and his stress on its mere 'usefulness':

He rejects the notion of such fundamental laws, as having any peculiar force and speaks with slight of those who 'ascribe a kind of transcendental authority or mysterious sanctity to the Constitution, as if it were founded on some higher original than that which gives force and obligation to the ordinary Statutes of the realm, or were inviolable on any other account than its intrinsic utility.' Now the persons who have ascribed and exalted authority to the English Constitution, have spoken of it with reverence, and have defended it as inviolable, are all the greatest statesmen, lawyers, and patriots, who have adorned this country; and in proportion to their ability, their legal knowledge, and their patriotism, they have been copious, earnest, and pointed, in appealing to the principles of the Constitution as something of paramount authority and value. They have ascribed to the Constitution, not so properly a 'mysterious sanctity' which Paley speaks of, as a moral sacredness: . . . When a writer is thus led by his doctrines to speak contemptuously of the emotions of moral reverence and affection which have thus prevailed for generations, in the nation and the race, he cannot be, to them, a moral teacher; and as far as he gains their attention, he can only perplex them.[61]

Whewell himself took a more organic, Burkean view of national history and the Constitution.[62] And he explained his own essential conservatism in terms of an unwillingness to rush into ill-thought-out 'progress', progress unconnected with the roots and traditions of the nation.

During the course of the first half of the nineteenth century, then, Cambridge University gradually turned away from the guidance of William Paley. Testimony to this change in attitude is provided not only in the philosophical writings of Cambridge dons but in the memoirs of undergraduates. When Maurice went to Cambridge in 1823 Benthamism was 'the prevalent faith among the clever undergraduates, especially at Trinity'.[63] By 1845, however, Charles Astor Bristed would describe the University's approach to ethics as of the 'anti-Paley or independent moralist' school.[64] Examination reforms also indicated that Paley's influence was receding: his works were gradually pushed out of the honours curriculum into the 'poll' or the 'Previous' examinations, and by the fifties only the *Evidence of Christianity* was retained in any form.

Had this gradual rejection of the influence of a distinguished alumnus been based on genuine, intellectually valid considerations? To the extent that scholars like Maurice, Hare, Thirlwall, and Grote had been influenced by Coleridge and a familiarity with the sophisticated theological thought of Germany, Cambridge's turning away from Paley represented a definite positive step, part of the process which would lead eventually to the development of the flexible and creative 'Broad Church movement'. And even the philosophically less sophisticated Sedgwick and Whewell were on solid ground in some areas, as when they objected to the non-organic view of political life which the early utilitarians had held. By and large, however, Cambridge dons seem to have rejected Paley not so much because they found him philosophically unsound as because his writings no longer appealed to their sense of what was seemly, to what one could call their aesthetics. Writing almost as embodiments of what we now might view as the 'Victorian Spirit', the Cambridge dons were determined that their ethical systems be not so much rigorously logical as obviously and solemnly righteous. The eighteenth-century *sang-froid* of Paley (who had once observed in some political connection that he could not afford to keep a conscience)[65] was no longer acceptable. The university clerics insisted that the tone of moral philosophy should be earnest and serious; and while they by no means wanted any drastic reforms in underlying social structure, they rejected the outward forms which would interpret man's behavior in what they called 'debased' ways. It is thus not surprising that Sedgwick and Whewell contributed little that was original to the progress of moral thought in England or that they ignored almost completely the more recent movements within utilitarianism. Nevertheless, by reflecting the mid-century attitudes of thoughtful Englishmen they stimulated responses in other thinkers more creative than they; even Mill cites his reaction to the writings of Sedgwick and Whewell, together with his much more famous essays on Coleridge and Bentham, as marking significant steps in his development of a personal view of utilitarian thought.[66]

Thus by rejecting the teachings of William Paley and by removing his works from the curriculum, Cambridge University gave an indication of where British thought was at mid-century, and helped clear the decks for the varied and more creative social philosophies which were to emerge.

CHAPTER 5

RELIGION AND LITERATURE: TOWARD THE BROAD CHURCH

Oxford and Cambridge had traditionally been viewed as 'Seminaries of Sound Learning and Religious Education',[1] and the exclusive legal connection between the old English universities and the Established Church was deeply rooted in British history. As the nineteenth century wore on, this relationship came ever more sharply into question. The Church itself was failing to satisfy the needs of an increasing number of people; the universities were patently doing an inadequate job of teaching theology and educating clergymen; and the exclusive admissions standards came more and more to be criticized for denying the benefits of 'national' institutions to a large segment of the nation. The process of 'opening' the old universities was a slow one, by no means completed by mid-century. But with respect to religion as in other matters, Sedgwick, Whewell, and their friends were tolerant and in favor of moderate reform. During their period of leadership Cambridge made a good beginning toward freeing itself from rigid sectarian control.

The earliest question of religious toleration to attract the University's attention had to do not with its own regulations but with the extension of general political rights, with Catholic emancipation. In the very early part of the century, with religious questions much disturbing popular opinion, the University twice refused to succumb to the hysterical cry of popery and elected public officials who were at least moderates on the Catholic issue.[2] The University as a whole was probably about as conservative as the country at large, mustering in 1812, for example, a small majority vote for a petition against Catholic relief. But the men who would lead later reform movements were already expressing religious toleration, opposing the sending of anti-Catholic petitions and supporting parliamentary candidates who were liberal on this issue.[3] And when the actual political decision to seat Catholics in Parliament was reached in 1829, the more liberal faction at Cambridge expressed strong support for the government.[4] Total open-mindedness towards papists was, however, by no means achieved during the early nineteenth century – most of even the liberal Cambridge dons were disgusted by Newman's conversion to Rome,[5] and as late as 1856 an alarmist flysheet described the possible opening of the University to Catholics as 'delivering up a principal fortress of the Reformation to the Church of Rome'.[6]

Catholic emancipation might be a straw in the wind, but of much more immediate concern to the Cambridge community was the issue of admitting non-Anglicans to university privileges, especially to the taking of degrees. Unlike Oxford, where undergraduates were required to subscribe the Thirty-Nine Articles at matriculation, Cambridge demanded no religious test upon admission, and so there had for some time been a handful of dissenters in attendance at the colleges. To take a degree, however, students had to swear that they were bona fide members of the Church of England, so that many practical benefits were denied to dissenters, even to those who had distinguished themselves in their academic careers.

The possibility of abolishing the religious tests raised several issues: first, what was the historical connection between the Establishment and the Universities? How much ought Cambridge to be bound by the will (and wills) of its founders? To an extent probably surprising to the modern reader, spokesmen on all sides of the issue assumed that the historical argument was an important one, and scholars for and against the admission of dissenters turned to the past for guidance.

On the one hand the Elizabethan statutes – to which most of the colleges traced either their foundations or their re-foundations[7] – very explicitly established a strong tie between the University and the Anglican Church.[8] Just as the newly established Church had been styled 'national', so were the universities 'national institutions', necessarily excluding those Englishmen who did not accept the political settlement of the religious controversy. On the other hand it could be argued that the founders of at least the pre-Elizabethan colleges (thirteen of those seventeen existing in 1840) had donated their money for the support not so much of the national Church as of the Christian – that is, in the middle ages, the Roman Catholic – Church. Was it just that the original beneficiaries of the founders should be systematically excluded from their benefits?[9] Furthermore, the concept of 'national' had changed since the time of the

Reformation. There was no longer an assumption that the body-politic must encompass a particular religious communion. Dissenters stressed the need to make available to the whole country the assets of these important historical institutions.[10] A dissenters' petition to Parliament in 1834, for example, mentioned exclusion from the universities along with

a want of general registration, difficulties in the solemnization of marriages, the difficulties in the burial of their dead, . . . and their liabilities to the payment of rates and other compulsory levies for the maintenance of the Established Church [as the] principal practical grievances under which they laboured.[11]

The rising tide of democracy made it seem likely that university privileges would be extended with or without university cooperation: 'Was it not better and wiser', argued Thomas Spring Rice, the Cambridge M.P., 'that those advantages which the Dissenters justly claimed should be freely and liberally conceded by the members of the University, than that they should be extorted from them by importunity and clamour?'[12]

No doubt the legal-historical argument for exclusion did have real force, for the various officers of the University and colleges had all sworn oaths to uphold the ancient constitution, oaths which really demanded that Cambridge degrees be reserved for Anglicans.[13] On the other hand it was apparent that many of the other oaths binding the University were unenforced and seriously outdated. (In large part the problem came from the fact that the early rules had been designed to restrain students of a much younger age; school-boy regulations obviously could not be, and were not, enforced for a student body made up of young men.) As W. J. Conybeare wrote in 1841:

It cannot be necessary, so soon after the appearance of Dr. Peacock's interesting work, to remind any member of the University, that our daily life here is one continued and systematic violation of the letter of the ancient statutes. Yet those statutes we are all sworn to obey. How do we reconcile that apparent inconsistency between our oaths and our conduct . . . [except by] understanding that we swear to obey the statutes only so far forth as they are enforced by the competent authorities? . . . It is surely singular that at the present moment, when so strong a light has been so lately thrown upon the history and character of our statutes, and when their total want of assimilation with our present conduct has been so forcibly proved, an isolated portion of these statutes should be brought forward as an authority for regulating detail in our practice.[14]

Although mid-century Cambridge men may not have said so explicitly, they were in the process of discovering, as Lewis Campbell would write of them fifty years later, 'that oaths and subscriptions imposed in one century can have no binding force in an altered world, but are an inert and fruitless burden on the consciences of succeeding generations'.[15]

A second, more practical, problem arose with the possibility of admitting dissenters: graduation and succeeding to the degree of Master of Arts implied not merely academic recognition but a permanent right to participate in the government of the University. Fellows of the colleges were elected from among the graduates, and the ecclesiastical livings which the colleges controlled were in turn doled out to the fellows. It seemed to many conservatives that to admit dissenters meant inevitable secularization and the disestablishment of the Church.

Other inroads of the Dissenters may be easily forseen. The Cambridge petitioners do not advocate any interference with the statutes of the colleges – colleges, therefore, are for the present to be allowed to close the door against the admission of nonconformists to fellowships ... But ... must not this barrier . . . give way before the spirit they are creating? Suppose a Dissenter to take the highest honours; let him be senior wrangler and medalist, or double first classman; with what grace can his college turn him adrift on the world without a provision, whilst it is at the same moment admitting to its preferments persons altogether his inferiors? . . . It is easy to imagine the blasts of Alecto which will be sounded upon this subject by all the popular organs of the day – from the hustings – from the House of Commons – from the newspaper office. Now we ask of those who, whilst they advocate the Dissenters' claims to degrees in the University, profess to patronage, where is the wisdom of thus driving the colleges into a corner – placing them in a position which cannot fail of exposing them to public obloquy?[16]

Christopher Wordsworth thought that to admit dissenters would be to change the whole nature of university government;[17] the Bishop of Exeter argued in the House of Lords that to open the universities was to 'persecute' the Church;[18] and in debate in the House of Commons the M.P. for Cambridge said that through such a move the House would 'take upon itself to unchristianize the country'.[19] In part what all this furor meant was that dons feared that the

extended church patronage presently in the gift of the universities
might be thrown open to the country at large, and that the very
comfortable way in which the colleges could make financial provi-
sions for their own members would be disrupted.[20] Furthermore,
as fellows, dissenters would be members of the Senate, and it was
widely assumed that they would work toward the secularizing of the
University. As the *Quarterly Review* prophesied:

It is our belief, therefore, that after the concessions proposed, not a great
many years would elapse before the universities would be made up of a
multitude of sects, amongst which the Church of England would be but
as one.[21]

Even supporters of the dissenters agreed that once admitted to
degrees they would have to be allowed to participate in the government of the University; but it was asserted that the colleges would
retain their control in religious matters and that the Church would
not be harmed in any substantial way. George Pryme argued in
Parliament thus:

Although the concessions prayed for would give the Dissenters a vote
in the Senate, and in the administration of the general affairs of the
University, yet the details of education, and matters of minor consideration, are entirely under the direction and control of the different colleges,
and are not governed by the senate of the University. The concession
would not, therefore, interfere in the least degree, with the course of
academical instruction and discipline of the University.[22]

Many conservatives expressed fear that the religious life of the
University would be disrupted by the intrusion of nonconformists;
the teaching of theology, it was asserted, would become impossible,[23]
college chapel would have to be abandoned,[24] and the students
would be troubled by painful religious strife and, eventually, skepticism.[25] Moderates like Sedgwick responded to this worry by assuring
the university community that the numbers of dissenters involved
would be small, that colleges could continue to regulate their own
internal practice, and that the important religious functions of the
University could continue unchanged:

A man is not to come up [enroll] as a Dissenter; he is not to be considered
as such by any official college act; he must conform to discipline, and we
give him a degree without exacting subscription. A moderate, well-
informed Dissenter will come up under such a system . . . and he will take
a degree. A bigot – a man who would haggle about organs and surplices –

will and must keep away, and we do not want him. A right to a degree without signing a test does not do away with the necessity of discipline, or of conforming to college rules; nor does it give . . . any right of admission [to the colleges] which is not sanctioned by the voluntary acts of the admitting officers . . . [Re: college chapel] A Dissenter knows our organization when he comes up, and if the advantages of our education have induced him to conform during the years past, *a fortiori* he will be willing to conform when he can thereby have also the advantage of a degree . . . Again, I affirm with perfect confidence that the operation of the Bill implies no change whatsoever in the college lectures. We have had amongst us during the last twenty years Roman Catholics, Methodists, Presbyterians, Quakers, Congregationalists of every shade, and they all attended lectures, and never, I believe made a single objection to a lecture given in College.[26]

More radical dons pursued a different line of argument, one which caused some embarrassment to their more moderate allies. Connop Thirlwall asserted that the admission of dissenters could do little harm to religious life at the University because religion was already at an extremely low ebb. He would insist

that our colleges are not theological seminaries: that they are so far from being dedicated exclusively or principally to the study of theology, that among all the branches of learning cultivated in them there is none which occupies a smaller share of our time and attention . . . I cannot even attach any great importance, in this respect, to that relation between the Tutor and his pupils . . . In whatever other point of view a college Tutor may be considered as standing in the room of a parent, I am afraid that it would be a somewhat exaggerated idea of the intimacy of this relation, to suppose that he commonly thinks it a part of his duty, to inquire into the state of his pupil's religious feelings or habits, or that their intercourse is one of the ordinary means by which religion is communicated to our students . . . [Even if the compulsory chapel service were perfectly decorous, which Thirlwall argued it was not] I should still think that the best which could be said of it, would be, that at the end it leaves everyone as it found him, and that the utmost religion could be hope from it, would be to suffer no incurable wounds.[27]

Undoubtedly there was much truth in Thirlwall's assertions; but most even of the reforming party felt that his washing of dirty linen in public was a bad tactic.[28] No doubt religious reform of the universities was also needed, but most dons did not want such improvement to come from outside, and to discuss questions of internal discipline along with the dissenters' grievances was to confuse the issue.

In any case, concern for the opening of the universities, whether or not coupled with general religious improvement, was a central part of the moderate reformers' program during the first half of the century. The issue came to public attention several times: in 1818–19 when James E. Smith, the president of the Linnean Society and a Fellow of the Royal Academy, was forbidden to deliver a course of botany lectures because he was a dissenter;[29] in 1827 when George Dyer published a study of the Cambridge statutes and argued for the admission of nonconformists;[30] in 1833 when the Regius Professor of Physic argued publicly that the exclusiveness of Cambridge was driving many very good prospective doctors to the University of London.[31]

In 1834 there was a 'furious discussion about the admission of dissenters into the university'.[32] Partly concerned lest the democratic spirit engendered by the Reform Bill should force public action and take the initiative away from the University and in part because of a general agitation in the country for the relief of religious disabilities, a group of Cambridge men began seeking reform. When two attempts to have the removal of subscription debated in the Senate were vetoed by the Caput, a group of sixty-two resident members of the University got up a petition to Parliament asking for the abrogation

by legislative enactment [of] every religious test exacted from members of the University before they proceed to degrees, whether of bachelor, master, or doctor, in Arts, Law, and Physic.[33]

Conservative members of the University responded by organizing a 'Declaration' asserting that they approved of the existing restrictions and would vigorously resist any effort to alter them. These two documents provided the occasion for extended discussion in both Houses of Parliament,[34] and after a short interval were followed by a Bill

to grant to His Majesty's subjects generally the right of admission to the English Universities, and to equal eligibility to Degrees therein, notwithstanding their diversities of religious opinion, Degrees in Divinity alone excepted.[35]

The Bill passed the House of Commons, but it was thrown out by the Lords on the second reading.[36] After the legislative defeat the debate lost much of its heat, but not before Connop Thirlwall had been forced to leave the University. Almost immediately, however, the Whig government appointed Thirlwall to an ecclesiastical living in Yorkshire, from which he went on to become the rather unorthodox Bishop of St David's and an influential member of the episcopal bench. Christopher Wordsworth, on the other hand, the extremely conservative Master of Trinity who forced Thirlwall out, found himself increasingly unpopular in his college[37] and not many years later resigned his office and went into obscure retirement. The future, obviously, belonged to the more liberal faction.

In 1835 the subscription issue was discussed again, at a more abstract level, by F. D. Maurice, who argued in a little book called *Subscription No Bondage*, that predefined religious guidelines could be an aid, not a hindrance, to general education. His argument, however, was mainly directed towards practice at Oxford (where students had to subscribe to the Articles on matriculation) and in any case was too subtle to have much practical effect.[38] Occasional ineffective efforts toward reform continued to be made, as when in 1842 Whewell as Vice-Chancellor proposed a Grace benefiting dissenters,[39] or when in 1843 W. D. Christie proposed another Bill

to abolish certain oaths and subscriptions in the Universities of Oxford and Cambridge, and to extend education in the Universities to persons who are not members of the Church of England.[40]

The Bill was defeated overwhelmingly on the first reading. Moderates at the University continued to be concerned for the removal of restrictions,[41] but it became increasingly clear that the problem was inextricably linked with a general reform of the University statutes, a reform which could not really be accomplished without the intervention of Parliament. The next two decades, therefore, were spent more in a general revision of university and college laws than in working for the admission of dissenters; it was not in fact until 1871 that all religious restrictions were finally removed from Cambridge regulations.

The early-nineteenth-century movement toward religious toleration in the University was in some ways paradoxical. The dons active in the campaign – Sedgwick, Airy, Whewell, Thirlwall, Maurice – were devout members of the Church of England, most of them in religious orders. None of them wanted to diminish the influence of the national Church, and none of them wanted to turn the University into a secular institution. They sincerely asserted again and again that to open Cambridge to non-Anglicans would necessitate neither a change in university government and practice, nor a transformation of the religious tone of the institution. What they proposed was a conservative reform. They would give the dissenters the real advantages of the right to degrees and hope that that would satisfy them; the legal connection between the University and the Church would be maintained.[42] In a process which, from hindsight, seems inevitable, however, the reform movement quickly overstepped the boundaries imposed by its early advocates. Once the obstacles of various antiquated statutes had been swept out of the way by the University Commission of the 1850s, a much more widespread religious tolerance seemed possible. Undergraduates were freed from religious tests in 1856; and almost immediately a movement to open fellowships and posts in university government began.[43] Some of the most influential and attractive scholars of the second half of the century – John Grote, Henry Fawcett, Leslie Stephen, Henry Sidgwick[44] – took up the cry of reform in a more extreme version. By the late sixties they had succeeded in crystallizing university opinion behind the concept of an almost completely open government. Such a government was established by the passage of the University Tests Act of 1871.[45]

A good measure of the continuity and evolution of feeling on this subject can be seen in Clark's description of Sedgwick's participation in a meeting in 1869:

Sedgwick, as one of the few survivors of those who had made an unsuccessful movement in the same direction in 1834, was of course invited to be present. It was a question respecting which his opinions had undergone no change, and he eagerly accepted the invitation. The first resolution was proposed by the Master of Trinity W. H. Thompson:

> That in the opinion of the meeting the time has come for settling the question of University Tests; that the mode in which the question is dealt with in the Permissive Bill introduced by Sir J. Coleridge [a Bill which would have given the colleges the right but not the obligation to open their fellowships] is open to grave objections; and that any measure designed to effect such a settlement should include an enactment that no declaration of religious belief or profession shall be required of any layman on obtaining a Fellowship, or as a condition of its tenure.

This was seconded by Sedgwick, who . . . ended with some such words as these: 'Though I have outlived my friends, and now belong to no party, I have not outlived my love of liberty. I believe that the removal of tests would tend to perpetuate our great institutions. Fears have been expressed of the possible predominance of Dissenters. That is a white-livered opinion. If Dissenters should command a predominance of the intellect of the nation, let them take the place to which they are entitled. I am a Churchman because I believe the Church of England to be right; but I deprecate the University hiding itself in any little nook of prejudice out of the general spirit of the community.' This was Sedgwick's last appearance on a public occasion in Cambridge.[46]

It could be argued, in contrast to Clark's assertion, that Sedgwick's opinions had undergone very considerable change, although to be sure gradual change, and that all the worst fears of the conservatives of 1834 had come to fruition. When the *Quarterly Review* in 1834 had warned that it would be impossible for the colleges to elect inferior Anglicans to fellowships, passing over the superior qualifications of outstanding dissenters, Sedgwick and his friends had responded confidently that by no means would such radical changes grow out of their reform program.[47] But by 1880 Benjamin Jowett, the Master of Balliol, Oxford, was writing to his M.P.:

I think that after provision has been made for the chapel services and the religious education of undergraduates, all clerical restrictions should be abolished.

It is an invidious thing, partaking of the nature of a bribe, to elect an inferior man because he is willing to take Orders, to reject a superior man because he is unwilling.

It is a bad thing both for the colleges and the clerical profession that the management of the colleges should pass into the hands of inferior men because they are clergymen . . . The attempt to maintain clerical restrictions is an anachronism in the present state of Oxford opinion.[48]

In the words of a twentieth-century historian of Cambridge:

These fears [of the early-nineteenth-century conservatives] may have been exaggerated, but they were not entirely without foundation; and it is not impossible that if the men who entertained them were alive today they might deplore the neglect of certain religious ordinances, and be unable to distinguish our religious peace from the peace of the tomb.[49]

Obviously it is impossible to resist the flow of historical change, and there were clearly many factors besides the abolition of university tests which contributed to the secularization of Victorian England. But it seems at least possible to conclude that those who genuinely wanted to preserve the status quo were right in trying vigorously to preserve it, and that the proverbial thin-end-of-the-wedge could indeed be a formidable instrument.

In the course of the debate about tests the issue of Cambridge's position as a theological seminary was raised several times (most frequently by those trying to show that Cambridge was so ineffective in this area that the admission of dissenters would make no difference). It was easy to show that early in the century theology was a comparatively insignificant part of the curriculum[50] and that even the inadequate arrangements which existed were frequently subject to abuse.[51] The mere contrast between reality and the conservative rhetoric about 'seminaries of sound learning and religious education' would have been bad enough; but in the light of the hard fact that throughout the century a large majority of alumni did indeed become Anglican clergymen,[52] the neglect of theological training became a real scandal.

Several factors combined to keep theology in the background. Probably most important was the preeminence of mathematics – it was very widely felt that mathematics was the particular pride of the University and that no other subject should be allowed to compete with it for the students' time or attention. Further, theology had always been provided for through university funds (the various professoriates) so that an attempt to strengthen it might seem to be a threat to college power;[53] certainly the colleges, especially the small ones, would find it difficult to provide adequate teaching staff for any kind of significantly diversified curriculum. Precisely because theology was a traditional part of the University it was bound about with ancient custom, much of it deleterious. The Regius Professorships of Divinity and Hebrew had been founded by Henry VIII in 1540, and over the intervening centuries much questionable practice had developed around them. The posts came to be attached to clerical livings, so that the professors were often absent from the University. Even when present they were sometimes ill-qualified.

It is not perhaps of much moment that the electors did not always conduct the examination of the candidates in the prescribed way and sometimes did not examine them at all [during the eighteenth century]; but the total neglect by the Professors of their obligation to lecture was a grave scandal, and there were other less serious infractions.[54]

The Lady Margaret Chair in Divinity, also founded during the

Reformation period, had become by the nineteenth century a nearly perfect sinecure;[55] while the late-eighteenth-century bequest of John Hulse was used only to maintain the nearly formal posts of Christian Advocate and Christian Preacher. Only the Norrisian Professorship, not founded until the end of the eighteenth century, was a genuine means for theological instruction, as the bishops required Cambridge candidates for ordination to certify that they had attended a certain number of the Norrisian lectures.[56]

The combination of these problems made it very difficult for the University to carry out an effective internal reform of the divinity curriculum. Although some of the original proposals for the classical tripos could have included significant amounts of theology, that reform when finally instituted in 1822 was very nearly purely literary.[57] Some outcry about the sorry state of Cambridge theology was raised in 1833–34, mainly in connection with the agitation to remove the tests,[58] but it was not until the 1840s that a systematic reform began. George Peacock's 1841 book on the university statutes called attention to the need:

At least one-half of the students in the university are designed for the church, and no provision (the lectures of the Norrisian professor alone excepted) is made for their professional education; this is a deficiency in our academical system, which, in the present state of public opinion on this important subject, it will be impossible long to overlook. We believe that there are few members in the university who are not prepared for the adoption of the most prompt and decisive measures for the effectual remedy of so great an evil.[59]

In the same year several members of the Senate proposed improvements in the theological curriculum. James Hildyard, a tutor at Christ's, preached a sermon in which he recommended that clergymen stay two extra terms after the B.A. to study theology, and that more voluntary lectures be provided for undergraduates.[60] Charles Perry, an assistant tutor at Trinity, agreed that postgraduate study should be instituted and would have been prepared to reduce the undergraduate residency requirement to expedite the young theologian's progress. Perry was also concerned that the practical aspects of the clerical role should be prepared for, and would have established a chair in 'Pastoral Theology' and instituted a kind of clerical internship after graduation, using the post of deacon for training.[61] There were even suggestions made that separate post-graduate theological colleges be established; removed from the University, such institutions could provide the concentrated training called for, while avoiding the bad influences and the 'low moral tone' of Cambridge.[62] Most Cambridge reformers, however, preferred to keep theological teaching within the University, where it traditionally belonged: there were many clerical candidates already there, the critical intellectual atmosphere mediated against extreme views or heresy, and the presence of non-clerical students was a 'liberalizing' force.[63]

But improvement was unquestionably necessary. During the next two years the University debated various aspects of the suggestions made by Perry, Hildyard, and others,[64] and in 1843 a Syndicate appointed 'to consider whether any and what steps should be taken to provide a more efficient system of theological instruction in the University' recommended a rather far-reaching reform.[65] The Previous examination and ordinary degree examination would be changed to include more theological material, and even the honours candidates would be required to answer a few questions on ecclesiastical history and moral philosophy. But more important, a voluntary post-graduate examination would be made available, through which clerical candidates could demonstrate a much more extensive familiarity with religious subjects. The success of such an examination obviously depended on the seriousness with which it was viewed by the church hierarchy; fortunately the bishops began requiring it of their applicants and it shortly 'ceased to be voluntary except in name'.[66] When by 1848, as part of a general effort to improve the effectiveness of the university professoriate, the Senate required candidates for the theological examination to have attended lectures of the divinity professors,[67] Cambridge was well on its way towards a respectable program of religious education. The establishment of a tripos in theology would have been a big improvement, but that would have to wait for a later day.

The general religious atmosphere at Cambridge is, of course, harder to describe than the specific legal structures in which it operated. Even with the new examinations and the increasingly open religious discussion generated by the dissenters question, Cambridge at no point in the early nineteenth century could be described as a center of religious ferment or enthusiasm.

There were, to be sure, some active High Churchmen in Cambridge during the middle part of the century. But whereas in

Oxford High Church sentiment led to Tractarianism, the Oxford Movement, and – ultimately for some – to Rome, in Cambridge its only concrete manifestation was a short-lived antiquarian society which fell into disrepute and was disbanded while trying to agree on a proper approach to the restoration of the Church of St Sepulchre.[68] To be sure, Charles Simeon and the Evangelicals represented a powerful though minority voice in Cambridge, especially during the early years of the nineteenth century. Simeon's church was usually full on Sundays and his rooms became the focus of a social group which spent many serious hours discussing religious questions. In 1811 with his help a group of undergraduates joined some of the senior members of the University in forming a society for the distribution of Bibles.[69] And Simeon used his influence on his young followers to develop an informal system of instruction in the art of sermon writing and preaching. Evangelicalism, however, was never the majority opinion in nineteenth-century Cambridge. By the 1840s the nickname 'Sim' was often used as a term of opprobrium; and the students of St Catharine's and Queens', where 'enthusiasm' was more common than at some of the other colleges, were frequently ridiculed for the intensity of their feelings.[70] Cambridge men by and large prided themselves on their cool-headed, dispassionate temperaments – nurtured, they would argue, by their solid, mathematically-based curriculum.[71]

On the other hand, there was a great deal of free and open discussion of religious topics. 'The Apostles', a very prestigious social club which numbered many of the brightest undergraduates among its members, had as its purpose the investigation and discussion of topics in 'higher philosophy'.[72] In arguing that religious discussion would not disturb the University, Connop Thirlwall described the Apostles:

You may be alarmed when I inform you that there has long existed in this place a society of young men . . . in which all subjects of highest interest, without any exclusion of those connected with religion, are discussed with the most perfect freedom . . . the members of this society for the most part, have been and are amongst the choicest ornaments of the University, and . . . some are now among the ornaments of the Church, and so far from having had their affections embittered, their friendships torn and lacerated, their union has been rather one of brothers than of friends.[73]

This group included during its heyday – the late twenties and the thirties – Alfred Tennyson, Richard Monckton Milnes (later Lord Houghton), John Sterling, John Kemble, Arthur Henry Hallam, and Frederick Denison Maurice, among others; it is not surprising that the conversation was brilliant, or that it touched upon the most profound subjects. But, no matter how fundamental, all topics were handled dispassionately and intellectually. Thirlwall and Hare (though as graduate fellows they served as 'advisors' rather than as active members) were instrumental in determining the direction of the society's investigations.

The members learned from these authorities never 'to take anything upon trust (always excepting the great mysteries of our faith, which rest on a different footing altogether)', according to Henry Alford. Such scepticism was, perhaps, necessary, because they discussed such weighty problems as 'the Origin of Evil', 'Ghosts', 'the Derivation of Moral Sentiments', 'Prayer', 'the Personality of God', and 'Is an Intelligible First Cause Deducible from the Phenomena of the Universe?'[74]

The *sang-froid* of Thirlwall and Hare in connection with theological questions has been mentioned above; and while most of the Apostles became committed leaders of the Church, their commitment exhibited a flexible open-minded character developed during their undergraduate days. With their liberal attitudes they formed the nucleus for a new central party within the Church; 'the Apostles Club was the cradle of the Broad Church movement'.[75]

What were the characteristics of their general theological position? In 1853 W. J. Conybeare[76] wrote an article in the *Edinburgh Review* which provided a clear definition of 'Broad Church':

Its distinctive character is the desire of comprehension. Its watchwords are Charity and Toleration. Its adherents love the Church of England for that very peculiarity which has most provoked the criticism of her detractors. She is reproached by Rome with Puritanism, by Geneva with Popery . . . Her catholic [Broad Church] sons, on the contrary, consider this balanced and compromising character as among her greatest claims to their admiration. If they wish for any change, it is only that the same principle should be pushed still farther. For they believe that the superficial differences between Christians are as nothing in comparison with their essential agreement; and they are willing that the portals of the church should be flung as widely open as the gates of Heaven . . . willing to own the Romanists as brethren [still] they are sincere and even fervent Protestants. But they conceive the essence of Popery to consist not in points of metaphysical theology, but in the ascription of magic virtue to outward acts; and against this idolatrous superstition they protest, whether it manifests itself in the Puritan or the Papist . . . A characteristic feature of their theology is the prominence which it gives to the idea of the *Visible Church* . . . They hold the Church to be a society divinely instituted for the purpose of manifesting God's presence, and bearing witness to his attributes, by their reflection in its ordinances and in its members . . . It will appear from what we have said, that the Broad Church are, to the middle of the nineteenth century, what the Low Church were to its beginning, – the originators of ecclesiastical reform, and the pioneers of moral progress . . . [Unlike the Evangelicals, however, the Broad Church] have so little organisation or mutual concert of any kind, that they can scarcely be called a party at all . . . The reason for this is not hard to find. It is always easier to keep together a body of partisans on a narrow than on a comprehensive basis. The watch words of party should be battle cries, not notes of peace . . . Critics of the Broad Church say they are so inclusive as to be unable to exclude anyone, even the Unitarian, the Jew, the Deist, and the Pantheist . . . But another and more serious objection remains. It is said that this easy comprehension leads too often to careless coldness; that universal toleration is usually associated with universal indifference. It cannot be denied that this charge contains some ground of truth.[77]

Because of the comprehensiveness of the Broad Church position, naturally enough its various adherents differed on theological points. But the Cambridge contingent, especially those who had been Apostles, shared several specific beliefs and predelictions. Under Hare and Thirlwall's influence they developed an appreciation for German theology and philosophy, and with that for a Platonic – as opposed to a roughly Aristotelian – orientation.[78] Niebuhr's *History of Rome*, which looked at traditional and often mythical materials in a new and skeptical way, kindled in many of them a vital interest in literary and historical criticism. Hare and Thirlwall translated Niebuhr, Milnes studied with him in Germany,[79] and Maurice said of his research

that Rome was a great ichthyosaurus, which Niebuhr, by help of different fossil remains, had in humble imitation of the geologists for the first time constructed.[80]

They read other Germans as well: Goethe was regarded by Maurice as 'among the wisest and the greatest of his age'[81] and Milnes 'was more deeply influenced by the writings of Goethe than by those of any other poet'.[82] They did not uncritically accept any idea just because it came out of Germany, however; their views on Hegel were mixed, and even Goethe was criticized by Maurice and Thirlwall for his excessive egotism.[83]

An aspect of German thought which would have very great impact on English ideas was represented by Thirlwall's translation of Schleiermacher's *Essay on St. Luke*. Influential in German intellectual circles the *Essay* raised a critical question which would trouble much of nineteenth-century literary and religious thought: to what extent ought the Bible to be read as a book of Divine Inspiration, literally true? Or ought it to be read, as Coleridge advised, 'as you would any other book'?[84] Schleiermacher himself discarded the orthodox view of scripture – and, for that matter, of the meaning of Jesus' life – and developed instead, a critical, scientific method of studying the Bible as one would any important work of classical antiquity.[85] That his critical conclusions were not always correct[86] was less important than his basic critical premise.

Not surprisingly this new approach was viewed with considerable alarm in conservative English circles. Hugh James Rose, the University Select Preacher, delivered a series of sermons attacking Schleiermacher and, by implication, Thirlwall.[87] And as late as 1848, Maurice noted that Thirlwall's reputation among High Churchmen was still tarnished because of his association with the German theologian.[88] Perhaps fortunately both the original work and the translation were extremely abstruse and difficult; probably for that reason the *Essay* never achieved a very wide readership.[89] But the critical premises which underlay it had been introduced to England. Thus when in 1835 D. F. Strauss published his *Leben Jesu*, presenting the story of Jesus as a human biography, there were literary and religious scholars in England able to come to grips with it. The publication in 1863 of Ernest Renan's *Vie de Jésus* or in 1865 of J. R. Seeley's *Ecce Homo* was a natural extension of the humanistic, scientific treatment of Biblical topics which began with German criticism in the early part of the century.[90]

The German influence was also 'Romantic'. Theologians, philosophers, political thinkers, and poets – they all stressed the importance of the individual, the need for a sense of community and historical continuity, the power of the inner, emotional man.[91] To some extent Cambridge men absorbed this influence directly from Germany,[92] but they were more fundamentally affected by the ideas of their own English Romantic poets. Milnes' biographer writes:

The young men of the University were living under the shadow of two great names, those of Wordsworth and of Shelley. Milnes throughout his life was proud of the fact that as an undergraduate he had done something to generate the enthusiasm for Wordsworth . . . There was something . . . in the moral spirit of Wordsworth, as well as of Shelley, which touched the hearts of the Cambridge youth of that period, and led them to revolt against the worship of Byron, which was then almost supreme in the literary world. [93]

Maurice counted himself a defender of Wordsworth's poetry,[94] and Hare viewed the Lake Poet with near reverence.[95] Nor was sympathy for the Romantic poets confined to the Apostles and the literary 'node' of the 'Cambridge network':[96] scientists like Sedgwick and Whewell formed personal friendships with Wordsworth and were very much impressed with his ideas and his poetic achievements.[97]

Without question, however, the most important English influence on Cambridge thought was Coleridge. Like his youthful disciples Coleridge was interested in German ideas[98] and in Romanticism. Like them he was committed to preserving the most important principles of the Christian tradition. His organic view of society appealed to the serious dons and students who were trying to move away from the extreme individualism of Locke and Paley. And his flexible, comprehensive theological views attracted their support as they formed themselves loosely into the Broad Church party.[99]

Julius Hare, for example, admired Coleridge very much and, at the poet's death in 1834, wanted Cambridge to establish a memorial prize for an essay in Christian philosophy:

[In advocating such a prize] I was influenced by two motives, the wish to see Coleridge's name associated with Christian philosophy, and the wish to have it openly recognized that philosophy and Christianity are not antagonist powers. Such an admission might do much towards the emancipation of our theology.[100]

Hare also associated Coleridge and Wordsworth with elevated political and social ideals; in 1838 he argued to Whewell that J. S. Mill had proved his merit by coming 'forward as a cordial admirer of Wordsworth, of Coleridge, of Plato, showing a great faculty for receiving their truths, though not indiscriminately'.[101]

Maurice was also very much a Coleridgean as a young man,[102] though in later life he developed a philosophy which was peculiarly his own.[103] He agreed with Coleridge that society was organic and interdependent,[104] and like Coleridge he risked being charged with heterodoxy as he struggled to reconcile religious truth with contemporary scientific, political, and critical ideas. A friend wrote to Maurice in 1863:

For more than a quarter of a century you have been helping Englishmen see through the theories and systems which have been invented to prop up, restore, develop or narrow the ancient edifice of their National Church; and amidst ceaseless comtumely and misrepresentation levelled against yourself, you have striven to teach, . . . as S. T. Coleridge taught before you, that the Bible and the Church of England, in all their comprehensiveness, can best bear witness for their own truth, and for God's providence, against infidelity and Pantheism.[105]

Milnes, Thirlwall, Sterling, and others of the Apostles' circle of course also liked Coleridge,[106] and again even the scientists – though by no means uncritical – felt that his influence was important.[107]

It should be noted, however, that while these German, poetic, Broad Church ideas were important in forming the thinking of individual Cambridge scholars, these influences at the University continued to be mainly extra-curricular, not official. The Apostles might debate German theology and higher criticism, but even the newly established Voluntary Theological Examination remained highly technical, not theoretical. Although certainly less true than when he wrote it, still by mid-century Maberley's charge was in some measure correct:

Put a Cambridge man in the Dead Sea of Criticism and he is in his element; lead him into the grand ocean of general knowledge but a few yards and he is out of his depth.[108]

Furthermore while as individual thinkers Cambridge men might be open-minded and sympathetic with the Broad Church, collectively and officially they were less tolerant. The Coleridge prize was not in fact established, partly because the University hesitated to seem to condone the poet's peculiar personal life.[109] And Maurice, who could have been one of the shining ornaments of the University, ran into a great deal of criticism and hostility because of his supposed heterodoxy.[110] The psychological ground was prepared for the more open attitudes of the second half of the century; the extremely controversial *Essays and Reviews*, published in 1859, would have two Cambridge dons amongst its authors,[111] and one of the most humanistic lives of Christ would be written by a man who later became the

Regius Professor of History.[112] But at a visible level the University's recognition of new theological currents was limited to a rejection of Paley and the establishment of a rather dry examination.

One final observation: the argument here presented has tended to blend literary, theological, philosophical and critical ideas together, as if these disciplines were not separate entities. Despite the fact that such amalgamation may be confusing to the modern reader, it seems justified and even necessary in terms of the thinking of these early-nineteenth-century scholars. To them, the various intellectual activities they undertook did blend – it was perfectly natural for Whewell to travel to Germany on a geological mission, learn German, translate a novel, and write English hexameters based on German poems.[113] This theme of the unity of truth runs throughout the various works produced by these thinkers; to fragment their ideas into 'disciplines' would have been to disrupt the integrity of their thought. A very practical letter from Hare to Whewell illustrated the theological 'relevance' they saw in literary criticism:

I am greatly in want of a copy of Sandyses' Translations of the Psalms, which I have vainly tried to get in London . . . Can you contrive to get me a copy out of the Trinity or University Library? . . . My reason for wanting it is that I am printing a Version of Select Passages from the Psalms. My original purpose was to make a few selections from the authorized versions for my own Church. But the first is generally so feeble and diluted, the second so tawdry and mawkish that I despaired of doing much good till I got hold of the Scotch Version, which, if it were not regardless of idiom and grammar and rhythm and meter, would be excellent. This led me to fancy that it would be possible with the help of these to produce something better than any of them, and that might endeavour to preserve as much as possible of the simplicity and dignity of the original, in the pure English of our Bible, yet without violating the genius of our language; and I have been trying on this principle to collect a version of all such passages as seemed in any way adapted for the worship of a Christian congregation. Should such an attempt be at all successful, and get ultimately sanctioned by authority, it seems to me that it would be the greatest benefit that could be conferred upon our Litergy.[114]

Many such attempts by Hare and his friends were 'successful'. Through their efforts they presented an integrated Christian world view which was at once secure and progressive.

CHAPTER 6

THE CHALLENGE OF DARWIN

In the natural sciences as in moral philosophy, mathematics, theology, and literature, the Cambridge dons were committed to presenting and defending a unitary vision of truth. No matter from what perspective they viewed the natural universe, they expected to see a coherent, consistent picture. And this consistency would not merely exist among the various sciences, but also between the sciences and the humanities. In particular natural theology and natural science were seen as two sides of a single coin. In each case the raw subject matter was nature: natural theology helped to reveal the existence and the aspects of nature's Creator, while science demonstrated the mechanisms by which the Creator chose to work.

As with the other university disciplines, Cambridge science saw a great deal of development and change during the first half of the nineteenth century. And like theology, literary criticism, and the very idea of a liberal education, science at mid-century was approaching a disintegrative intellectual crisis – in this case one which can be at least symbolically tied to a specific event, the 1859 publication of *The Origin of Species*. It is tempting to assert that Darwin destroyed the Christian faith of the earlier age: to say that by replacing an intervening anthropomorphic God with an impersonal evolutionary force, by rejecting the creation story of Genesis, and by describing a nature-red-in-tooth-and-claw instead of one full of evident beneficence, he had made intellectually untenable the old Christian cosmogony. This would be over-simple and wrong. There were as many Christians in the English intellectual community after 1859 as before. What Darwin's work had done was wrest apart two previously united aspects of truth. Henceforth, although it would still be possible to be religious and a scientist, the two parts of life would be kept in different compartments. Some of the underlying principles of natural theology were absorbed into biology; and, stripped of its specifically Christian content, natural theology as a discipline ceased to exist.[1] Pure theology – study of the ideas growing out of divine revelation – was put into another category altogether.

Until the crisis was upon them, however, the 'conservative reformers' of Cambridge worked in science as in other fields – to produce, articulate, and defend a coherent, unified world-view. It has been noted above that while Sedgwick, Whewell, and the others rejected William Paley's utilitarian view of moral philosophy, they did not at all turn away from his natural theology. Indeed, the broad belief that the investigation of nature could provide a firm base for religious faith lay behind much of the scholarly activity of the age. The eighth edition of the *Encyclopaedia Britannica* spelled out clearly the relationship between the study of nature and the study of Scripture:

the attempt to present the entire body of . . . theology in one continuous whole, necessarily involves the statement both of the doctrines of natural and those of biblical theology . . . It is . . . undeniable that there are some principles of theology which may be called *natural;* for though it is in the highest degree probable that the parents of mankind received all their theological knowledge by *supernatural* means, it is yet obvious that some parts of that knowledge must have been capable of proof purely rational, otherwise not a single religious truth could have been conveyed through the succeeding generations of the human race, but by the immediate inspiration of each individual . . . whatever propositions relating to the being and attributes of the first cause and the duty of man can be demonstrated by human reason, independent of written revelation, may be called *natural theology,* and are of the utmost importance, as being to us the first principles of all religion. Natural theology, in this sense of the word, is the foundation of the Christian revelation; for without a previous knowledge of it, we could have no evidence that the Scriptures of the Old and New Testaments are indeed the Word of God.[2]

The eighth Earl of Bridgewater, Francis Henry Egerton, died in 1829. His will directed the commissioning of eight scientific treatises, to demonstrate

the Power, Wisdom, and Goodness of God, as manifested in Creation, illustrating such work by all reasonable arguments, as for instance, the variety and formations of God's creatures in the animal, vegetable, and mineral kingdoms; the effect of digestion, and thereby of conversion;

the construction of the hand of man, and an infinite variety of other arguments; as also by discoveries ancient and modern, in arts, sciences, and the whole extent of literature.[3]

These essays, written by eight eminent scientists, provide a convenient summary of the whole discipline of natural theology. Surprisingly popular, all of the treatises went through numerous printings in the next few decades, Whewell's work on Astronomy and General Physics seeing nine editions by 1864. They showed, at great length and with infinite detail, the marvelous adaptation of nature to man's needs, and thus demonstrated the beneficence of God. Their general orientation is well illustrated by the title Thomas Chalmers gave to his treatise: *On the Power, Wisdom, and Goodness of God as Manifested in the Adaptation of External Nature to the Moral and Intellectual Constitution of Man*. It is easy, from a post-Darwinian perspective, to ridicule these essays, and indeed the whole natural theology tradition which they represent.[4] We are accustomed to thinking of eyes existing in response to light and not light for the benefit of eyes. But it would be a serious error to assume that in their own time the Bridgewater Treatises were trivial or naive, or that they appealed only to the ignorant. Whewell's essay, for example, was appreciated not only by the public but by his scientific friends at Cambridge and elsewhere.[5] And reviews of the treatises in contemporary journals, while sometimes critical of the organization of the essays, did not question the underlying premise of the usefulness of natural theology.[6]

With the viewpoint represented by the Bridgewater Treatises the Cambridge scientific community was quite comfortable. Sedgwick was an ardent spokesman for the relationship between science and religion:

The religion of nature and the religion of the Bible are . . . in beautiful accordance; and the indications of the Godhead, offered by the one, are well fitted to give us a livelier belief in the promises of the other . . . Are we to believe that there can be such beautiful and harmonious movements in the vast mechanism of nature, and yet think that the Spirit of God hath not brooded over them, and that his hand hath not guided them? Can we see in every portion of the visible world the impress of wisdom and power, and yet believe that things were not foreseen in the Divine mind, and these ends not contemplated before he called the universe into being?[7]

Herschel and Babbage wrote treatises explicitly extolling science as a source of religious inspiration.[8] Whewell, in addition to the Bridgewater Treatise, published in 1845 and 1854 *Indications of the Creator* and *Of the Plurality of Worlds*, both works essentially on natural theology. And even Maurice, though not a scientist, wrote to a friend in 1840:

I am sure that Nature is a teacher, and a great teacher . . . It contains at least a prophecy of what we want; and though it does not contain God, as the Pantheists would have us believe, it witnesses to us that He is; and not merely that He is in some relation to us.[9]

There were several axioms which underlay the discipline of natural theology. Nature was orderly. But the laws which governed natural phenomena were only viewed as descriptions of collections of related events, not as 'ideas' or 'vital forces' which in themselves had any organizing power.[10] Nature was beneficent. Natural theologians, of course, were fond of displaying specific examples of benevolence; but more than that, even when the evidence apparently spoke to the contrary, there was a general faith that 'nature does nothing in vain' and that 'whatever is, is right'.[11] Much energy was expended in explaining the existence of evil and demonstrating that from the proper perspective even apparent pain is part of a higher good.[12] Nature was purposive. The basic analytical tool of natural theology was to display the 'usefulness' of various natural objects, to show through examination of adaptations that the natural world was contrived and hence had a contriver. Essentially the discipline was teleological – it explained existence by reference to ends or purposes. And the suitability – in an infinite variety of cases – of structures to their purposes made convincing the argument for design and a designer. Because it was so well-contrived, nature was in balance and in harmony; this meant in turn that it was essentially static and unchanging. In the act of creation God had made organisms and their environments suitable to one another; there was no real room therefore for a concept of change through adaptation. Furthermore, if the laws of nature were uniform, they would be uniform through time.[13] In some ways the world natural theology presented can be understood in terms of the concepts of the Great Chain of Being: nature was plentitudinous, nature was continuous, nature was arranged as a unilinear gradation.[14]

The discipline itself demanded intellectual rigor. Its practitioners were not to make any claims on it beyond what it could legitimately provide:

if any man ever proposed to prove as much [Kant had argued that natural theologians claimed to reveal God's essential nature] by the argument from design, he is to be censured for using that argument beyond its competency. We are content to have it proved to us that there is a world-builder, and to Him, assured of his existence, we turn, if haply He will speak to us and tell us more of himself than we can gather from the mere study of his works. Thus natural theology hands over its students to the teaching of Scripture.[15]

Furthermore, it was to be pursued in a scrupulously scientific fashion; as the *Quarterly Review* observed in 1834:

Natural theology is an inductive science. Our knowledge of the existence and attributes of God, as far as that knowledge is traceable by the light of nature, is acquired by an intellectual process strictly analogous, and exactly similar, to the intellectual process by which we acquire our knowledge of the laws of the physical world; but if the inductive philosophy is to be applied to theology, all metaphysical arguments from first causes, and from the supposed nature of things, must be banished as contrary to the rules of sound investigation; and all the principles from which we reason must themselves be *facts*, ascertained by experience, and true in all the actual circumstances to which they can be traced. By this reasoning, Newton discovered the true system of the heavens; and it is only by this reasoning that the theist can ascertain, from the light of Nature, the existence and the attributes of Him who made the heavens. The proof of a divine intelligence ruling over the universe is as full and, as perfect as the proof that gravitation extends throughout the planetary system.[16]

As a last general characteristic, natural theology was convincing. The 1854 *Encyclopaedia Britannica* article on theology examined all of the various traditional proofs of the existence of God: the historical (that God must exist because man has always in all cultures believed in Him), the physical (that whatever exists must have a cause, the uncaused cause we call God), the ontological or psychological (that we can conceive an all-perfect being indicates that He exists), and the teleological or argument-from-design. In each case but the last the author reveals the weaknesses or the fallacies in the argument, but of teleology he writes:

When we see two or more objects fitted to each other, so as thereby to secure a definite end or result, we are constrained to assume the agency of an intelligent mind by which the end was contemplated, by which the fitness of the given adaptation to secure that end was foreseen, and by which the objects themselves were adapted to each other, so as to accomplish what was thus designed, as well as of a power sufficient to effect the contemplated arrangement. This is an assumption we make *irresistibly; we cannot consider the facts without making it*. Now, the universe, subject to our scrutiny is full of such instances . . . The inference is *irresistible*. There must have presided over the formation of this vast and everywhere well-ordered scheme a high intelligence by which it was conceived and planned, and a mighty power by which the whole was carried into effect.[17] [italics mine]

The science from which natural theology drew most of its illustrations – and out of which came, eventually, its own destruction – was geology. From the beginning of the century until Darwin's publication, students of geology were embroiled in a series of controversies and crises, most of them connected at least in part with the relationship between science and religion.[18] First came a debate about the origin of the earth. 'Neptunists', basing their interpretation on the work of Abraham Werner, argued that the earth had precipitated and condensed out of primordial waters. 'Vulcanists', led by James Hutton, argued that the earth's central heat played a more fundamental formative role. Furthermore, the Neptunists felt that creation had occurred relatively quickly, through forces different from those now in operation; Vulcanists perceived endless, unchanging processes, with 'no vestige of a beginning, no prospect of an end'.[19] By the 1820s the water/heat conflict had been resolved, pretty much in favor of the Vulcanists, and a new controversy developed, between the 'catastrophists', led by William Buckland, and the 'uniformitarians', led by Charles Lyell. As their names imply, the first group believed that the earth had been formed through a series of dramatic, short-lived geological events, of which the Noachian deluge was probably the last example; while the uniformitarians thought that – given vast expanses of time – the earth had assumed its present shape through the very gradual action of processes still operating. By the forties the main features of uniformitarianism in turn had come to represent geological orthodoxy, only to find the field disturbed by the beginnings of the controversy over evolution.

Note that none of the geological schools was committed to an exactly literal interpretation of Genesis. In each conflict there was, to be sure, a conservative and an advanced camp, with the conservatives tending to interpret the geological record in a way at least metaphorically compatible with the Biblical creation story, the advanced groups generally ignoring revelation in their scientific formulations. And from each controversy the advanced camp emerged victorious, as an intervening deity seemed a less and less important element in scientific explanation. It would be wrong however, to view the Vulcanists, the uniformitarians and the evolutionists as sophisticated, secular scientists and the Neptunists, catastrophists and opponents of evolutionary theory as reactionary, semi-hysterical country parsons. Reactionary religious fundamentalism did indeed exist in England, but its advocates condemned all geologists equally, no matter to which school they belonged.[20] Within the geological discipline itself there was a general belief – in all camps – that revealed religion and science both contained truth and that their truths were interrelated. The cyclical arguments which, it can now be seen, were part of a trend toward secularism, seemed at the time to be purely scientific controversies, conducted rigorously about inductive method and the proper interpretation of data.

Scholars from Cambridge were in the thick of the fray. Adam Sedgwick was elected in 1818 to the Woodwardian professorship of geology. At the time of his election he knew nothing of the discipline,[21] but he quickly set about studying and making observations and soon became a highly respected member of the scientific community.[22] William Whewell had been a member of the Royal Society since 1820 and in 1828 was elected to the Cambridge professorship of mineralogy. He wrote to his sister that he had 'for some years been employing himself a good deal on matters connected with this subject',[23] a claim which his geology field trips, experiments, and papers on crystallography seem to support.[24]

At this stage in their careers both men were essentially empiricists, given to observing and describing rather than to theorizing. Whewell's first mineralogical treatise was called *An Essay on Mineralogical Classification and Nomenclature; with Tables of the Orders and Species of Minerals*. And throughout his life Sedgwick's major works remained descriptive;[25] he distrusted those who took the dangerous position of viewing 'all things through the distracting medium of an hypothesis'.[26] Nevertheless, they were not free from general biases, finding themselves in the successive controversies as outspoken champions of the more conservative camps. Sedgwick in particular was committed to the doctrine of catastrophism. His Wernerian prejudices, which he seems to have held when he first entered the discipline, were set aside easily enough,[27] for the fire/water controversy had almost subsided by 1818.[28] And when the evidence seemed conclusive he even came to distrust the geological argument for the Mosaic deluge, making a public recantation in his Presidential Address to the Geological Society:

there is, I think, one great negative conclusion now incontestably established – that the vast masses of diluvial gravel, scattered almost over the surface of the earth, do not belong to one violent and transitory period . . . We saw the clearest traces of diluvial action, and we had, in our sacred histories, the record of a general deluge. On this double testimony it was, that we gave a unity to a vast succession of phaenomena . . . and under the name of diluvium, classed them all together.

To seek the light of physical truth by reasoning of this kind, is, in the language of Bacon, to seek the living among the dead, and will ever end in erroneous induction . . . Having been myself a believer, and, to the best of my power, a propagator of what I now regard as a philosophic heresy, . . . I think it right, as one of my last acts before I quit this Chair, thus publicly to read my recantation.[29]

But Sedgwick did not reject other catastrophes just because he rejected the Flood. He still – like Buckland, Murchison, Conybeare, and others – [30] saw in the geological record a series of enormous, cataclysmic events, events which left whole species of plants and animals extinct. What struck Sedgwick and his colleagues was the violence and discontinuity with which nature (or Providence) seemed to work; in 1827, for example, he wrote of the strata of magnesium limestone:

After the production of the rocks of a carboniferous order, the earth's surface appears to have been acted upon by powerful disturbing forces, which, not only in the British Isles, but through the greater part of the European basin, produced a series of formations of very great extent and complexity of structure . . . We have no right to assume, nor is there any reason to believe, that such disturbing forces acted either uniformly or simultaneously throughout the world.[31]

And when Lyell published his uniformitarian *Principles of Geology* in 1830, Sedgwick led in the attack on its fundamental idea:

According to the principles of Mr. Lyell, the physical operations now going on, are not only the type, but the measure of intensity of the physical powers acting on the earth at all anterior periods; and all we now see around us is only the last link in the great chain of phaenomena, arising out of uniform causation, of which we can trace no beginning, and of which we see no prospect of the end . . . we all allow, that the primary laws of nature are immutable – that all we now see is subordinate to those immutable laws – and that we can only judge of effects which are past, not by the effects we behold in progress . . . But to assume that the secondary combinations arising out of the primary laws of matter, have been the same in all periods of the earth, is, an unwarrantable hypothesis with no *a priori* probability . . . If the principles vindicated in Mr. Lyell's work be true, then there can be no great violations of continuity either in the structure or position of our successive formations. But we know that there are enormous violations of geological continuity: and . . . of this we are certain, that they have been produced by forces adequate to the effects and coextensive with the phaenomena.[32]

Whewell also preferred catastrophism to Lyell's new uniformitarian doctrine. In a review in the *British Critic* he wrote:

Mr. Lyell throws away all such crutches [cataclysmic geological events]; he walks alone in the path of his speculations; he requires no paroxysms, no extraordinary periods; he is content to take burning mountains as he finds them; and with the assistance of the stock of volcanoes and earthquakes now on hand, he undertakes to transform the earth from any one of its geological conditions to any other. He requires time no doubt; he will not be hurried in his proceedings. But if we will allow him a free stage in the wide circuit of eternity, he will ask no other favour . . . Common readers will probably not be disposed to consider as requiring any refutation, a theory which asserts that the elevation of the Andes from the bed of the Pacific is a phenomenon 'of the same kind' as those which happen in our time.[33]

The Cambridge scholars' most intense feelings were reserved for the third geological controversy of the nineteenth century – the argument over the evolution of biological species. As early as 1831 when he criticized Lyell's theory of gradual geological development over long periods of time, Sedgwick saw and was disturbed by the fact that such a process could apply to the biological world as well:

may I remind you, that in the very first step of our progress [in geological research] we are surrounded by animal and vegetable forms, of which there are now no living types. And I ask, have we not in these things some indication of change and of an adjusting power altogether different from what we commonly understand by the laws of nature? Shall we say with the naturalists of a former century, that they are but the sports of nature? Or shall we adopt the doctrines of spontaneous generation and transmutation of species . . .?[34]

It was in 1844, with the publication of *Vestiges of the Natural History of Creation*, that Sedgwick's full powers as a controversialist were brought into play. Written for a popular audience by not a scientist but an anonymous literary critic, the *Vestiges* was an attempt to apply the principles of uniformitarianism to biology. The author, Robert Chambers,[35] wanted to show that all of the universe – organic as well as inorganic – had been created in an orderly, lawful, systematic manner, and that its development had not required the miraculous intervention of God. The fossil record, he thought, revealed a picture of progressive development within animate creation, with the lowest levels containing primitive specimens and higher strata more advanced forms. It seemed to him foolish to assume that 'creative fiats were required for each new class, order, family, and species of organic beings', ridiculous to suppose that

the external Sovereign arranges a planetary or astral system by dispositions imparted primordially to matter; but [that] he has to give a particular heed to the formation of the few corals and shell-fish in the Cambrian seas; he has by a new fiat to add fish, afterwards reptiles – birds – mammifers; and not only these great classes, but each particular species of which those classes are composed![36]

Instead it seemed clear that 'species were introduced upon our globe by virtue of primordial arrangements having that object in view, and in which Deity was only present and active in the sense that he is in all the phenomena of nature'.[37]

Such a view was, of course, intolerable to many English scholars on theological grounds. But the *Vestiges* was also a very bad work of science, and as such it was attacked by scientists of all schools, catastrophists and uniformitarians alike. Sedgwick led the assault. Both his concern for scientific truth and his commitment to the argument-from-design made Sedgwick feel very intensely about the *Vestiges*. As he wrote to Sir Charles Lyell:

I do from my soul abhor the sentiments, and I believe I could . . . crush the book by proving it base, vulgar in spirit, (not so in dress and manner, and there is the mischief of it, but I would [strive] to strip off the outer coverings and show its inner deformity and foulness,) false, shallow, worthless, and, with the garb of philosophy, starting from principles which are at variance with all sober inductive truth. The sober facts of geology shuffled, so as to play a rogue's game; phrenology (that sinkhole of human folly and prating coxcombry); spontaneous generation; transmutation of species; and I know not what; all to be swallowed, without tasting or trying, like so much horse-physic! Gross credulity and rank infidelity joined in an unlawful marriage and breeding a deformed progeny of unnatural conclusions.[38]

In an article in the *Edinburgh Review* Sedgwick combined a solid grasp of scientific data with the vehemence growing from his religious feelings to write a critique of the *Vestiges* which most contemporaries regarded as devastating. Darwin wrote to Lyell of the review, 'It is a grand piece of argument against mutability of species, and I read it with fear and trembling.'[39] And in 1850 Sedgwick added an introduction to the fifth edition of his *Discourse on the Studies of the University* in which he continued his assault on the Chambers book.[40] His objections were of several types: he was outraged at the author's obvious lack of scientific training, believing at first even that the book was based 'on the science gleaned at a lady's boarding school'.[41] Even more he was offended by the *Vestiges'* modes of reasoning – analyses based on mere apparent resemblances,[42] hypotheses built on other hypotheses not yet proved,[43] evidence of the most questionable sort,[44] abandonment of the inductive method.[45] In attacking Chambers' central point Sedgwick raised what was really the basic argument against the developmental theory: how could tiny, imperceptible changes over so long a period of time have taken place without leaving any sign of ambiguity between species? What, in other words, was the mechanism for this assumed developmental process? Until that question could be answered no evolutionary theory would be convincing.[46] Examining in detail the geological evidence from a region in South Wales Sedgwick asked:

What are the fossil species of this system, and what is their arrangement? We reply, not in any order representing what we call a natural scale . . . Some of the old species are found straggling through the upper system; but as a group the species are new and characteristic; and their arrangement seems to have been chiefly determined by the successive physical conditions at the bottom of the old ocean. Are, then, the new species derived from the old by a gradual transmutation or development from one series to another? We reply, no; because the new species, as a general rule, are as sharply defined as the old; and show no gradations leading to any ambiguity.[47]

Perhaps most of all Sedgwick was offended by what he called Chambers' 'rank, unbending, and degrading materialism'.[48] Particularly troubling was the *Vestiges'* treatment of the human mind. By viewing man as a natural part of the animal kingdom and his brain as a physical organ, more highly developed but similar to that of a monkey, Chambers had portrayed man's mind as material, not spiritual. The *Vestiges* did not avoid this issue: while individual men might seem to be independent and capricious, in the aggregate they could be studied statistically and their behavior be seen to obey systematic laws.[49] In Chambers' words, 'The difference between mind in the lower animals and in man is a difference in degree only'[50] so that 'the distinction usually taken between physical and moral is annulled'.[51] Not surprisingly, this sort of reasoning seriously disturbed Sedgwick, and it need not be argued that he was deluded by blind religious sentiment or anthropocentricism. In 1845 sound reasoning and public opinion would have agreed with Sedgwick that Chambers was irrational to ask his readers to believe that

there is no essential difference between man and beast . . . that the buzzing of bees, the gabbling of turkeys, and the jabbering of apes, are phenomena of the same order – differing only in degree – with the highest symbolical representations of human thought, and the highest recorded abstractions of pure intellect.[52]

Although they expressed themselves with less vehemence, other members of Sedgwick's scientific circle agreed with him in disliking the *Vestiges*.[53] Henslow, the botanist, wrote to Whewell in 1847: 'Sedgwick put the same quere [*sic*] to me as you have done respecting the "transmutation" of species – and my reply must be the same – No Botanist, so far as I am aware, gives any credit to the tale.'[54] Whewell himself gathered together some extracts from earlier writings

in which, as he considered, the opinions of the author of the *Vestiges* had been anticipated and condemned . . . he attached great importance to the fact that the passages thus selected had presented themselves spontaneously in the course of his philosophical reflections, and had not been produced with any specially controversial object.[55]

He called his little book *Indications of the Creator*, and his correspondence shows that his friends found it an effective reply to the

Vestiges.[56] Like Sedgwick, Whewell thought that the critical issue was man's place in nature:

I have attempted to show that, dim as the light is which science throws upon creation, it gives us reason to believe that the placing of man upon the earth (including his creation) was a supernatural event, an exception to the laws of nature. The Vestiges has, for one of its main doctrines, that this event was a natural event, the result of a law by which man grew out of monkey . . . Nor do I see how the development of the different kinds of animals, on his plan, is to be performed, even in our imagination, without Lamarck's process of appetencies operating, or something of the same kind. As to his special form of the doctrine of the development of species, I have answered it in the preface; that is, I have shown that it is contrary to the established doctrines of geology and physiology.[57]

Whewell's most important work on natural theology and popular science was *On the Plurality of Worlds*, first published in 1853. Although it was not directed specifically against the evolutionary argument, the book was a clear statement of the old world-view which the *Vestiges* had so severely challenged. In considering whether astronomy and the other sciences indicated the existence of additional forms of intelligent life in the universe, Whewell was basically asking whether it was reasonable to view man as the highest point of God's creation. To him the answer was unquestionably a resounding 'yes'. First he asserted that the geological and paleological evidence was extremely unclear about the evolutionary or 'progressive' theory of the development of species.

Not entire resemblance, but universal difference is what we discover; not the repetition of exactly similar cases, but a series of cases, perpetually dissimilar, presents itself; not constancy, but change, perhaps advance; not one permanent and pervading scheme, but preparation and completion of successive schemes; not uniformity and a mixed type of existence, but progression and a climax [man].[58]

But even those geologists

who hold that, in other ways, the course of change has been uniform; – that even the introduction of man, as a new species of animal is only an event of the same kind as myriads of like events which have occurred in the history of the earth; – still allow that the introduction of man, as a moral being, is an event entirely different from any which had taken place before; and that this event is, geologically speaking, recent.[59]

It was man's moral and intellectual nature which made him unique, and to Whewell – even should some general evolutionary theory be shown to be correct – it would always remain inconceivable that man's nature could be understood as a natural outgrowth of mere animal existence.

For the introduction of reason and intelligence upon the Earth is no part nor consequence of the series of animal forms. It is a fact of an entirely new kind. The transition from brute to man does not come within the analogy of the transition from brute to brute. The thread of analogy, even if it could lead us so far, would break here. We may conceive analogues to other animals, but we could have no analogue to man, except man. Man is not merely a higher kind of animal; he is a creature of a superior order, participating in the attributes of a higher nature.[60]

God clearly had intervened in a very special way to create man; there was no reason to believe that intelligent life would have evolved naturally.[61] And if God had been satisfied to have man exist only during such a tiny proportion of the whole of time ('He has made their period, though only a moment in the ages of animal life, the only period of intelligence, morality, religion'),[62] He might well have also been satisfied to provide only one tiny planet with the special blessing of intelligent life.[63] Whewell's analysis was extremely complex, ranging over biology, geology, astronomy, and natural theology and covering several hundred pages. But in the end he produced a coherent argument for the uniqueness of man, against the existence of intelligent life elsewhere. His essay was successful, as contemporary doggerel had it, as

> A book meant to show
> That throughout all infinity
> There's nothing so grand
> As the Master of Trinity.[64]

More nearly definitive as a statement of Whewell's purely scientific views on these difficult questions was his *History of the Inductive Sciences*, first published in 1837 and reissued, more or less unrevised, in 1847 and 1857. With respect to catastrophism and uniformitarianism Whewell was prepared to blend the two doctrines together, granting the immensely long time periods demanded by Lyell but still insisting that some geological events had surely been of a very dramatic sort.

In reality, when we speak of the *uniformity* of nature, are we not obliged to use the term in a very large sense, in order to make the doctrine at all tenable? It includes catastrophes and convulsions of a very extensive and intense kind; what is the limit to the violence which we must allow to these changes? In order to enable ourselves to represent geological causes as operating with uniform energy through all time, we must measure our time by long cycles . . .[65]

Furthermore, Lyell saw slow cyclical movement but nothing which could be called progress;[66] but Whewell, who gave considerable credence to the nebular hypothesis about the formation of the universe, thought that the astronomical analogy might at least tend to support a progressive view:

consider our knowledge of the heavens as a palaetiological science; – as the study of a past condition, from which the present is derived by causes acting in time. Is there then no evidence of a beginning, or of a progress? What is the import of the Nebular Hypothesis? A luminous matter is condensing, solid bodies are forming, are arranging themselves into systems of cyclical motion; in short, we have exactly what we are told, on this [the astronomical] analogy, what we ought not to have; the beginning of a world.[67]

With respect to the question of transmutation of species Whewell was very direct. He saw the problem as a clear dilemma:

either we must accept the doctrine of the transmutation of species, and must suppose that the organized species of one geological epoch were transmuted into those of another by some long-continued agency of natural causes; or else, we must believe in many successive acts of creation and extinction of species, out of the common course of nature; acts which, therefore, we may properly call miraculous.[68]

The first doctrine would force us to abandon 'that belief in the adaptation of the structure of every creature to its destined mode of being'[69] – that is, the concept of final cause. In any case 'full and careful consideration from eminent physiologists' revealed that:

Indefinite divergence from the original type is not possible; and the extreme limit of possible variation may usually be reached in a brief period of time: in short, *species have a real existence in nature*, and a transmutation from one to another does not exist.[70]

On the other hand Whewell readily admitted that natural science could by itself offer no evidence as to the action of an intervening, miraculous creative force.

When our thoughts would apprehend steadily the creation of things, we find that we are obliged to summon up other ideas than those which regulate the pursuit of scientific truths; – to call in other powers than those to which we refer natural events . . . [Theology and geology may present us with a converging vision of how creation occurred.] But such a train of thought must be pursued with caution . . . The two sciences may conspire, not by having any part in common; but because, though widely diverse in their lines, both point to a mysterious and invisible origin of the world . . . Science has presented no really satisfactory theory explaining the creation of species: the bare conviction that a creation of species has taken place, whether once or many times, so long as it is unconnected with our organical sciences, is a tenet of Natural Theology rather than of Physical Philosophy.[71]

He posed the problem clearly and left it there.[72]

When Darwin published in 1850, answering the questions which Sedgwick, Whewell and their friends had so explicitly asked, the Cambridge community was in general outraged. Darwin sent Sedgwick a copy of his book and received an honest, warm, and extremely critical letter in reply:

Parts of it I admired greatly, parts I laughed at till my sides were almost sore; other parts I read with absolute sorrow, because I think you have utterly *deserted* – after a start in that tram-road of all physical truth – the true method of induction . . . Many of your wide conclusions are based upon assumptions which can neither be proved nor disproved.[73]

To his other correspondents Sedgwick was even more outspoken.[74] And he lost no time in issuing a public, purely geological rebuttal at an 1860 meeting of the Cambridge Philosophical Society; his biographer notes that 'the general sense of the meeting was unquestionably . . . on Sedgwick's side'.[75] Furthermore, even though Darwin's theory gained much ground in scientific circles as the years went by, Sedgwick remained unconverted; in 1865 at the age of eighty he wrote:

the Geological Society is partly in fetters . . . some of its leading men are led by the nose in the train of an hypothesis – I mean the development of all organic life from a single material element by natural specific transmutation . . . Darwin has made this theory popular, but he has not added one single fact that helps it forward; and I think that it appeared (about sixty-five years since) far better in the poetry of the grandfather, than now in the prose of the grandson.[76]

Whewell did not play so public a role in opposing the *Origin*, but he agreed with Sedgwick in thinking Darwin's book to be pernicious. He and his friends were shocked by the Oxford meeting of the British Association where T. H. Huxley so roundly attacked Bishop Wilberforce; Whewell wrote of it to his old friend J. D. Forbes:

It is very poor that Huxley was very bitter against the Bp. of Oxford . . . Perhaps the Bp. was not prudent to venture into the field where no eloquence can supersede the need of precise knowledge. The young naturalists declared themselves in favour of Darwin's views, which tendency I saw already at Leeds two years ago. I am sorry for it, for I reckon Darwin's book to be an utterly *unphilosophical* one.[77]

Opinions of the rest of the Cambridge circle were probably less significant, but they were also by and large negative. Darwin sent a copy of his book to Herschel, anxious to hear whether it would 'produce any effect on such a mind'. Later he wrote to Lyell:

I have heard, by roundabout channel, that Herschel says my book 'is the law of higgledy-piggledy.' What this exactly means I do not know, but it is evidently very contemptuous. If true this is a great blow and discouragement.[78]

J. S. Henslow had been a good friend and collaborator of Darwin's, but he was able to muster only a weak and partial acquiescence to the views expressed in the *Origin;* he did, however, at least chair the heated Oxford meeting of the British Association with impartiality.[79] And William Hopkins, the beloved and very successful Cambridge mathematics coach, wrote a critical review in *Fraser's* which Darwin said was 'thought to be the best which has appeared against us'.[80]

Because they rejected the 'correct' answers to questions they themselves had asked, it has been commonplace to regard these older scholars as inadequate scientists, or at least as men misled by their religious convictions.[81] But any real attention to their scholarly work shows at once that they were as careful of their methods and as thoughtful in their use of evidence as any of their younger antagonists.[82] They were leading members of a serious scientific community;[83] indeed they were in friendly contact with precisely those scientists of whose ideas they disapproved.[84] Their language – especially Sedgwick's – when criticizing opposing views was often strong, but this seems to have been more a matter of style than an expression of real rage.[85] And though unquestionably troubled by some of the new scientific questions these university men continued to live their scholarly lives in a quiet and civilized way, by no means in a frenzy of religious hysteria.

Furthermore, while it is true that religious considerations seem to have influenced conservative Cambridge scientists like Whewell and Sedgwick, advocates of more advanced geological views were also operating in the context of natural theology. In his assessment of the *Vestiges* Sedgwick did mention God frequently and attacked Chambers' degraded view of the Deity.[86] But Chambers, too, made frequent references to Providence and indeed seemed to feel that his interpretation of nature would elevate, not debase, God in men's eyes.[87] John Playfair and James Hutton, representatives of the more liberal Vulcanist doctrine in the early fire/water controversy, were in complete agreement with the more conservative Neptunists that science, rightly understood, would demonstrate the wisdom and goodness of God.[88] Lyell was at least sensitive to the religious feelings of his scientific colleagues, trying hard to couch his essentially materialistic, anti-miraculous doctrine in language designed not to give offence.[89] And Henslow apparently felt no hypocrisy in publicly defending even Darwin by

refusing to allow that he was guided by any but truthful motives, and declaring that he himself [Darwin] believed he was exalting and not debasing our views of a Creator, in attributing to him a power of imposing laws on the Organic World by which to do his work, as effectually as his laws imposed on the inorganic had done it in the Mineral Kingdom.[90]

Modern scholars disagree about why some nineteenth-century scientists accepted Darwin's thesis while others rejected it. There is a tendency to assume that those who accepted the *Origin* were somehow brighter than their more conservative fellows.[91] But historians who avoid this pitfall and credit Sedgwick and his friends with ample ability, still often emphasize their concern that God play a directing role in the universe. Charles Gillispie, for example, divides those scientists who were interested in natural theology into two camps – those

who subscribed to the idea that science is the witness of a divine plan for the universe, took a uniformitarian position and argued that God's provision for the laws of nature is immutable and that science proves their divine origin by demonstrating the self-sufficiency and invariability of their operation and not by finding evidence of exceptional and miraculous interventions, which, in fact, have never occurred.

And on the other hand

the tradition [in which he would place Sedgwick and Whewell] which held that science discovers a Deity who is not only a first cause but also an active governor of His creation, directly participating in its development, continually adapting means to benevolent ends, and by so doing demonstrating His perpetual watchfulness over its behaviour and that of its inhabitants.[92]

Gillispie's contention is that this latter camp was disturbed by progressive geological theories because they pushed the superintending Deity into the background of his creation.[93] Even Walter Cannon, who is extremely (and, I think, properly) sympathetic to the scientists of the Cambridge circle, argues that they were influenced significantly by religious concerns when they rejected Darwin's hypothesis:

The natural theologians had accepted a set of postulates which, they believed, relied upon the best scientific principles to show that the world is both purposeful and historical. They were shocked to find that the animate organization in this world could be explained by natural selection as easily as by reference to God, that indeed natural selection must operate whether God does or not.[94]

No doubt religious preconceptions did do a lot to influence the frame of mind in which various scholars received new scientific ideas. But in presenting them as the really sophisticated thinkers they surely were, it is necessary to view their intellectual world from a slightly different perspective. They believed in the unity of truth. No matter how complex the question raised, no matter how far from the path of received opinion new methods or new discoveries might take them, they were confident that all of man's knowledge would weave together into a consistent whole. It was the fragmenting of knowledge into 'disciplines' with limited 'proper spheres' that they were resisting – they wanted to maintain an integrated world of truth. In their own words:

Herschel – '[Scientists and natural theologians err when they try to make scientific evidence correlate too closely with scriptural testimony.] To persons of such a frame of mind it ought to suffice to remark, on the one hand, that truth can never be opposed to truth, and, on the other, that error is only to be effectually confounded by searching deep and tracing it to its source . . . truth is single, and consistent with itself.'[95]

Henslow – 'It has often appeared to me, that the study of God's word alone may not always be sufficient to protect some of us against the morbid imaginings of these uncertain days; and I therefore the more rejoice to find the Natural Sciences at length taking firmer root in the seat of sound learning and religious education than they have hitherto obtained.'[96]

After attacking the *Vestiges*, Sedgwick – 'For our own parts we trust, in all good hope, that human knowledge will go on in the right road of sober Inductive Truth; and if that be its direction, we can look for no consequences but such as will tend to the good of the human race . . . we must seek knowledge at the fountain head – in the order of nature – and in an humble contemplation of her works; so we may rise, step by step, to a more lofty knowledge.'[97]

Although warning against intellectual pride, Whewell – 'It may be urged that all truths must be consistent with all other truths, and that therefore the results of the geology or astronomy cannot be irreconcilable with the statements of true theology. And this universal consistency of truth with itself must be assented to; but it by no means follows that we must be able to obtain a full insight into the nature and manner of such consistency. Such an insight would only be possible if we could obtain a clear view of that central body of truth, the source [God] of the principles which appear in the separate lines of speculation.'[98]

Babbage felt that even miracles were just the working out of a higher law, imperfectly understood,[99] and he closed his essay on natural theology with these words:

Any theory on whatever subject, that is really sound, can never be inimical to a religion founded on truth; and any that is unsound may be refuted by arguments drawn from observation and experiment, without calling in the aid of revelation. If we give way to a dread of danger from the inculcation of any scriptural doctrine, or from the progress of physical or moral science, we manifest a want of faith in God's power, or in his will, to maintain his own cause. That we shall indeed best further his cause by fearless perseverance in an open and straight course, I am firmly persuaded; but it is not only when we perceive the mischiefs of falsehood and disguise, and the beneficial tendency of fairness and candour, that we are followers of truth: the trial of our faith is, when we *cannot* perceive this: and the part of the lover of truth is to follow her at all seeming hazards, after the example of Him who 'came into the world that we might bear witness to the Truth'.[100]

When writing of ideas which have since become problematical

or which segments of the modern intellectual community have come to reject, it is common to describe earlier thinkers as having 'believed' or 'believed in' a particular set of doctrines. It seems more accurate to speak of 'knowledge' than of 'belief' – Sedgwick, Whewell and the rest of the Cambridge network did not 'believe' that the universe was governed by law, that it had been designed by a Designer, that man was the highest ornament of creation, and that God was still immanent in his world: they knew these things. If Darwin's theory conflicted with these facts the theory was not threatening or frightening; it was necessarily and logically wrong. All truth was one; it could not be in conflict with itself.

As Whewell wrote in 1853:

[Even if new scientific facts come forth which force new theories to be accepted] still the argument from the design which appears in the parts of which we most clearly see the purpose, would not lose its force. If, for instance, it should be made apparent, by geological investigations of the extinct fossil creation, that the animal forms which have inhabited the earth, have gradually approached to that type in which the human form is included . . . still the evidences of design in the anatomy of man are not less striking than they were, when no such gradation was thought of. And what is more to the purpose of our argument, the evidences of the peculiar nature and destination of man, is shown in other characters than his anatomy, – his moral and intellectual nature, his history and capacities – stand where they stood before; nor is the vast chasm which separates man, as a being with such characters as these latter, from all other animals, at all filled up or bridged over.[101]

Or in Sedgwick's words to Darwin:

There is a moral or a metaphysical part of nature as well as a physical. A man who denies this is deep in the mire of folly. 'Tis the crown and glory of organic science that it *does*, through *final cause*, link material to moral; . . . you have ignored this link; and if I do not mistake your meaning, you have done your best in one or two pregnant cases to break it. Were it possible (which, thank God, it is not) to break it, humanity, in my mind, would suffer a damage that might brutalize it, and sink the human race into a lower grade of degradation than any into which it has fallen since its written records tell us of its history.[102]

These scientists were willing to be flexible in their interpretation of inessential aspects of revealed religion – they could set aside the Flood, they could explain miracles by reference to a higher vantage point, they could be supportive of their colleagues in the humanities, doing scriptural criticism and analytical theology. But they simply could not conceive of truths which would force them to set aside the fundamental bases of their faith. An occasional subtle thinker like Maurice could step back and incorporate even Darwinian theory into his profoundly Christian world-view,[103] but for most of the Cambridge circle such accommodation was simply not possible.

There is an ironic quality about the role played by these conservative scientists in the geological controversies. At each step they more clearly than anyone else formulated the questions which each new thesis would raise, presenting the problems they perceived as insuperable obstacles to the acceptance of the new theory. And the answer to each question in turn sparked the next controversy, until the final answer was utterly intolerable. In 1831 Sedgwick objected to Lyell's uniformitarianism by pointing out that such a principle would raise the 'doctrines of spontaneous generation and transmutation of species, with all their train of monstrous consequences'.[104] When Chambers did, in fact put forward those doctrines in the *Vestiges*, Sedgwick ridiculed the work because it provided no mechanism by which species could be transmutated.

The theory of Lamarck, though baseless as the fabric of a crazy dream, is better framed than the one before us. It gives us, at least, a comprehensive cause of organic changes from one species to another; while our author talks only of *development* – a word without sense or significance, if he fail to give us any material facts to gloss its meaning.[105]

And when Darwin in turn did provide a mechanism – Natural Selection – Sedgwick replied that to accept such a theory would be to reject the doctrine of final cause, to sever the tie between the moral and the material. Such a severance Darwin's immediate disciples and the scientists of the post-Darwinian period were prepared to accept. It was a division which the creative, thoughtful, and conservative (in the best sense of the word) scholars of Cambridge simply could not stomach. The answers to Sedgwick's questions – and he spoke for his whole circle, not just himself – spelled the end of the integrated world-view he so much believed in and wanted to sustain.[106]

In 1851 Whewell delivered a paper to the Cambridge Philosophical Society on 'The Transformation of Hypotheses in the History of Science'.[107] In it he described the natural conservatism of the scientific community, the tenacity of old views, and the ways in which older scholars try to amalgamate new and old doctrines without sacrificing any central precepts.

when a prevalent theory is found to be untenable, and consequently, is succeeded by a different, or even by an opposite one, the change is not made suddenly . . . at least in the minds of the most tenacious adherents of the earlier doctrine; but is effected by . . . a series of transformations of the earlier hypothesis . . . and thus, the defenders of the ancient doctrine are able to go on as if still asserting their first opinions.[108]

To some extent the conservative scientists of Cambridge were willing to attempt this sort of accommodation, to redefine terms and to assert that they and the Darwinians still interpreted nature the same way; Sedgwick wrote to Darwin, for example:

As to your grand principle – *natural selection* – what is it but a secondary consequence of supposed, or known, primary facts . . . For you do not deny causation. I call (in the abstract) causation the will of God; and I can prove that He acts for the good of His creatures. He also acts by laws which we can study and comprehend. Acting by law, and under what is called final cause, comprehends, I think, your whole principle.[109]

But in the end such efforts would not suffice – Sedgwick and Darwin really were not talking the same language.[110]

Perhaps the senior scholars were simply too old to adjust. For in his essay Whewell also noted that to some extent scientific opinions must be

ascribed to the lasting effects of education and early prejudice. The old opinion passes away with the old generation: the new theory grows to its full vigour when its congenital disciples grow to be masters. John Bernoulli continues a Cartesian to the last. Daniel, his son, is a Newtonian from the first.[111]

He might describe the process academically, but it was not pleasant to experience it personally. Whewell wrote to Forbes in 1860:

It is a wrong business when the younger cultivators of science put out of sight and deprecate what their predecessors have done; but obviously that is the tendency of Huxley and his friends.[112]

When Darwin published in 1859 they were all – Sedgwick, Whewell, Herschel, Babbage, Conybeare, Henslow, Hare – if still alive, in their sixties or seventies. Within fourteen years they were all dead. And with them passed away a coherent world revealed and held together by the mutual action of religion and science.

CHAPTER 7

THE DISINTEGRATION OF AN IDEAL

Even while their academic disciplines were undergoing development and sometimes crisis, the dons of Cambridge managed to articulate a stable university ideal which they were determined to uphold: the ideal of a liberal education. Their concern to make orderly and then to vindicate their educational program grew at least in part out of their 'Victorian' morality – it was their duty, enforced by their oaths, to make the University genuinely into a 'seminary of sound learning and religious education'. Unlike their eighteenth-century counterparts, they took their duty seriously. Furthermore, interest in educational theory was fashionable. Thinkers outside the Cambridge community – J. S. Mill, T. H. Huxley, John Henry Newman, Edward Pusey, and Mark Pattison[1] – also wrote treatises on the subject during the middle part of the century. Another reason why the concept of a liberal education was so appealing at Cambridge was that it meshed neatly with the other intellectual principles which the university dons held dear. It was the pedagogical expression of their commitment to a unitary world of truth.

Their educational program had several components, the most obvious being the curriculum. The principles on which a liberal curriculum should be based were clearly spelled out in Whewell's educational treatises[2] and in Sedgwick's *Discourse on the Studies of the University*. Because mathematics develops the reasoning power and ancient literature heightens taste and connects men with all the best wisdom of the past:

The study of elementary mathematics . . . along with the study of classical authors, ought to be imperatively required by all Universities. To separate these studies, and to allow students to neglect one of them . . . is to abdicate the functions of education altogether. Universities' business is the general cultivation of all the best faculties of those who are committed to their charge, and the preservation and promotion of the general culture of mankind . . . To neglect to demand a combination of these two elements, would be to let slip the only machinery by which Universities, as the general cultivators of the mind, can execute their office.[3]

In principle the curriculum as analysed by Sedgwick was, indeed, based on these two main disciplines, 'the study of the laws of nature' and 'the study of ancient literature', along with a third component, not nearly so strenuously pursued, 'the study of ourselves, considered as individuals and as social beings'.[4]

For several reasons actual curricular practice deviated widely from the ideal. Cambridge served two really quite separate groups of students, 'classmen' and 'passmen' – that is, honours candidates and students taking only the ordinary degree. From the beginning of the century there had existed for honours students a rigorous mathematical examination and after 1822 a similarly exacting test in classical literature. For the really good students, then, improving the curriculum (in terms of the liberal ideal) required little more than tinkering with these two triposes – extending the length of the examinations, making subject matter more comprehensive, adjusting the relationship between the two disciplines, seeing that Sedgwick's third component (the social sciences) was taught in a reasonable way without distracting students from their real specialties.

The poll examination was a much more difficult problem. The standard required of passmen at the beginning of the century was appallingly low, and little that the reformers did during the next fifty years had much effect. Looking back at the end of the period Leslie Stephen[5] discussed the weakness of the ordinary degree program; his criticisms would have been applicable at nearly any point in the previous half-century. In the first place, the pass students (usually about two-thirds of the undergraduate body)[6] simply were not very bright.

A young Englishman at a University is remarkably like a young Englishman anywhere else, – that is to say, he is full of animal spirits, a thoroughly good fellow, and intensely and incredibly ignorant.[7]

Second, the University's commitment to classics and mathematics, while maybe reasonable at the honours level, inflicted upon these unenthusiastic young men two of the most demanding and – to the uninspired – distasteful subjects possible. Third, in addition to being what Stephen called 'singularly repulsive to the general public',[8] the subjects were utterly useless in preparing students for later life.

We have got to think of education here so much as a means of training rather than as a means of giving useful information, that we have almost come to dislike any system of education by which useful information is conveyed. At least, I can only thus account for the favour extended to the Poll. Every one admits that it does not give one any mental training of the least value. But it seems to be considered as a negative merit that it does not try to teach anybody anything he can ever want to know afterwards.[9]

Finally, in a society and institution where competition – or 'emulation', as it was called at Cambridge – was widely used as a spur to achievement, no effort was made to get pollmen to feel competitive. All prizes and ranking systems were reserved for honours students; of pollmen: 'Their wisest ambition is to be last amongst those not actually disqualified.'[10]

Various suggestions were put forward during the course of the century for improving the ordinary degree. It was suggested that some sort of university entrance examination be instituted. But as admission to Cambridge was determined by admission to a particular college, and as this right was jealously guarded by the individual houses, no progress was made toward excluding 'young men quite unfit to profit by a sojourn at the University'.[11] It was also argued that an examination of some sort was needed early in the undergraduate program, to discourage students from remaining idle until their final year. Instituting this reform was comparatively easy – after 1824 all students had to undergo a 'Previous' examination within two years of their arrival at the University. Setting up the examination and making it an effective instructional device were two separate matters, however. To counterbalance what had come to be viewed as an overemphasis on mathematics, the subject matter of the Previous was to be limited to classics and a smattering of theology.[12] It was then used as a sort of qualifying test; those who did well on it were allowed to sit for honours, while bad papers pushed their authors automatically into the ranks of the poll. But critics immediately pointed out that the standard on the Previous was too low to give honours candidates an adequate acquaintance with the humanities; indeed, the examination eventually came to be viewed merely as a distraction and nuisance to students who should really have been concentrating on their mathematics.[13] As for pollmen, noted J. H. Monk, the dull and the indolent, knowing that there is to be no further call upon them for either divinity or classics, will think they have finally got rid of these subjects and that the renewal of their acquaintance with Euclid and algebra may safely be postponed till the ultimate examination approaches.[14]

The examination was modified in 1842,[15] in 1849, and in 1854,[16] but at no point did it become more than an irritant to honours candidates and a burdensome hurdle to pollmen.

The ordinary degree examination itself faced many of the same problems and experienced very nearly the same dreary history. In 1822 a university Syndicate recommended that the pass examination consist of papers on Euclid, simple arithmetic and algebra, Paley's *Evidences* and *Moral Philosophy*, Locke's *Essay on Human Understanding*, the first six books of the *Iliad*, and the *Aeneid*.[17] Trivial adjustments were made in the examination scheme in 1828, 1836, and 1843,[18] but at no point was the subject matter substantially changed or the standard significantly raised. In 1845 Alexander Thurtell, a tutor at Caius, circulated a flysheet in which he asserted that the standard on arithmetic questions was 'really a disgrace to the University'. He went on:

The Algebra is, by the majority of students, either almost entirely neglected, or so little attended to, as to lead to no useful result. I believe that very few of those who pass the Examination could make any use whatever of Algebra, even in the simplest employment of it in any scientific study they might take up.[19]

During the first half of the century – so long as the classics-and-mathematics view of liberal education held sway – no attempt was made to make the poll examination cover subjects more congenial to its victims. As the Cambridge University Commission Report of 1852 noted:

Mathematics and Greek and Latin still form a considerable part of it [the ordinary examination]. But these are subjects in which time had long since shown that most of this class of students did not possess the desire or the aptitude to excel. If their tastes and talents had inclined that way, the majority of them would no doubt have been found in the career of competition for mathematical and classical honours. For five weary terms [since taking the Previous] they have been compelled to continue a course of reading, which, whatever attractions, whatever benefits, it may have for others, is to them irksome, and, need we hesitate to add, little better than unprofitable.[20]

But even the Commissioners' recommendations for change could not override long-established prejudice; even in the 1860s the examination subjects remained the same and the standard remained low.

It is clear, then, that for the majority of students there was considerable disparity between the ideal liberal education and the actual Cambridge curriculum. For the honours programs the story was significantly different, although these examinations, too, faced difficulties. It has been discussed above how the program of study and testing in mathematics was gradually reformed throughout the first half of the century, so as to maintain the rigor necessary for mental discipline while introducing undergraduates to the best modern mathematical concepts. By the 1850s or 60s almost no one in or outside the University would have seriously criticized the concept of the mathematical curriculum. In 1863 Leslie Stephen wrote:

I believe there is no better intellectual training than that which is necessarily undergone by a man who takes good . . . mathematical honours.[21]

Whether the program was balanced, whether it approached Whewell's ideal of a liberal education, was another matter. In principle both mathematics and literature, both reason and taste, had to be cultivated to develop the whole man. But aside from the very limited amount of classics contained in the Previous, mathematics honours candidates could very nearly afford to concentrate all their attention on their preferred discipline.[22] To some extent this comparative neglect of classics could be justified because most of the public schools the students had attended before Cambridge had very much stressed classical studies,[23] but it seems strange that the University would be satisfied to let the schools do its work in this important area. Whewell's attitude was not clear. He was adamant about not allowing classicists to graduate without mathematical training; Winstanley assumes that this was because inwardly he was unimpressed with the value of a university classical program.[24] Whewell's educational treatises do not support this interpretation; in his 1845 book he expressed concern that the mathematicians were not receiving an adequate classical training[25] and he was a member of several syndicates which tried to raise the classical standard of the Previous examination. Sedgwick similarly paid lip-service to the value of a balanced curriculum, but his real enthusiasm was also clearly reserved for the mathematical part of the program.[26] No doubt the tendency of any academic system to be self-perpetuating was in part responsible for the dons' lack of concern for the narrowness of the mathematics program. They had attended Cambridge before even the classical tripos had existed; they had been successful at the mathematical examination[27] and in their later scholarly careers; it was therefore difficult to admit that a significantly different scheme would be better. There was also the traditional Cambridge veneration for mathematics – the discipline of Newton, it was the only subject which had kept the university program respectable during the 'dark ages' of the eighteenth century. In any case' so long as a student showed himself really talented in mathematics, he was unlikely to find himself much molested by other subjects even in a reforming Cambridge committed to liberal education.

The one degree program which seemed really consistent with Whewell's expressed ideal was classical honours. By the early 1820s the reforming spirit, which had manifested itself in mathematics in the Analytical Society, had also surfaced with respect to literature. The Master of Trinity, Christopher Wordsworth, and the Regius Professor of Greek, J. H. Monk, managed in 1822 to rally university support for the establishment of a voluntary tripos or honours examination in classics. Candidates first had to have earned honours in the mathematics tripos; they then would write a four day examination in which

translations shall be required of passages selected from the *best* Greek and Latin Authors, as well as written Answers to questions arising immediately out of such passages. No original composition, either in Greek or Latin, shall be required.[28]

Examinees would be divided into three groups and their names published in order of merit. In general the University seemed pleased with the new program. At the larger colleges there had long been sophisticated tutorial instruction in the classics, and an 1843 Syndicate expressed satisfaction with university tuition in the subject.[29] It is true that Sedgwick – and presumably some of his colleagues – felt that the classical examination erred in stressing literary accuracy and the cost of understanding the basic ideas presented;[30] a step towards remedying this problem came in 1849 when a paper in ancient history was added to the examination.[31] But to at least one student the classical training at Cambridge seemed to be ideal: Bristed felt that it stressed 'thoroughness and accuracy' and that a classics student was so well trained that throughout his life his Greek and Latin would never be forgotten. 'He remembers and knows what he studied at College, better than he does anything else except his immediate daily occupation.'[32]

Concern did begin to develop about the imbalance of requiring classicists to gain mathematical honours while mathematicians were not required to pursue classics. In 1848 honours triposes were established in the moral sciences and the natural sciences,[33] and in each case to attend them candidates had only to have passed the Previous examination. It therefore hardly seemed reasonable to continue to require an honours degree in mathematics from the classics candidates; yet the struggle over decoupling the two older triposes was surprisingly brisk. In 1849 the most the reformers could accomplish was to allow students who had either received mathematical honours or a first class ordinary degree[34] to become candidates for classical honours. In 1854 it was finally agreed that classicists, too, could proceed directly to their tripos after having taken only the Previous examination.[35]

The principle of combining mathematics with classics as the basis of a liberal education is an interesting one, one which people other than Whewell espoused.[36] In reviewing Whewell's *Liberal Education in General* an article in *Fraser's Magazine* said:

We all know what is intended when we speak of liberal or general education; we know that it implies a training of the human mind as such, – that it presumes a cultivation of our habits of thought without any reference to the specific occupation or profession for which we are destined, or which we are led to embrace . . . We accept the conclusion . . . of Dr. Whewell's assertion, that 'inasmuch as, in a good education, we must educate the Reason as well as the Literary Taste, we require of our students a mathematical, combined with a classical culture' . . . To insist that the classical scholar should also be in some sort a mathematician is undoubtedly a reasonable demand, . . . but it would be better far if the University would begin to require, also, that all mathematicians should be competently advanced in literary education, and that up to a certain point the claims of philology and exact science should be accurately balanced.[37]

The argument for the efficacy of mathematics does not perhaps seem completely convincing to the modern reader, for it was based on a Lockean view of learning psychology which has largely been superseded. And, indeed, in its own day there were many and vocal critics of mathematics as a mental exercise. The Hamilton articles of the 1830s were especially critical of precisely this aspect of the Cambridge curriculum.[38] There were classicists at Cambridge who rejected Whewell's claims,[39] and by the sixties the mystical power of mathematical study was a subject for open debate, if not ridicule:

A man must have a strange belief in the efficacy of mathematics who holds that a mere speaking acquaintance with its technical terms for a few years exercises a mysterious influence on a man's mind.[40]

The argument for classical study seems somehow to be still attractive, in part no doubt because the claims made for it lay more on the value of its content than on its worth as intellectual gymnastics.

The cultivated world, up to the present day, has been bound together, and each generation bound to the preceding, by living upon a shared intellectual estate. They have shared in a common development of thought, because they have understood each other. Their standard examples of poetry, eloquence, history, criticism, grammar, etymology, have been a universal bond of sympathy, however diverse might be the opinions which prevailed respecting any of these examples. All the civilized world has been one intellectual nation; and it is this which has made it so great and prosperous a nation. All the countries of lettered Europe have been one body, because the same nutriment, the literature of the ancient world, was conveyed to all, by the organization of their institutions of education. The authors of Greece and Rome, familiar to the child, admired and dwelt on by the the aged, were the common language, by the possession of which each man felt himself a denizen of the civilized world; – free of all the privileges with which it had been gifted from the dawn of Greek civilization up to the present time.[41]

Whewell was writing of ideal cases, of course, and even in his own day his description was so far removed from practical reality as to be almost ludicrous. Still, there is something pleasantly appealing about this vanishing vision, unrealistic and elitist as it obviously was.

By the middle of the century the central role of classics, like mathematics, was beginning to come under attack. Earlier scholars, even those who, like Thirlwall and Hare, were ardent advocates of the study of modern languages, had accepted without question that the classics should provide the foundation for further literary study. But as other subjects – notably science – became available and as modern languages became more and more important in understanding new discoveries in various scholarly fields, many thoughtful dons came to feel that too-exclusive concentration on the dead languages was a luxury the University could ill afford.[42] With the development of a variety of major 'lines' or fields, classics gradually became an optional part of the university program and after a much more than decent interval even the admission requirement of proficiency in Latin and Greek was abandoned.[43] But at mid-century the traditional combination of classics and mathematics – even if assailed – still held pride of place in the Cambridge curriculum.[44]

A liberal education involved more than just the subjects to be taught; it also implied a specific method of teaching. The basic subjects were to supply not information but mental habits and discipline. These habits could not be gained by mere passive attendance at lectures; they had to be developed through exercise, like that available in the collegiate tutorial system. Whewell put a great deal of emphasis on the importance of this 'practical' education, as he called it, feeling strongly that the subjects which students learned through recitation and practice were of more fundamental value than those which they absorbed only through memory.[45] He also distinguished between 'direct' and 'indirect' teaching – the former being that offered for its own sake, the latter employing tests and prizes so as to spur ambition. For a long time college lectures had been examples of direct teaching, offering courses of instruction which had

no reference to . . . public University trials; and which were selected by the authorities of the College, because they were considered as valuable for their own sake, and proper parts of a liberal education. But though this is still the case, a strong disposition has manifested itself of late years . . . to give a complete preponderance to the indirect system; – to conduct our education almost entirely by means of examinations, and to consider the lectures given in the Colleges as useful only in proportion as they prepare the student for success in the examinations.[46]

Indeed, for reasons which can easily be understood, Cambridge had come to depend more and more on the university examination system. Reforms of curriculum, improvements in instruction, changes in general educational philosophy – all had been articulated through revisions of the examination structure. Whewell pointed out that this was an efficient system for reform,[47] and it is clear that by changing examinations the University could change instruction without interfering in the internal affairs of the colleges.

But the disadvantages of excessive examining were great. From very early in the century many thoughtful dons were concerned that the emphasis on examinations was getting out of hand. Objections were raised even to the establishment of the classical tripos,[48] and by the forties most serious scholars felt some misgivings about the extreme dependence on competition. Hare wrote to Whewell in 1841 strongly advising against establishing a tripos in theology:

Emulation [competition] has done enough harm already; in heaven's name let us not extend it any further. We should try to teach people that knowledge is to be pursued for its own sake, . . . and not for the prizes attacht to it. Until we do this we produce nothing strong or lasting. When the stimulus is taken away, the student turns to something which will afford him a substitute for it. The only truly powerful influence, by which men's minds and characters are lastingly affected, is personal, that of mind on mind, of moral character on moral character.[49]

DeMorgan was also extremely critical of all the examining at Cambridge; he called the mathematics tripos 'the great writing race', and tried to prevent the same system from developing at his own University College, London.[50] And Whewell himself clearly recognized the evils which grew from such excessive dependence on systems of testing.[51] Much of the academic legislation during these years dealt with methods of 'bracketing' the candidates for honours – that is, ways of ranking and grading the students. Like latter-day quarrels over letter versus number grades, or pluses and minuses, these debates seem trivial; but beneath the technicalities lay real concerns – how to be fair while at the same time diminishing the emphasis placed on competition and examination.[52]

There were, to be sure, some people who explicitly endorsed the principle of using examinations to stimulate effort – William Hopkins argued in an 1842 pamphlet that without examinations most students would refuse almost completely to do any work.[53] More convincing than overt argument, however, was the pattern university reform followed. More, not fewer, examinations grew up during the middle part of the century; as Maurice had observed, whenever reform was spoken of a new tripos was the first remedy suggested. During Leslie Stephen's period as a don excessive examination was as much a problem as ever:

Put heavy premiums on two or three selected studies, confine all effort as much as possible to them, and appeal only to the most material motives, and you may, it is true, produce a very energetic competition for certain honours, but you cannot expect that the standard of intellectual cultivation prevalent at the University at large will be very enlightened or elevated.[54]

Such criticisms notwithstanding, English university education has not even in modern times turned away from the final examination as one of its most important educational mechanisms.[55]

A very troubling side effect of the increasingly powerful examination system was the development of a concomitant 'evil' – private tuition. The 'public' tutors in the colleges had a wide range of responsibilities towards their students, mainly administrative or related to discipline, so that to expect really intensive instruction from them was unrealistic. As competition in the various examinations became really vigorous, it therefore was common for a student to hire a private tutor to direct his reading. Such tutors were almost always Cambridge M.A.s living in the town; the best ones were often first rate scholars.[56] There were real advantages to private tuition: even opponents of the system admitted that the colleges, especially the small ones, did not have adequate teaching staffs.[57] Students received personal attention and instruction and often formed friendships with their coaches. Private tuition employed the 'practical' or active method of teaching which Whewell so much valued, for students were called on to work up and present certain problems or passages to their coaches. The long vacations were effectively utilized through reading parties. And it was even regarded as a benefit that private tuition allowed the wealthy to avail themselves of a privilege inaccessible to other students.[58]

On the other hand, there was no question that the system encouraged 'cram'. The coach's job was to help his student get a good place in the tripos, and to a large extent he did this by second-guessing the examiners and predicting what topics would be covered.[59] It was widely believed that the tutors taught only material likely to be examined on, so that the evils of excessive examination – narrowness, shallowness – were exacerbated.[60] And there is no doubt that with most of the real instruction being conducted on an unofficial basis, the colleges were necessarily losing much of their significance as educational centers. Nevertheless, so long as the other basic features of the Cambridge system remained the same, private tuition was almost certain to continue to exist.[61]

Proposals for alleviating the effects of the practice varied. The most obvious remedy would have been to improve collegiate instruction, presumably by requiring all fellows to teach.[62] But fellowships through the years had come to be viewed as rewards for undergraduate excellence, not contracts for future service; they did not even require residence in Cambridge. Unless there was outside interference or the colleges voluntarily chose to reform themselves along those lines, university fellows could not very practicably be viewed as a pool of private instructors. Other reformers suggested that the private tutors be somehow brought into the public system. Colleges could simply hire some of the private tutors as members of their own staffs;[63] or the University could allow coaches to establish regulated boarding houses where students could live and study more cheaply than in the regular colleges.[64]

To some extent all of the instructional problems mentioned – dependence on examinations, 'excessive emulation', private tuition – were reflections of a larger organizational problem. If the colleges had been performing their functions adequately – if they had required all fellows to teach and thus provided reasonable instruction, if they had used entrance examinations to exclude students obviously unfit, if they had developed programs of sensibly related college lectures and examinations – then it would have been possible for the collegiate foundations to provide the liberal education which Cambridge in principle so much cherished. Conservative reformers indeed would have liked to look to the colleges for solutions, and in the case of the larger foundations such hope was not entirely misplaced. St John's and Trinity had both had entrance examinations and coordinated annual lecture/examination programs since the beginning of the century; and Whewell was able to convince himself, at least, that the role of public tutor had the potential for being very effective.[65] But the small colleges were too much in need of students voluntarily to institute entrance examinations and too poorly supplied with senior scholars to provide adequate courses of instruction.

Thus it became increasingly clear that real reform was going to have to depend on leadership from the central University.[66] But in several ways the central University was the rival, not the ally, of the colleges. The seemingly simple matter of establishing university hostels, for example, would have allowed the central organization to compete with the smaller units for members, while at the same time usurping the right, traditionally held by the colleges, of providing a setting for familial discipline. New university examinations, whether honours or ordinary, Previous or entrance, forced the colleges to change their instructional systems, sometimes in directions they were not prepared to go.[67] And to finance an active university role in undergraduate instruction posed a troublesome problem. Since the colleges were rich but relatively ineffectual while the University was impoverished but potentially very powerful, plans to increase university activity often seemed to carry with them a threat of possible 'usurpation' of collegiate resources.[68] Many dons, therefore, who on other grounds actively wanted instructional reform, became alarmed at the prospect of increasing university power.

Furthermore, in an almost essential way university instruction was really inimical to liberal education. College teachers were 'tutors', classes were small, and instruction was personal and 'practical'. University teachers, on the other hand, were 'professors'; they taught through lectures not tutorials, and their subject matter was 'speculative' or 'progressive',[69] not fixed and stable. Some of the most talented men in the University were the professors, and at least after the first quarter of the century many of them had come to take their teaching responsibilities seriously. But they were mainly specialists in disciplines other than classics and mathematics, so that attempts to make better use of the professorships automatically involved a reorientation of the curriculum. The report of an 1848 syndicate appointed 'to afford greater encouragement to the pursuit of those studies for the cultivation of which Professorships have been founded in the University' began:

The Syndicate admitting the superiority of the study of Mathematics and Classics over all others as the basis of General Education, and acknowledging therefore the wisdom of adhering to our present system in its main features, are nevertheless of opinion that much good would result from affording greater encouragement to the pursuit of various other branches of Science and Learning which are daily acquiring more importance and a higher estimation in the world, and for the teaching of which the University already possesses the necessary means.[70]

Through its more efficient use of university professors, there were really two things this syndicate was attempting to do, both threatening to the traditional liberal ideal. They wanted to offer some subjects to pollmen which would capture their interest, even at the sacrifice of insistence on classics-and-mathematics. And they wanted to begin encouraging the development of various new disciplines, to turn Cambridge toward 'research' even if at the expense of elementary education. Pressure to move in the first direction, to broaden the basis of the ordinary degree, came from many sources. Critics from outside the University had, of course, been saying for a long time that the curriculum was too narrow.[71] But gradually even moderates within Cambridge were coming to recognize the futility and even cruelty of insisting that all undergraduates pursue a course in which they had little interest or ability. Whewell was prepared to see the 'progressive' subjects introduced into the curriculum – indeed, he was an active member of most of the syndicates which established new triposes, improved theological instruction, and encouraged the work of the professors, though he continued, of course, to insist that such subjects should be studied in connection with a solid preparation in the basic courses.[72] And other dons who remained committed to the basic premises of liberal education still advocated widening the curricular options for the pollmen;[73] a letter from Hare to Whewell perhaps sums up this new 'softened' attitude as well as any published pamphlet:

There is another remark in your former letter, with reference to the degree in wch students may be allowed to follow the bent of their own genius. This, you say, is not to *educate*. It may not be to *instruct:* But as you know I am fond of following an etymological clew; and to *educate* seems to me to be to bring out that which is in a man. And this is the business of education, to protect from stunting and blighting influences, and to cherish and develope the innate life, giving it room to spread all its branches around, and to put forth all its leaves, its own leaves, not another tree's leaves.

All these things you of course know and assent to; and I know not why I have thought it necessary to urge them, except that some of your conclusions seem to militate against them. In the service of truth, one must bring out truisms, when they are wanted.[74]

To encourage diversification the University began by requiring all pollmen to attend a series of lectures from at least one of the university professors. This made the curriculum more flexible in principle but hardly significantly affected the level of education of the ordinary degree students.[75] Of the three bodies of teachers at Cambridge – the college tutors, the private tutors, and the professors

– university organization rendered those with the broadest view and the greatest ability the least effectual.

Such distinguished men as Professor Sedgwick have done what they have done in spite of their position rather than by force of it . . . [With the requirement that pollmen attend at least one course of professorial lectures] the ablest men obtainable – and there are many distinguished professors at Cambridge – are set to talk ABC to lads whose whole soul is in cricket and boating, and whose theory of learning is to pass the barriers of the examination at the smallest possible expenditure of brains.[76]

Nevertheless, there was a general feeling that something was being done for the pollmen, and that although the traditional liberal courses were becoming less important, still a general education was being offered as part of the ordinary degree. Looking back from 1854 Whewell summed up what he regarded as the major direction that reform of the poll degree had taken:

The tendency of [recent] legislation has been, to separate the different Lines of Study from each other more and more, so far as Candidates for *Honours* are concerned; but to require a greater and greater number of different subjects from Candidates for the *Ordinary* degree . . . I conceive this practice – so long pursued by the University – of dealing in a different way with those who are and those who are not Candidates for Honours, to be perfectly well-founded, wise, and confirmed by experience. Those who have such an amount of preparatory knowledge, love of study, ability, ambition, as to become Candidates for Honours, may *perhaps*, derive mental advantage from being left to pursue their favourite study undisturbed by other requirements . . . But those who have no love of study or of distinction which can compete with their love of amusement or idleness, or who, from want of preparation or ability, have no chance of obtaining an honour, derive the greatest advantage which they are capable of receiving here, from being required to prepare themselves, to a moderate extent, in *several* subjects. This they can do; though they cannot make any considerable proficiency in any subject; and the accumulation of subjects may be made to occupy their time, as no single subject could do; especially if one of the conditions be attendance at public Lectures.[77]

A second reform carried out at the same time was more to the point: the Syndicate established honours triposes in natural sciences and in moral sciences. Candidates had to have passed the Previous; they would then write examinations on anatomy, physiology, chemistry, botany, geology and comparative anatomy or on moral

philosophy, political economy, modern history, general jurispru-
dence, and the laws of England. The examinees would in each case
be arranged into three classes of merit, but they would still have to
pass the ordinary examination in order to receive their degrees.[78]
Lacking an honours degree in mathematics as a prerequisite, the
new triposes were not immediately viewed with a great deal of
respect. They were certainly better than the old poll degree, but they
hardly carried with them the prestige of the traditional triposes.
Even while recommending that his friends vote for the new programs
Whewell admitted that the proposals were weak.[79] And throughout
the next decade the University was troubled that the examinations
were not rigorous enough to deserve being considered honours
triposes, while at the same time they undercut the traditional
education program.[80]

Part of the trouble was merely structural: the new triposes did
not lead to degrees and they required too many examinations too
close together. But in part the difficulty was one of philosophy – these
new fields were essentially different from the old ones. They conveyed more information than training; they could not really hope
to provide comprehensive education; in their effort to be broad they
were painfully shallow. The disciplines encompassed in these new
triposes were 'sciences', not 'science'. To try to unify them was to
make them trivial. W. G. Clark wrote in 1860:

It seems to me impossible that these Triposes can ever work so long as
candidates are encouraged to take up for examination so many subjects
at once. Each of these subjects affords ample matter for the study of a
life-time. When a man of two-and-twenty is encouraged to attempt
proficiency in all, what other result can be looked for than . . . 'a shabby
superficiality'? I trust that in future no honours will be given in either
Tripos except to such persons as have shown a real, profound knowledge
of some one subject: that no candidates shall be required to take up for
examination more than one subject . . .[81]

Pressure to divide the disciplines into individual subjects came
from still another direction, from within the sciences themselves.
The scholars who taught the various courses in the new triposes were
by mid-century mostly serious specialists. They were painfully aware
of the disparity between the level of academic work going on in the
British Universities and abroad,[82] and they wanted Cambridge to
commit its curriculum and its financial resources to the support of

scholarship in their various fields.[83] The complete story of the development of the individual disciplines – or as it might be put, the fragmenting of the curriculum – belongs to the second half of the century and is carefully and interestingly told in Sheldon Rothblatt's *The Revolution of the Dons*. It is enough to note here that improving the professoriate, broadening the curriculum, and strengthening the central University were all steps which would logically lead to a different kind of academic program, one quite incompatible with the unified vision of liberal education espoused during the early part of the century.

The ideal itself did not immediately disappear. Even the older triposes gave up any pretense of presenting a balanced program; in 1854 the Senate agreed to let candidates sit the classics honours examination without any higher qualification in mathematics than that guaranteed by the Previous.[84] On the other hand there were continued efforts to make the Previous into a meaningful test and to require through it that men receive something of a general education before they began on their separate lines of specialized study.[85] Essentially what the University seemed to be saying was that the old liberal curriculum ought to be pushed back into a student's earlier years, that it was really an elementary course upon which the more specialized disciplines ought to be based. There was really nothing revolutionary in this idea – during the period when the *trivium* and *quadrivium* had been the first part of a university training, students had been much younger boys; it was in some ways reasonable to let liberal education be the task of the schools or of the very early undergraduate years.[86] There were at least two difficulties in this approach – scholars might agree that general education should come first and specialized work later, but it was not easy to decide on the optimum age for each type of study. To Whewell, university undergraduates still seemed very young and in need of civilizing; when he talked about 'mature scholarship' he obviously meant what would today be at least post-graduate work. Critics of the Cambridge system, on the other hand, pointed out that the level at which the traditional courses were taught was so puerile as to make discussions of ideals of liberal education meaningless. The second difficulty grew, out of the complex relationship between the universities and the preparatory schools, especially the prestigious public foundations. The University could theorize about leaving elementary education to the schools.[87] But the two sets of institutions were interrelated in such a way as to make such an expectation quite unrealistic. Schools taught what they thought the colleges wanted students to know; once the traditional subjects came to be seen as unimportant at the universities they would inevitably decline in significance at Rugby, Harrow, and Eton.[88]

Whewell and some of the other conservative reformers tried to escape this dilemma by relying on their old favorite, collegiate instruction. Final degrees would be regulated by the University and an invigorated professoriate would assume an increasing share of the instruction in specialized disciplines. But college tutorials and lectures would continue to provide training and information of great value, laying the basis for a general education.[89] No doubt partly because he was becoming more conservative as he grew older but also because of his faith in the inherent worth of the college system, Whewell was a spirited opponent of proposals in the fifties which attempted to strengthen the University at the expense of the colleges. In 1857 he outlined what he perceived to be the theory and principle of collegiate government:

the constitutions and practice of our Colleges as they have existed since the Great Reformation . . . have been reasonable in theory and beneficial and effective in practice. Their revenues have been employed in maintaining a body of Fellows, whose office it has been to give instruction to the Students or Pupils belonging to the College, and to fill, as vacancies occurred, the Vicaries and Rectories of which the College was Patron. So long as the Fellows remained in College discharging the former class of duties, they were required to remain unmarried, because the whole scheme of College life was conceived as caenobitic or gregarious. The whole College was one Family. The ultimate destination of the Fellows was Holy Orders, because they were to be the Incumbents of the Colleges Livings. [At times there were more Fellows than college offices or livings available and such Fellows might be pursuing a profession elsewhere.] Yet such Fellowships were far from being without their effect in promoting the business of the College. Since Fellowships could be held on such loose conditions, they were objects of competition to many who did not intend to enter Holy Orders or to exercise the office of College Teachers: and the body of competitors for College Honours and Emoluments thus increased, formed a nucleus of zealous students who made zeal in study habitual and general in the College.[90]

Richard Sheepshanks, who though not residing at Cambridge had continued to take an active interest in university affairs, agreed with

Whewell as to the value of collegiate instruction;[91] and G. B. Airy, by now Astronomer Royal, was also very much concerned that the influence of the colleges not be diminished.[92]

With respect to instruction, however, there was a certain sense of futility about it all. That no real effort was made to decrease the significance of the examinations meant that university control was bound to increase and the influence of collegiate instruction to decline. A convenient symbol for this movement was provided by King's College. Since its foundation King's had been allowed to grant Cambridge degrees without having its students in any way examined by the central University;[93] Graces about examinations as late as 1849 contained the proviso 'That the foregoing Regulations shall not interfere with the composition between the University and King's College'.[94] But by the fifties the Fellows and Scholars of King's had come to realize that taking the university examinations was a valuable privilege, not an onerous obligation; by their free will in 1851 they relinquished 'all right and title whatsoever to be exempt from the ordinary examination of the University'.[95] Furthermore, even though their public statements about the colleges might be optimistic, the conservative reformers recognized that the difficulties under which the colleges labored were real and not likely to disappear. In a depressing confidential letter to Forbes in 1855 Whewell wrote about the possibility of appointing James Clerk Maxwell to a Trinity fellowship:

But I should like to know that he would be willing to labour in college as a mathematical lecturer for some years when he is elected. I have been much plagued by all my mathematical lecturers running away from the College to other employments – retaining their Fellowships of course. If I were to say all that I know from experience of the working of our Fellowships system in this way, it would be a stronger weapon in the hands of our Reformers than I choose to give them.[96]

Maxwell was, in fact, elected to a fellowship, served the College for only one year, and then departed to London and 'other employment'. He did return to Cambridge in 1870, but it was as a university professor – the organizer of a program in experimental physics and the head of the newly established Cavendish Laboratory.[97]

There was one aspect of Cambridge education which remained longer in the hands of the colleges, and in a way it was as central to the concept of liberal education as were classics and mathematics: moral guidance. In the early years of the century there had been no doubt that colleges should serve in *loco parentis*, and early university records are full of regulations affecting students' personal and social lives.[98] The control of student debt was regarded as the special function of the college tutor, and at various times townsmen were 'discommuned' (cut off from all trade with the University and their establishments declared out-of-bounds to undergraduates) for allowing students to run up excessive bills.[99]

More important than these strictly disciplinary functions were the colleges' religious responsibilities to their students. It is very unclear that collegiate efforts in this area had much impact, but that college officers by and large viewed these obligations seriously is unquestionable. An undated[100] 'Memorandum for the Tutors' from Whewell spelled out the familial relationship and responsibilities which were to be undertaken by the college and students. Regulations included daily chapel (twice on Sunday), regular attendance at dinner in hall, being in college by ten o'clock at night ('If out after twelve, to give explanation to the Tutor or Dean'), faithful attendance at lectures, and gaining permission to leave Cambridge for any reason. Whewell then went on to list other examples of practices which tutors should urge upon their pupils 'as the opportunity offers':

To behave reverently in chapel, and to make it a place of devotion, using the prayer book, etc. To attend at least one sermon at St. Mary's every Sunday. To join in the Communion when administered in College. To conform to the College course of reading, and [not] allowing their reading with Private Tutors to interfere with it. To avoid giving heed to statements of their companions as to what is unsanctioned or expected: – as for instance that they need attend chapel only some smaller number of times: – that they may go without their gowns when they please, except at official times: – That they may at their pleasure omit dining in hall except so far as to keep the greater part of the Term: – That they may go any distance from Cambridge without leave (for example to London): That they may dress as fantastically as they please. All such practices, whether noticed in the offices or not, are violations of proper College Habits. If such transgressions are overlooked there is by this means the opportunity given to the student to show that he conforms to college habits willingly, and not from compulsion only.

The Tutors will judge which sections of this advice to give in their Public Lectures and which in private. The Tutors, including the Assistant Tutors, will of course promote the observance of these Rules by their example and by the tenor of their conversation.[101]

132

That the college should serve as a substitute family and provide religious guidance continued to be believed well past the middle of the century. Airy in 1859 objected to allowing masters of colleges to be laymen because it was his belief,

A belief which (so far as I can learn) has been entertained by the wise and good in almost all ages of the world, that no scheme of Liberal Education in its best sense can be successfully carried out except as an institution of religious character, and under the superintendence of persons ostensibly connected with religion by the tie of ecclesiastical ordination.[102]

Airy also felt that all students, including religious dissenters, should continue to be required to attend college chapel:

all will hear what concerns all, and what is indispensable for the welfare of the future man that the present boy should hear: that man is feeble and erring; that omnipotence is, as we trust, merciful though just; and that a deeply grounded feeling of religious humility is the only foundation upon which dignity of character can be built.[103]

And Robert Potts, in suggesting a series of subjects for a possible entrance examination, selected his readings in part in terms of their moral value.[104] More and more, however, the overseeing of students' private conduct receded into the background of college business. University records almost ceased to discuss matters of student discipline, and Sheepshanks in 1854 advised that the college should simply tell parents that it would refuse to play nursemaid to unruly boys.[105] With the general admission of dissenters – and with the disintegration of any uniform religious view among the fellows – religious instruction and guidance gradually became very much diluted; by the end of the century even the collegiate role of moral guide had nearly been abandoned.

There were a number of people outside the Cambridge community who continued to believe in the broad concept of a liberal education. There might be disagreement about what should constitute the core courses. But that there should exist an educational system which would bring out the best of each man's abilities and prepare him not for a profession but for life was an ideal widely and vigorously espoused by scholars of various academic persuasions.[106] Mill would have prescribed a course based on ancient literature, history, philosophy, the social sciences, and some mathematics.[107] Newman advocated a traditional classical curriculum with theology as a basic component.[108] And Huxley wanted a university to offer moral and social science, physical science, modern literature, and history.[109] But they all agreed that some organized curriculum ought to be presented to all undergraduates and that in pursuing it students would at least be exposed to a liberal education.

But for reasons which should by now be clear, the University of Cambridge in the second half of the nineteenth century was simply not going to be able to fill this need. In order to make their program conform more nearly to their own ideal the earlier reforming dons had come to depend on the central University; this meant an emphasis on 'subjects' instead of 'general education' and on an active professoriate. And this in turn had spelled the beginning of the end of the familial, 'permanent', 'practical' system of instruction which the colleges had provided and on which their concept of liberal education had so much depended. Even more important, the coherent body of thought on which their pedagogical principles rested had disintegrated. No longer agreed as a group about the meaning of the Christian message, they found their new Broad Church principles (or in some cases overt agnosticism) put their program of moral instruction on a very insecure basis. Furthermore, religion and science had been wrested apart; it was increasingly difficult, and eventually impossible, to present their students with an all-encompassing, unified vision of the universe.

In many ways the Cambridge of the second half of the century was a very exciting, creative place. Academic disciplines were pursued rigorously, brilliant specialized scholars were educated, and a wide-reaching intellectual vitality developed which had earlier – for a large part of the university population, anyway – been quite impossible to attain. Cambridge became an effective research institution of the modern type. There also developed a new kind of moral vitality. Friendly relationships between students and thoughtful, accepting dons like Leslie Stephen, Henry Sidgwick, and J. R. Seeley became a basis for personal ethical growth which was perhaps more meaningful than that gained from the formal religious guidance of half a century before. 'Muscular Christianity' provided a healthy and constructive outlet for the energies of non-reading men, who previously had pretty much been left to their own devices. And the University gradually made its resources available to classes of English citizens – especially women and non-Anglicans – who had hitherto been excluded from it.[110]

Nevertheless, the older, disappearing Cambridge had also had a great deal to recommend it. When it worked well the old system had been capable of helping men develop the ability to reason and to make sound aesthetic judgments. It had laid a firm base on which students could go on to build their own specialized educations. Cambridge men were initiated into an intellectual world based on unified truth, their Christian faith confirmed and its complete compatibility with physical knowledge demonstrated. A good Cambridge graduate of the early nineteenth century was literate, accurate, critical, and competent. And, most of all, he was confident – confident that he was in honest contact with the universe and the forces that governed it. One could hardly ask more of his Alma Mater.

NOTES

1. The widespread recognition of the loneliness of college life can be illustrated in the correspondence between William Whewell and Julius Hare, two devoted Cantabrigians and dedicated scholars. Hare agreed with Whewell that 'college rooms are no home for declining years'. See pp. 205 ff. in Janet Stair Douglas' *Life and Selections from the Correspondence of William Whewell, D.D.*, London, 1881. And in his otherwise eulogistic *Ode to Trinity College* (London, 1812) a former undergraduate, George Pryme, included this verse:

   > Here the unfriended churchman pines
   > And half the bliss of life resigns
   > Bound by those harsh monastic rules
   > Accurst remains of popish schools.   (p. 21)

   For the eccentricity of extreme hypochrondia see John W. Clark and T. McKinney Hughes, *The Life and Letters of Adam Sedgwick*, Cambridge, 1890.
2. See Kenelm Digby, *The Broad Stone of Honour*, Cambridge, 1822, pp. 262 ff.; J. Pycroft, *The Collegian's Guide, or Recollections of College Days*, London, 1845, p. 64; Robert Southey (published under name of Don Manuel Alvarez Espirella), *Letters from England*, London, 1808, pp. 274 and 275.
3. Victor Aime Huber, *English Universities*, London, 1843, vol. II, pt 1, pp. 319–324. Huber is particularly useful, as here, when he discusses the social value of the eighteenth-century English university system.
4. See Robert Southey, *Letters from England*, p. 237. Edward Gibbon (*Memoirs of my Life*, New York, 1969, p. 48), as is well known, dissented from this widespread satisfaction with the Universities. He regarded his fourteen months at Oxford as 'the most idle and unprofitable of my life'.
5. William Whewell, *Of a Liberal Education in General*, London, 1845, p. 161.
6. T. G. Bonney, *A Chapter in the Life History of an Old University*, London, 1882, pp. 12–13.
7. See Whewell's survey of recent changes in Cambridge examinations (*Of a Liberal Education*, pp. 178–196).
8. A useful summary of the state of British science during this period can be found in 'The Scientific Spirit in England,' vol. I, pp. 226–301, in J. T. Merz' *A History of European Scientific Thought in the Nineteenth Century*, London, 1904.
9. *Edinburgh Review*, vol. XI, no. 22, Jan., 1808, p. 249; vol. XIV, no. 28, July, 1809, p. 429; vol. XV, no. 29, Oct., 1809, p. 40.
10. Edward Copleston, an Oxford don, responded in two short books, *A Reply to the Calumnies of the 'Edinburgh Review' against Oxford* and *A Second Reply to the 'Edinburgh Review'*, both published in 1810.

11. By 1842 Trinity College had an income of £45,209, of which £5,000 was spent directly on tuition costs. (See V. A. Huber, *English Universities*, vol. II, pt. 3, pp. 576–580, which provides a statistical survey of the revenues and expenditures of the colleges of both old universities.) St John's took in £34,020, spent £2,200 on tuition; St Catharine's – a poor college – took in £5,621 and spent £850 on tuition. The difference in each case went to support senior members of the Colleges, often in what could quite legally be total idleness. On Trinity's income earlier in the century see 'Trinity College in the Age of Peel', *Ideas and Institutions of Victorian England*, ed. R. Robson, London, 1967, p. 316.

12. See Albert Mansbridge, *The Older Universities of England*, Boston, 1923, p. 130. Or D. A. Winstanley, *Early Victorian Cambridge*, Cambridge, 1955, pp. 155–156.

13. W. Cockburn, *Strictures on Clerical Education at the University of Cambridge*, London, 1809, p. 34.

14. Charles Henry Cooper, *Memorials of Cambridge*, Cambridge, 1861, vol. I, pp. 351–352, vol. II, pp. 339–342.

15. R. M. Beverley's pamphlet, *A Letter . . . on the Present Corrupt State of the University of Cambridge*, London, 1833, closed with such a threat, but there were also loyal sons of Cambridge who would gradually come to advocate governmental interference and reform – see George Peacock, *Observations on the Statutes of the University of Cambridge*, London, 1841, pp. 96 ff.

16. A series of *Edinburgh Review* articles in the 1830s argued that in the past the colleges had intentionally seized power from the central University and had systematically perverted the traditional Cambridge constitution. See W. Hamilton, 'On the State of the English Universities', *Edinburgh Review*, vol. LIII, no. 106, June, 1831, p. 384. This conspiracy-of-the-colleges view of university history was widely held (see for example, James E. Smith, *Considerations Respecting Cambridge . . .*, London 1818) although the changes involved had been quite obviously evolutionary and had occurred over a period of several centuries.

17. See M. Lawson, *Strictures on the Rev. F. H. Maberley's Account of 'The Melancholy and Awful Death of Lawrence Dundas, Esquire'*, London, 1818. Lawson showed clearly that Maberley's treatment was unnecessarily harsh.

18. Maberley, *The Melancholy and Awful Death of Lawrence Dundas, Esquire*, London, 1818, p. 11.

19. 'I can scarce conceive, had the University wished to lead her members to the commission of fornication, and indeed produce a lascivious spirit throughout the kingdom, that it would have hit upon a more notable experiment than the exhibition of pictures of naked women, beautifully painted.' *Ibid.*, p. 27.

20. See J. D. Campbell, *Samuel Taylor Coleridge*, London, 1894, p. 28.

21. This suggestion was contained in the Maberley pamphlet; an anonymous *Letter to Lord Holland on the Regulation of Undergraduate Expense and Moral Improvement* (signed 'Thrasybulus', Oxford, 1837) also advised the old universities to establish a *Censor Morales*, 'a conservator of morals, whose office should be strictly, under his oath, to repress all vice, and to encourage all virtue', p. 12.

22. See Southey, *Letters from England*, p. 179, and Winstanley, *Early Vic. Camb.*, pp. 415–416.

23. The arrangement with the 'fellow commoners', for example, was designed as much for the benefit of the fellows, who enjoyed mingling with the soon-

to-be-famous, as for the undergraduates. See Winstanley, *Early Vic. Camb.*, p. 415.

24. See R. Robson, 'William Whewell, F.R.S., Academic Life', *Notes and Records of the Royal Society of London*, vol. XIX, Dec., 1964, p. 172.

25. Coaches and students often vacationed together in remote districts; such 'reading parties' were a normal and very pleasant part of a serious student's training. The friendship engendered by the coach/student relationship is well exemplified in the life of Henry Fawcett, who – blinded in a hunting accident while an undergraduate – received greatest consolation and encouragement not from his friends but from his mathematics coach, William Hopkins. See Leslie Stephen, *Life of Henry Fawcett*, London, 1885, pp. 48–51.

2. REFORM FROM WITHIN

1. See *Edinburgh Review*, vol. XI, no. 22, January, 1808, p. 249; vol. XIV, no. 23, July, 1809, p. 429; vol. XV, no. 29, October, 1809, p. 40; vol. XVI, no. 31, April, 1810, p. 158.

2. See William Hamilton, *Discussions on Philosophy, Literature, Education and University Reform*, a collection of his *Edinburgh Review* articles; London, 1852.

3. An Oxford don, Edward Copleston, responded to Smith with *A Reply to the Calumnies of the 'Edinburgh Review' against Oxford, containing an account of the Studies pursued at the University*, Oxford, 1810. And William Whewell's treatise *On the Principles of English University Education*, London, 1837, was written largely in refutation of Hamilton's criticisms.

4. See Charles Lyell, *Travels in North America in the Years 1841–42*, New York, 1845, especially Chapter XIII.

5. See A. P. Stanley, *The Life and Correspondence of Thomas Arnold*, 5th edition, London, 1845.

6. On Jowett see Geoffrey Cust Faber, *Jowett, a Portrait with Background*, London, 1957.

7. On Mark Pattison see the very helpful *Mark Pattison and the Idea of a University* by John Sparrow, London, 1967.

8. See D. A. Winstanley, *Early Vic. Camb.*, pp. 86, 94–95. Winstanley refers to a bill in the Lords, introduced by Lord Radnor in 1837, to appoint a commission inquiring into the state of the colleges and halls of Oxford and Cambridge, as well as an attempt by Radnor in 1835 to present a bill abolishing the religious tests. See Hansard, 3rd series, vol. XXXVII, cols. 1001–1043; vol. XXVIII, col. 642; vol. XXIX, cols. 496–537. Also see James Heywood, *Academic Reform and University Representation*, London, 1860, for a thorough survey of governmental action for university reform, and L. Campbell, *Nationalization of the Old English Universities*, London, 1901.

9. Hansard, vol. CX, cols. 691–765. See Winstanley, *Early Vic. Camb.*, pp. 220–225. Lord John Russell had attended neither Oxford nor Cambridge and was generally regarded as actively hostile toward them.

10. R. M. Beverley, *A Letter to His Royal Highness, the Duke of Gloucester, Chancellor, on the Present Corrupt State of the University of Cambridge*, London, 1833.

11. Edward Pusey and John Henry Newman, two of the most influential members of the early Oxford Movement, both were serious educational theorists. See Pusey's *Collegiate and Professional Training and Discipline*, Oxford, 1854, and Newman's *On the Scope and the Nature of University Education*, London, 1965.

12. The connection between the 'Broad Church' movement and various efforts at university reform will be examined later; suffice it to say that men like Coleridge, Tennyson, Maurice, and Kemble were satisfied neither with the anachronistic privileges of the universities nor with the simplistic outworn eighteenth-century theology which they were taught.

13. See Kingsley's satirical novel *Alton Locke*, London, 1850, for a biting assessment of Cambridge-as-it-was.

14. Especially useful on Simeon is Charles Smyth's *Simeon and Church Order*, Cambridge, 1940. See also H. C. G. Moule, *Charles Simeon*, London, Inter-Varsity Fellowship, 1965, and *Memoirs of the Rev. Charles Simeon, M.A.*, eds., William Carus, Robert Carter, New York, 1847.

15. On Huxley see Cyril Bibby's 'Thomas Huxley and University Development', in *Victorian Studies*, vol. II, no. 2, 1958, p. 97. Matthew Arnold and Leslie Stephen were two other 'free-thinkers' with important influence on educational developments.

16. See Frederick Denison Maurice, *Life of F. D. Maurice*, London, 1884, especially Chapters I, II, III, and VI of vol. II.

17. One of Mill's most useful statements about English education can be found in his 'Article I – Civilization', published in the *London and Westminster Review*, vol. XXV, no. 1, 1835, p. 1.

18. A poet and rector of the University of Glasgow, Campbell was also an active early supporter of the University of London.

19. A radical M.P. who, among other things, continually agitated for more technical education and for greater public attention to the education of the working classes. In 1850 he carried a bill establishing free public libraries.

20. The book was called *Alma Mater, or Seven Years at the University of Cambridge*, London, 1827.

21. L. Wainewright, *The Literary and Scientific Pursuits which are encouraged and enforced at the University of Cambridge*, London, 1815; Edward Copleston, *A Reply to the Calumnies*, 1810.

22. See Thomas Turton, *Thoughts on the Admission of Persons without regard to their Religious Opinions to Certain Degrees in the Universities of England*, Cambridge, 1834. Turton later became the Bishop of Ely.

23. On Christopher Wordsworth's conservatism see Chapter V, 'Christopher Wordsworth', in Winstanley's *Early Vic. Camb.*, pp. 58–82.

24. See M. Holroyd, *Memorials of the Life of George Elwes Corrie*, Cambridge, 1890. In 1847 Corrie campaigned for Lord Powis to be University Chancellor because of Powis' 'well-known attachment to our Institutions', particularly the episcopacy (p. 247).

25. W. Dalby, *The Real Question at Issue between the Opponents and Supporters of a Bill now before the House of Commons*, London, 1834, p. 22.

26. See *Report of H.M. Commissioners Appointed to Inquire into the State, Discipline, Studies, and Revenues of the University and Colleges of Cambridge*, State Papers, vol. LXIV, 1852, pp. 2–12. The Masters of Magdalene, Clare, Caius, Corpus Christi, King's, Queens', St Catharine's, Trinity, and Downing all included this theme in their responses to the Commissioners' request for cooperation.

27. Quoted in Holroyd, *Life of Corrie*, p. 79. See also Douglas, *Life of Whewell*, p. 497.

28. Both Whewell and John Sterling criticized Connop Thirlwall for *publishing* his opinions of compulsory chapel, not for simply holding them. See John Connop Thirlwall, Jr, *Connop Thirlwall*, London, 1936, pp. 76, 80.

29. Hare, together with Thirlwall, had been publicly attacked for translating

Georg Niebuhr's *History of Rome*; Maurice would throughout his life be accused of heterodoxy because of his interest in non-traditional sources of theology. The dangers of 'German rationalism' were pointed out energetically by the theologian Hugh James Rose. As Select Preacher at Cambridge in the early thirties he delivered a series of discourses 'intended to forewarn and forearm the Church of England against the rationalistic criticism of the continent'. (*D.N.B.*, vol. xvii, p. 240.) See Hugh James Rose's *The State of the Protestant Religion in Germany*, Cambridge, 1824.

30. Babbage was an outstanding if somewhat eccentric mathematician who later invented a primitive calculating machine. After graduating in 1814 he was a Fellow of the Royal Society and for a time the Lucasian Professor of Mathematics at Cambridge. Babbage was a friend of John Herschel's; together they introduced 'continental' mathematical techniques to the University. See *Charles Babbage and his Calculating Engines*, eds. Philip and Emily Morrison, New York, 1961. This book is mainly a collection of Babbage's own writings, including parts of his autobiography.

31. Hopkins entered Cambridge at the age of thirty and graduated as seventh wrangler in 1827. Because he was married he was excluded from the normal fellowship structure and settled in Cambridge as a private mathematics 'coach'. He had an outstanding reputation as a 'wrangler maker', having among his students Stokes, Thompson, Tait, Fawcett, Clerk-Maxwell, and Todhunter. He was also a geologist of some note.

32. Hildyard graduated in 1833; he was a classicist and served as a lecturer and tutor at Christ's. His main reforming efforts were directed toward improving collegiate tuition.

33. Crowfoot graduated at Caius in 1839 and was immediately elected a fellow of his college and of King's. He also was active in improving the college instructional system.

34. In explaining William Whewell's achieving only the *second* wranglership, his biographer Todhunter said that he had failed to concentrate adequately on mathematics. 'Mr. Whewell's own taste would naturally lead him to the *more varied study* which has always been encouraged at Trinity College; that great foundation can, without danger, *pay less exclusive* regard to *mere* academic triumphs than its smaller rivals' (italics mine). Isaac Todhunter, *William Whewell*, London, 1876.

35. For a concise life of Herschel see N. S. Dodge, 'Memoir of Sir John Frederick William Herschel', *Smithsonian Institution Annual Report*, 1871, p. 109.

36. See Pryme, *Ode to Trinity College*.

37. See *D.N.B.* article, vol. xiii, p. 622.

38. See Clark, *Sedgwick*.

39. See *Romilly's Cambridge Diary 1832–43*, ed. J. P. T. Bury, Cambridge, 1967.

40. John Herschel, the astronomer mentioned above, was first in both contests. See Alexander MacFarlane, 'George Peacock', in *Lectures on Ten British Mathematicians*, New York, 1916, pp. 7–19.

41. See 'Archdeacon Hare's Last Charge', A. P. Stanley, *Quarterly Review*, vol. xcvii, 1855, p. 1.

42. Trinity College MSS, Add. Ms. a. 213[89].

43. See MSS letters to Whewell, 1842 and 1854. Trinity College MSS, Add. Ms. a. 213[89–90].

44. After he had published a collection of German stories in 1851 his friend Thirlwall, no unproductive scholar himself, wrote to Whewell: 'I do not know more whether to admire or envy you for being able to find time to do

such things when I can hardly contrive to read them.' Trinity College MSS, Add. Ms. a. 213[183].

45. Sydney Smith was credited with having originated this quip; see Todhunter, *Wm Whewell*, vol. I, p. 410.

46. Trinity College MSS, Add. Ms. a. 208[124]. Sir John Herschel concurred in Lyell's praise of Whewell's universal mastery of human knowledge; Todhunter, *Wm Whewell*, vol. I, p. 1.

47. *Ibid.*, vol. I, p. 6. See also Douglas, *Life of Whewell*, p. 22.

48. Thirlwall was at various times the junior bursar, junior dean, head lecturer, and assistant tutor at Trinity, and he served as the university examiner in classics in 1828, 1829, 1832, and 1834. See Thirlwall, *Connop Thirlwall*.

49. For Airy's life see *The Autiobiography of Sir George Biddle Airy*, edited by Wilfrid Airy, Cambridge, 1896.

50. J. F. W. Herschel, *A Preliminary Discourse on the Study of Natural Philosophy*, London, 1830, p. 10. See p. 82 of Walter Cannon's 'Scientists and Broad Churchmen: An Early Intellectual Network', *Journal of British Studies*, vol. IV, no. 1, 1964, pp. 65 ff. This whole article is an excellent survey of the backgrounds and attitudes of these men.

51. Except for a very small uninfluential group interested in restoring Gothic architecture. See Eliot Rose's 'The Stone Table in the Round Church and the Crisis of the Cambridge Camden Society', *Victorian Studies*, vol. X, no. 2, 1966, pp. 145 ff.

52. Thirlwall, *Connop Thirlwall*, p. 137.

53. On Hare's character see the obituary article written by A. P. Stanley in *The Quarterly Review*, vol. XCVII, 1855, p. 1.

54. Trinity required that all fellows take orders within seven years of proceeding to the M.A. or else forfeit their fellowships. Whewell, Sedgwick, and Thirlwall all postponed their decisions until the eleventh hour. See Clark, *Sedgwick*, vol. I, p. 151; Todhunter, *Wm Whewell*, vol. I, p. 8; Thirlwall, *Connop Thirlwall*, pp. 17, 39.

55. Letter to William Ainger, Dec. 15, 1834, quoted in Clark, *Sedgwick*, vol. I, pp. 434–435.

56. See Douglas, *Life of Whewell*, p. 201.

57. Walter Cannon, 'Scientists and Broad Churchmen', p. 76.

3. MATHEMATICS – THE CORE OF 'PERMANENT STUDIES'

1. Matthew Mowbray, *Autobiography of a Cantab.*, Cambridge, 1842, pp. 106–107.

2. Walter William Rouse Ball, *A Short Account of the History of Mathematics*, London, 1940, pp. 438–443.

3. Babbage quotes his own 'wicked pun' at p. 25 of his *Passages from the Life of a Philosopher* (reprinted in P. and E. Morrison's *Charles Babbage and his Calculating Engines*, New York, 1961). Descriptions of the formation of the Analytical Society can be found in Ball's book mentioned above, in Carl B. Boyer's *A History of Mathematics*, New York, 1968, pp. 621–622, and in most of the biographies of the mathematicians involved. Modern scholars agree that the organization was an important means toward bringing Britain into contact with modern mathematics – Boyer calls it 'the turning point' which let British mathematics 'emerge from the web of provincialism' – p. 621.

4. 'The treatise may be considered as one which, in conjunction with the

publications of Peacock and Herschel, introduced the continental mathematics, in order to replace the system of fluxions which had so long prevailed at Cambridge.' Todhunter, *Wm Whewell*, vol. I, p. 13.

5. Peacock wrote to a friend: 'I assure you that I shall never cease to exert myself to the utmost in the cause of reform, and that I will never decline any office which will encrease my power to effect it. I am nearly certain of being nominated to the office of Moderator in the year 1818–1819, and as I am an examiner in virtue of my office, for the next year I shall pursue a course even more decided than hitherto, since I shall feel that men have been prepared for the change, and will then be enabled to acquire a better system by the publication of improved elementary books. I have considerable influence as a lecturer, and I will not neglect it. It is by silent perseverance only, that we may hope to reduce the many-headed monster of prejudice and make the University answer her character as the loving mother of good learning and science.' Quoted at p. 11 of MacFarlane's *Ten British Mathematicians*.

6. See Merz, *History of Scientific Thought*, vol. II, pp. 630–631.

7. See Ball, *History of Mathematics*, pp. 438–439. 'The complete isolation of the English school and its devotion to geometrical methods are the most marked features in its history during the latter half of the eighteenth century; and the absence of any considerable contribution to the advancement of mathematical science was a natural consequence. One result of this was that the energy of English men of science was largely devoted to practical physics and practical astronomy, which were in consequence studied in Britain perhaps more than elsewhere.'

8. For a clear brief survey of Herschel's astronomical contributions see Dodge, 'Herschel', p. 113. Also see Merz, *History of Scientific Thought*, vol. I, pp. 229, 238, 285, 324.

9. Dodge, 'Herschel', pp. 116, 132.

10. *A Preliminary Discourse on the Study of Natural Philosophy*, facsimile of 1830 edition, New York, 1966, pp. 11–12.

11. Airy, *Autobiography*, p. 113.

12. Ball, *History of Mathematics*, p. 442.

13. Airy, *Autobiography*, p. 3.

14. When he became aware that he could not beat Herschel in the tripos, Babbage gave up all efforts to achieve an honours degree and 'went out in the poll', thus setting aside any hope of a college fellowship. After graduation he married immediately and moved to London, where he set to work on various physical experiments. See Chapters III and IV in Maboth Moseley's *Irascible Genius*, London, 1964. Also see chapters IV and V in Babbage's *Passages from the Life of a Philosopher*, pp. 22–52.

15. These efforts culminated in his publication of *A History of the Inductive Sciences* (1837, three editions by 1857) and *The Philosophy of the Inductive Sciences* (1840, three much altered editions by 1860).

16. Isaac Todhunter, Whewell's biographer, writes of his research on the tides: 'the main object of Mr Whewell's researches is to obtain an accurate knowledge of the *facts* of the Tides . . . Hence there is little reference to mathematical formulae in the memoirs . . .' *Wm Whewell*, vol. I, p. 76.

17. See George Peacock, *Treatise on Algebra*, 1830, reprinted from the 1842 edition, New York, Scripta Mathematica, 1940. Assessments of Peacock's work can be found in Boyer, *History of Mathematics*, pp. 621 ff.; in Ball, *History of Mathematics*, p. 441; and in Merz, *History of Scientific Thought*, vol. II, pp. 640, 654, 670.

18. See Boyer, *History of Mathematics*, p. 633; MacFarlane, 'Augustus DeMorgan' in *Ten British Mathematicians*, pp. 25 ff.
19. For lists of their scholarly writings see the individual Victorian biographies of these mathematicians. Whewell, for example, wrote articles on geometry, crystallography, mechanics, dynamics, scientific notation, political economy, geology, mineralogy, tidal motion, physics, glaciers, optics, and the history and philosophy of science. He submitted them to a number of different journals, including the *Cambridge Philosophical Transactions*, the *Edinburgh Journal of Science*, the *Journal of the Royal Institution*, the *Philosophical Magazine*, and the *Transactions of the British Association*. The *Catalogue of the Royal Society* lists more than 150 scientific papers written by Herschel for the scholarly journals.
20. J. F. W. Herschel, *A Treatise on Astronomy*, London, 1833, p. 5.
21. *Ibid.*, p. 6.
22. For example, Airy's *Mathematical Tracts*, 1826, or Whewell's *Elementary Treatise on Mechanics*, 1821.
23. See Merz, *History of Scientific Thought*, vol. I, pp. 120, 325; vol. II, pp. 569–570.
24. The Analytical Society was founded in 1812 by Peacock, Babbage, and Herschel. See Morrison, *Babbage*, p. 24. The Philosophical Society was the creation in the main of Whewell, Peacock and Sedgwick (1918). See Todhunter, *Wm Whewell*, vol. I, p. 12, and Clark, *Sedgwick*, vol. I, pp. 203–205. The British Association for the Advancement of Science grew directly out of a suggestion made by David Brewster in a review of a book by Babbage (see Merz, *History of Scientific Thought*, vol. I, p. 238). All of these scholars served as officers or reporters during the early years of the British Association. See Herschel's 1845 Address as President (republished in his *Essays from the Edinburgh and Quarterly Reviews*, London, 1857, pp. 634 ff.) and Peacock's very important report to the mathematical section on algebra and the current state of continental mathematics, 1833. (See Merz, *History of Scientific Thought*, vol. II, p. 640.)
25. In a speech to the British Association in 1869 J. J. Sylvester observed that by most English mathematicians Euclid had long been ranked 'as second in sacredness to the Bible alone, and as one of the advance outposts of the British Constitution'. *Report of the British Association*, London, 1870, p. 8. In a letter to a friend written in 1884 Airy said: 'I do not value Euclid's Elements as a super-excellent book of instruction – though some important points are better presented in it than in any other book of geometrical instruction that I have seen. But I value it as a book of strong and distinct reasoning, and of orderly succession of reasonings. I do not think that there is any book in the world which presents so distinctly the "because . . . therefore . . ." And this is invaluable for the mental instruction of youth.' *Autobiography*, p. 357.
26. Whewell, *Thoughts on the Study of Mathematics as a Part of a Liberal Education*, Cambridge, 1835, p. 7.
27. A. Thurtell, privately printed letter dated Nov. 19, 1845, Cambridge University Papers DC 5300.
28. Whewell, *Of a Liberal Education*, pp. 40–41. In a letter to Whewell, Herschel wrote: 'As regards a University course of Mathematics – I rather hold to examining in subjects than in books. But I agree with you that a tendency to *appear* familiar with the *latest* novel ideas (improvements though they may be) is too much a besetting sin . . .' Oct. 5, 1845, Trinity College MSS, Add. Ms. 207[67]. Or see DeMorgan's biography, p. 285: 'Mathematics is becoming too much of a machinery, and this is especially the case with reference to the

elementary students. They put data of the problems into a mill, and expect them to come out ground at the other end – an operation which bears a close resemblance to putting in hempseed at one end of a machine, and taking out ruffled shirts ready for use at the other end. This mode is, no doubt, exceedingly effective in producing results but it is certainly not so in teaching the mind and in exercising thought.'

29. Airy, *Autobiography*, p. 274.
30. Quoted in MacFarlane's *Lectures on Ten British Physicists*, New York, 1919, pp. 107–108. MacFarlane comments: 'Here we note a want of confidence in mathematical deduction which appears to have been characteristic of Airy and his generation of mathematicians.'
31. Boyer, *History of Mathematics*, p. 622.
32. On the lack of communication among various scholars trying to 'lay the foundations' for complex mathematics see Merz, *History of Scientific Thought*, vol. II, pp. 709–710: 'This feeling [of uncertainty about rigorous definitions of the foundations of mathematics] had led . . . to many isolated attacks and half-philosophical discussions by various writers in this country and abroad. Many of them remained long unrecognized; such were the suggestive writings of Hamilton, DeMorgan, Peacock in England, Bolanzo in Bohemia, Bolyai in Hungary, Lobatchevski in Kasan, Grassman in Stettin. Most of these were unknown to each other.'
33. DeMorgan, S. E., *A Memoir of Augustus DeMorgan*, London, 1882, p. 328.
34. See Merz, *History of Scientific Thought*, vol. II, pp. 648–650, 708–710.
35. MacFarlane, *Ten British Mathematicians*, p. 25.
36. *Ibid.*, p. 27.
37. Quoted in MacFarlane, pp. 25–26. See also Boyer, *History of Mathematics*, pp. 633–634, who asserts that with DeMorgan and with Boole (who extended and completed the work of DeMorgan) 'for the first time the view is clearly expressed that the essential characteristic of mathematics is not so much its content as its form. If any topic is presented in such a way that it consists of symbols and precise rules of operation upon those symbols, subject only to the requirements of inner consistency, this topic is part of mathematics.'
38. See MacFarlane, *Ten British Mathematicians*, pp. 29–30.
39. Quoted in *A Memoir of Augustus DeMorgan*, p. 115, from Mill's 'On Berkeley's Life and Writings', *Fortnightly Review*, Nov. 1871.
40. DeMorgan, *DeMorgan*, p. 159.
41. See Walter Cannon, 'Scientists and Broad Churchmen', p. 65.
42. Todhunter, *Wm Whewell*, vol. I, p. 93.
43. 'Article VII', *Edinburgh Review*, vol. LXII, no. 126, Jan. 1836, p. 409.
44. Whewell, *On the Principles of English University Education*, London, 1837. See p. 38 e.g., where he decries too exclusive dependence on any single subject, in this case classical literature. At pp. 60 ff. he is critical of the University's examination system: 'Such examinations may be necessary, but they can never be more than a necessary evil; and that system would indeed, be unworthy of a great and highly-civilised nation, whose machinery of education was all of this structure.' He goes on to talk of the advantages of college lectures, the tutorial system, etc. And on p. 73 he talks about the need to reduce the influence of private tutors who 'coached' or 'crammed' the students.
45. *Travels in North America in the Years 1841–42; with Geological Observations on the United States, Canada, and Nova Scotia*, New York, 1845. After describing American universities, especially Harvard, Lyell inserted a somewhat

extended discourse on the history and 'peculiarities' of the English universities. See vol. I, pp. 208–251.

46. This specific point – the detrimental effect of the collegiate 'usurpation' of the instructional function – had been raised by both Hamilton and Lyell, as well as by less important critics of the university system. See Hamilton 'Article VI', *Edinburgh Review*, vol. LIII, no. 106, June, 1831, p. 384; and Lyell, *Travels*, pp. 219 ff.

47. Whewell, *Of a Liberal Education*, p. 154.

48. *Ibid.*, pp. 8, 10. Or again: '. . . if men come really to understand Greek or Geometry, there is then, in each study, a real intellectual culture, however unwillingly it may have been entered upon . . . No education can be considered as liberal, which does not cultivate both the Faculty of Reason and the Faculty of Language; one of which is cultivated by the study of mathematics, and the other by the study of classics. To allow the student to omit one of these, is to leave him half educated. If a person cannot receive such culture, he remains, in the one case, irrational, in the other illiterate, and cannot be held up as a liberally educated person. To allow a person to follow one of these lines of study, to the entire neglect of the other, is not to educate him. It may draw out his personal propensities; but it does not draw out his general human faculties of Reason and Language. The object of a liberal education is, not to make men eminently learned or profound in some one department, but to educe all the faculties by which man shares in the highest thoughts and feelings of his species. It is to make men truly men, rather than to make them men of genius, which no education can make them.' Pp. 106–107.

49. Whewell, *Thoughts on the Study of Mathematics*, pp. 5–6.

50. *Thoughts*, pp. 39–40.

51. *Principles*, p. 45.

52. *Of a Liberal Education*, p. 18.

53. A modern interpreter of Whewell, Robert E. Butts, calls him 'a great and sincere champion of induction as the method of accumulating scientific facts', 'Professor Marcucci on Whewell's Idealism', *Philosophy of Science*, vol. XXXIV, no. 2, June, 1967, p. 179. His contemporary biographer, Todhunter, actually felt that Whewell overemphasized the significance of the 'intuitive guess' of induction and often misinterpreted scientific thought in his zeal to encourage the development of the 'inductive science'. See *Wm Whewell*, vol. I, pp. 107–108. Todhunter points out a variety of instances in which Whewell credited to induction discoveries or ideas which resulted either from deductive thought or from a combination of the two modes. For a very simple, clear and balanced presentation of Whewell's view of the roles of induction and deduction see pp. 325–329 of his Bridgewater Treatise, *Astronomy and General Physics considered with Reference to Natural Theology*, London, 1834.

54. *Principles*, pp. 14–15; *Thoughts*, pp. 45–46.

55. See *Of a Liberal Education*, pp. 21–22, on the absolute necessity of the basic 'permanent' studies preceding a student's undertaking to comprehend the modern 'progressive' disciplines.

56. For a clear assessment of Whewell's indebtedness to Kant see Butts, 'Professor Marcucci', pp. 175–183. See also the Introduction (pp. 3–29) to Butts' *William Whewell's Theory of Scientific Method*, Pittsburgh, 1968.

57. Butts, *Wm Whewell's Theory*, p. 6. The Whewell quotation is from 'Second Memoir on the Fundamental Antithesis of Philosophy', *Transactions of the*

Cambridge Philosophical Society, vol. VII, pt. V, 1848, pp. 33–35. His contemporaries regarded Whewell as something of an expert on Kant. In an April 3, 1863, letter DeMorgan wrote: 'Did *I* provoke you to an ontological discussion? . . . I asked you, who are Kantescient, whether you knew of a certain speculation in the later editions of Kant; and you say No. I am pretty sure you would have remembered it at once if it had been there.' DeMorgan, *DeMorgan*, p. 317.

58. *Of a Liberal Education*, p. 96.
59. Classics and mathematics really were 'traditional' – in a sense they were nothing more than the medieval *trivium* and *quadrivium* in nineteenth-century dress.
60. *Thoughts*, p. 37.
61. *Principles*, pp. 133–134.
62. 'I have always thought a rapid change of the books read among us to be a serious evil . . . Your Tracts are hard enough to occupy several generations of tutors and pupils before they are thoroughly mastered and made familiar. They are now well established among us, and, if they continue to be so for ten or twenty years longer, they will do us far more good than any other books can do, . . . even [some] by you.' Quoted in Todhunter, *Wm Whewell*, vol. II, p. 282.
63. See *Of A Liberal Education*, p. 141. Unfortunately Whewell seems to have been more perceptive about these difficulties in principle than in practice. His own text-books were so often altered in form as to be very confusing. Of *The Elementary Treatise on Mechanics* Todhunter wrote: 'But the great objection to the work is the perpetual alteration which deprived it of all stability and permanence. No sooner had teachers become familiar with one edition than another would appear in which the subject had been rather revolutionized than modified . . . It is scarcely possible for an author to retain the unwavering confidence of his readers when his own opinions are in constant fluctuation.' Vol. I, p. 20. Todhunter was also critical of Whewell's effectiveness as an examiner, accusing him of sometimes proposing 'problems which he himself had not fully worked out, and which were in fact too difficult for complete solution'. Vol. I, p. 407.
64. *Principles*, pp. 49–51. In his *Travels in North America* Sir Charles Lyell was very critical of Whewell's excessive insistence on 'obedience and deference to authority, . . . held forth as if they were the chief and almost sole moral virtues to be instilled into the minds of young academicians', and in his treatment of university students 'more as boys and children than as young men on the very point of entering on their several duties in life . . .' Vol. I, p. 242. Whewell was undaunted, however, and insisted again in *Of a Liberal Education*, 1845, that the respectful principle of undergraduate education was sound. (See *Of a Liberal Education*, pp. 116–131.)
65. *Principles*, pp. 5–7.
66. *Of a Liberal Education*, pp. 111–112.
67. See 'Mr. Lyell on English Universities', especially sections 131–2, 141–6, *Of a Liberal Education*, pp. 119–131.
68. For Sir William Hamilton's argument, see 'Article VI', *Edinburgh Review*, vol. LIII, no. 106, June, 1831, pp. 384 ff. Also see Lyell, *Travels*, vol. I, Chapter XIII, pp. 208–251. George Peacock, *Observations on the Statutes*, p. 146, also presents this argument.
69. See Camb. Univ. Papers, DC 5300, Apr. 8, 1843. A similar proposal was put forward three years later – see Camb. Univ. Papers, DC 5300, Mar. 7, 1846.

Todhunter, *Wm Whewell*, vol. i, p. 153, associated Whewell and Peacock with these proposals.

70. Camb. Univ. Papers, Cam. a. 500.5^{123}, Oct. 16, 1848: 'with a view to encourage attendance at the Lectures of the Mathematical Professors, and to secure a correspondence between those Lectures and the Mathematical Examinations of the University; and also as a means of communicating to the students themselves, from a body of experienced Examiners and Lecturers, correct views of the nature and objects of our Mathematical Examinations . . . a Board of Mathematical Studies shall be established; whose duty it shall be to consult together from time to time on all matters relating to the actual state of Mathematical Studies and Examinations in the University; and to prepare annually and lay before the Vice-Chancellor a Report, to be by him published to the University in the Lent or Easter Term of each year'. For a narrative of the various structural reforms of the University courses during this period see Chapter x, 'Internal Reform', in Winstanley, *Early Vic. Camb.*, esp. pp. 208–213.

71. *Of a Liberal Education*, p. 137.

72. One of the side effects was the very pervasive evil of private tuition. Tutors made it their business to 'cram' their students in precisely the subject matter which they thought would 'pay' in the examinations; a good tutor was obviously, therefore, much more important to an ambitious student's success than were his more detached, official university teachers.

73. Camb. Univ. Papers, Cam. a. 500.5^{96}, Feb. 25, 1843. Whewell, as Vice-Chancellor, was chairman of the syndicate.

74. *Thoughts on the Study of Mathematics*, p. 44.

75. Book N, pp. 186–190, June 4, 1827: a committee required a longer period for the tripos, with 'elementary' subjects to occupy the first few days. Pp. 376–377; Apr. 6, 1832: an outline of the examination work provided for no calculus on the first day, a small amount on the second and third days, advanced topics on the fourth and fifth days. Book *Ξ* pp. 21–23, Feb. 22, 1837: the mathematics requirements for the ordinary degree were spelled out explicitly, with an emphasis on basic concepts; and a May 13, 1846 entry noted that students should be able to make their reasoning explicit and not just produce correct results.

76. Charles Astor Bristed, *Five Years in an English University*, New York, 1852, vol. i, p. 76.

77. *Ibid.*, vol. ii, pp. 119–126, 173.

78. See Winstanley, *Early Vic. Camb.*, pp. 67–71.

79. *Ibid.*, pp. 216–217.

80. Sedgwick was specifically critical of Lyell for accepting Darwin's theories, feeling that Darwin was operating solely on the basis of theory, unsupported by evidence. 'Darwin has made his theory popular, but he has not added a single *fact* that helps it forward.' Clark, *Sedgwick*, vol. ii, p. 411. Sedgwick himself was very much an 'experimental' or 'observational' scientist; he became very dissatisfied with his lectures when he got to be too old to do the relevant field work: '"Tis poor work to be retailing other men's adventures', he wrote in 1858. *Ibid.*, vol. ii, p. 348.

81. '. . . in this, as in every other field of labour, no man can put aside the curse pronounced on him – that by the sweat of his brow he shall reap his harvest . . . his way is steep and toilsome, and he must read the records of creation in a strange, and to many minds, a repulsive language, which rejecting both

the senses and imagination speaks only to the intellect', *A Discourse on the Studies of the University*, Cambridge, 1833, 1st edition, p. 9.

82. *Ibid.*, p. 10.

83. Trinity College MSS, Add. Ms. a. 207[67].

84. F. Whaley Harper, flysheet, Oct. 25, 1848, Camb. Univ. Papers, DC 5300. As late as 1859 another don, J. B. Mayor, argued that the preliminary training in mathematics and classics ought to precede any advanced work in other disciplines; see *Open letter to the University*, Camb. Univ. Papers, DC 5650, Dec. 3, 1859.

85. *Cambridge Advertiser*, Mar. 7, 1849, 'The New Honours Triposes,' J. R. Crowfoot.

4. REACTION AGAINST PALEY AND THE BENTHAMITES

1. See the Introduction, p. xii, in Frederick Ferré's edition of Paley's *Natural Theology*, New York, 1963. A recent useful book on Paley and his thought is D. L. LeMahieu's *The Mind of William Paley*, Lincoln, Nebraska, 1976.

2. See, for example, William Paley, *A View of the Evidences of Christianity*, London, 1791, 5th edition, vol. II, p. 135. 'In collecting these examples, I have done no more than epitomize the first volume of the first part of Dr. Lardner's Credibility of the Gospel History. And I have brought the argument within its present compass, first, by passing over some of his sections in which the accordancy appeared to me less certain, or upon subjects not sufficiently appropriate or circumstantial; secondly, by contracting every section into the fewest words possible, contenting myself for the most part with a mere *apposition* of passages; and, thirdly, by omitting many disquisitions, which, though learned and accurate, are not absolutely necessary to the understanding or verification of the argument.'

3. See Charles C. Gillispie, *Genesis and Geology*, Cambridge, Mass., 1951, p. 39.

4. Paley, *Evidences of Christianity*, vol. I, p. 320.

5. An important point. Paley, of course, was familiar with many miraculous narratives which grew up at some point distant in time or space from the events described. The presence *at the scene* of the early Christian witnesses very much strengthened their case.

6. See *Evidences*, vol. II, pp. 133 ff.

7. *Ibid.*, pp. 289 ff.

8. Paley, *Natural Theology*, pp. 3–4.

9. *Ibid.*, pp. 46 ff.

10. *Ibid.*, p. 53.

11. *Natural Theology*, p. 68. In fact only a tiny percentage of snakes are poisonous, though their reputation protects all others of their genus.

12. *Ibid.*, pp. 63 ff.

13. Paley, *Principles of Moral and Political Philosophy*, Boston, 1825, p. 62. 'So then actions are to be estimated by their tendency to promote happiness. Whatever is expedient is right. It is the utility of any moral rule alone which constitutes the obligation of it.'

14. Bentham, of course, did not view his and Paley's work as at all equivalent, as he seldom recognized his own debt to any other writers. But he stressed his particular disagreement with Paley on the issue of eternal sanctions.

15. See Ernest Albee, *A History of English Utilitarianism*, London, 1957, pp. 163 ff.

16. Ben Ross Schneider, Jr, *Wordsworth's Cambridge Education*, Cambridge, 1957, p. 181. The *Principles* had been first published in 1785.

17. Camb. Univ. Papers, Cam. a. 500.5^{28}, 1822.
18. Camb. Univ. Papers, DC 1350, May 1822.
19. Camb. Univ. Papers, Cam. a. 500.5^{24}.
20. Camb. Univ. Papers, Cam. a. 500.5^{24}.
21. Adam Sedgwick, who would be one of Paley's sternest critics, began his attack by saying how much he had been impressed by Paley when he was an undergraduate; and Charles Darwin, who would reduce the Paleyan arguments to rubble, also admitted having been very much struck by the force of his reasoning. See Francis Darwin, ed., *The Life and Letters of Charles Darwin*, London, 1911, vol. II, p. 15.
22. Trinity College MSS, Add. Ms. a. 53$^{1-5}$.
23. Sedgwick, *A Discourse on the Studies of the University*, 5th edition, Cambridge, 1850, p. 314.
24. *Discourse*, 1st edition, pp. 18–19. See also Note C in the Appendix to the first edition which praises Paley's *Natural Theology* extravagantly, and at length. A facsimile first edition is available (New York, 1969) with an introduction by Eric Ashby and Mary Anderson.
25. *Ibid.*, p. 35.
26. *Ibid.*, p. 35.
27. 'I think it incontestably true, that for the last fifty years our classical studies . . . have been too critical and formal; and that we have sometimes been taught, while straining after an accuracy beyond our reach, to value the husk more than the fruit of ancient learning: and if of late years our younger members have sometimes written prose Greek almost with the purity of Xenophon, or composed iambics in the finished diction of the Attic poets, we may well doubt whether time suffices for such perfection.' *Ibid.*, p. 32.
28. See John Stuart Mill, 'Professor Sedgwick's Discourse on the Studies of the University of Cambridge', *London Review*, April 1835; reprinted in (and here cited from) *Dissertations and Discussions*, London, 1859. See particularly vol. I, pp. 114–121. See also 'Sedgwick on Cambridge Studies', *British Quarterly Review*, vol. XII, 1850, p. 360.
29. *Discourse*, 1st edition, pp. 48–49.
30. *Ibid.*, p. 49.
31. 'Every political, as well as moral principle, practically involves the determination of the will, and thereby becomes at once separated from the class of investigations in which we consider the immutable relations of physical phenomena. That the will is influenced by motives, no one pretends to deny – on that subject enough has been said before: but to compare that influence to a physical effect, is only to confound things essentially different, and must ever end in metaphysical paradox or practical folly.' *Ibid.*, p. 71.
32. *Ibid.*, p. 57.
33. See *Moral Philosophy*, pp. 169–173, where in dealing with the subject of 'revenge' Paley cites Christ's preaching on the subject and describes the benefits to society and the individual which derive from a forgiving spirit.
34. 'Utilitarian philosophy in destroying the dominion of the moral feelings, offends at once against the law of honour and the law of God. It rises not for an instant above the world; allows not the expansion of a single lofty sentiment; and its natural tendency is to harden the hearts and debase the moral practice of mankind. If we suppress the authority of conscience, reject the moral feelings, rid ourselves of the sentiments of honor, and sink (as men too often do) below the influence of religion: and if at the same time, we are taught to think that utility is the universal test of right and wrong; what is

there left within us as an antagonist power to the craving of passion, or the base appetite of worldly gain?' *Discourse*, 1st edition, pp. 64–65.

35. *Ibid.*, p. 76.
36. *Ibid.*, p. 72.
37. *Ibid.*, p. 73.
38. *Ibid.*, p. 76.
39. *Ibid.*, p. 77.
40. Coleridge, *Aids to Reflection*, p. 363, quoted in Charles R. Sanders' *Coleridge and the Broad Church Movement*, Durham, N.C., 1942, p. 49. See Sanders for a useful discussion of the Coleridgean influence on the universities and on English thought in general.
41. Hare's reverence for Coleridge and his agreement with him on the defects of utilitarianism were testified to by his attempt to have a prize in Christian philosophy established at Cambridge in the poet's honor; see Trinity College MSS, Hare to Whewell, 1834, Add. Ms. 206[116]. See also Sanders, *Coleridge*, pp. 126 ff.
42. Their assessments of Hegel differed. In 1849 Hare wrote to Whewell: '. . . with all my repugnance to many of his [Hegel's] notions, I have never read twenty pages of him, without feeling that he was a very great thinker and writer'. Trinity College MSS, Add. Ms. a. 64[114]. Thirlwall, on the other hand, wrote: 'My own examination of certain portions of Hegel's works . . . has impressed me with the deepest conviction, that he is, to say the least, one of the most impudent of all literary quacks.' (Oct. 31, 1849, Thirlwall to Whewell, Trinity College MSS, Add. Ms. a. 213[180].)
43. An extremely useful new book on this group is Peter Allen's *The Cambridge Apostles, the Early Years*, Cambridge, 1978.
44. See Sanders, *Coleridge*, p. 186. See also Olive J. Brose, *Frederick Denison Maurice, Rebellious Conformist*, Athens, Ohio, 1971, p. 15.
45. See Thirlwall, *Connop Thirlwall*, p. 58.
46. Hare to Milnes, August 5, 1837, Trinity College MSS, H.11[62]. A later and significant contributor to this Cambridge rejection of utilitarianism was the young Trinity fellow and later Knightbridge Professor of Moral Philosophy, John Grote. Writing partly in response to Mill's defense of utilitarianism, Grote developed the early Cambridge objections to Benthamism, basing his argument on a Kantian view of the intuitive nature of man's moral sense. Though his major writings really fall outside the period of this essay, he illustrates the continuity of the philosophical objection to the utility theory, an objection which lasted from the Apostles of the thirties right through to the last part of the century. See Lauchlin D. MacDonald's *John Grote: A Critical Estimate of his Writings*, The Hague, 1966, esp. pp. 215 ff. See also Grote's *Examination of the Utilitarian Philosophy*, London, 1870, and *A Treatise on the Moral Ideals*, Cambridge, 1876.
47. See *Astronomy and General Physics, considered with Reference to Natural Theology*, Whewell's contribution to the Bridgewater Treatises, published in 1834. E.g. 'One of the great uses to which the vegetable wealth of the earth is applied, is the support of man, whom it provides with food and clothing; and the adaptation of tribes of indigenous vegetables to every climate has, we cannot but believe, a reference to the intention that the human race should be diffused over the whole globe.' P. 67. Also see *Of the Plurality of Worlds*, published in 1854 and designed to show that the earth was the central point of God's creation.
48. January 4, 1838, Trinity College MSS, Add. Ms. a. 206[171].

49. Whewell, *Elements of Morality, Including Polity*, New York, 1845, vol. II, p. 394.
50. *Ibid.*, vol. I, p. 395.
51. Whewell, *Lectures on the History of Moral Philosophy in England*, Cambridge, 1852, p. 155.
52. *Elements*, vol. I, p. 389. See also p. 228: '[Utilitarians] contend that pleasure is universally and necessarily the object of human action; and that human pleasures do not differ in kind, but only in intensity and duration: so that, according to these teachers, there is no difference of superior and inferior, between the pleasures of appetite, the pleasures of affection, and the pleasures of doing good. Hence, say they, the only difference in the character of actions, is their being better or worse means of obtaining pleasure. But the universal reason of man assents to the opposite doctrine . . . [If we believe as the utilitarians do] we obliterate the difference between man and brute beasts.'
53. *Ibid.*, p. 390.
54. [This argument] 'is an irrelevant truism. "We cannot calculate *all* the consequences of any action." If Dr. Whewell can point out any department of human affairs in which we can do *all* that would be desirable, he will have found something new. But because we cannot foresee everything, is there no such thing as foresight?' John Stuart Mill, 'Dr. Whewell on Moral Philosophy', first published in *The Westminster Review*, Oct. 1852 and reprinted in *Dissertations and Discussions*.
55. 'The question *Why?* respecting human actions, demands a reason, which may be given by a reference from a lower Rule to a higher. *Why* ought I to be frugal or industrious? In order that I may not want a maintenance. *Why* must I avoid want? Because I must seek to act independently. *Why* should I act independently? that I may act rightly.
    'Hence, with regard to the Supreme Rule, the question Why? admits no further answer. Why must I do what is right? Because it *is* right. Why should I do what I ought? Because I ought. The Supreme Rule supplies a reason for that which it commands, by being the Supreme Rule.' *Elements*, vol. I, p. 64.
56. Mill, of course, recognized this, and in his later works he moved more and more toward an integrated, societal view of morality.
57. *Elements*, vol. II, p. 74.
58. *Ibid.*, pp. 234–235.
59. See *Lectures*, pp. 178–179.
60. Paley begins his section on property thus: 'If you should see a flock of pigeons in a field of corn; and if (instead of each picking where and what it liked, taking just as much as it wants, and no more) you should see ninety-nine of them gathering all they got into a heap; reserving nothing for themselves but the chaff and the refuse; keeping this heap for one, and that the weakest perhaps, and worst pigeon of the flock; sitting round and looking on all the winter, whilst this one was devouring, throwing about, and wasting it; and if a pigeon, more hardy or hungry than the rest, touched a grain of the hoard, all the others instantly flying upon it, and tearing it to pieces: If you should see this, you would see nothing more than what is every day practised and established among men.' Paley, *Moral Philosophy*, p. 82. Compare to Whewell's '. . . there should exist a Right of Property: for without the establishment of such a Right, the possession of any objects of desire would . . . give rise to Fear and Anger; and to an agitation of men's minds, in which rational and moral action could not take place. But a Right of

Property once established, there may be a state of repose, in which the Reason and the Moral Sentiments can act.' *Elements*, vol. I, p. 67.

61. *Ibid.*, p. 233.
62. See *Elements*, vol. II, pp. 237 ff. In the *Lectures*, pp. 254 ff. he, quite rightly according to modern critics, attacked Bentham's failure to consider national differences and historical development.
63. Quoted by Sanders, *Coleridge*, p. 186.
64. Bristed, *Five Years in an English University*, vol. II, p. 117. Bristed was a wealthy American who attended Cambridge between 1840 and 1845. Written with the objectivity (and some of the misapprehensions) of an outsider, his work is an invaluable source for the morals and manners of mid-century Cambridge.
65. Cited in Schneider, *Wordsworth's Cambridge Education*, p. 195.
66. In the introduction to his collected *Dissertations and Discussions* Mill wrote that he had not tried to correct over-emphases but had rather let the various essays balance each other. 'Thus, the review of Mr Sedgwick's Discourse, taken by itself, might give an impression of more complete adhesion to the philosophy of Locke, Bentham, and the eighteenth century, than is really the case, and of an inadequate sense of its deficiencies; but that notion will be rectified by the subsequent essays on Bentham and on Coleridge. These, again, if they stood alone, would give just as much too strong an impression of the writer's sympathy with the reaction of the nineteenth century against the eighteenth: but this exaggeration will be corrected by the more recent defence of the "greatest happiness" ethics against Dr. Whewell.' Pp. iv–v.

5. RELIGION AND LITERATURE: TOWARD THE BROAD CHURCH

1. See the sermon with this title preached on Commemoration Sunday, 1839, at Trinity College. Joseph W. Blakesley, Cambridge, 1839.
2. See Clark, *Sedgwick*, vol. I, pp. 88–89, 108, on the election in 1807 of Lord Euston to Parliament and the 1811 election of the Duke of Gloucester as Chancellor of the University.
3. In 1812 Sedgwick was active in two unsuccessful campaigns to defeat university petitions against Catholic relief. He referred to the first senate action (April 20, 1812) as 'that absurd petition' (Clark, *Sedgwick*, vol. I, pp. 118, 126–127); in fact the Senate House votes were very close in both cases. In 1822 Sedgwick actively, but again unsuccessfully, campaigned for a pro-Catholic M.P., James Scarlett (Clark, *Sedgwick*, vol. I, p. 257). Whewell wrote to his aunt in 1821 that he had opposed a university address against Roman Catholics and deplored 'the anti-papist bigotry' of Cambridge. See Douglas, *Life of Whewell*, pp. 73–74.
4. The social circle of students centering around John Kemble and Monckton Milnes organized an undergraduate petition to Parliament favoring Catholic emancipation. See Trinity College MSS, Houghton 13[116]. Sedgwick, this time successfully, led in opposition to another anti-Catholic petition; Clark, *Sedgwick*, vol. I, pp. 335–337.
5. For Thirlwall's reaction see pp. 203–207 of Thirlwall, *Connop Thirlwall*. Hare was also much offended by the Romanist extremes of the Oxford Movement – see letter to Whewell from Hare quoted at p. 203 of *Connop Thirlwall*. Sedgwick wrote to a friend: 'You will have heard that Newman and more than twenty others of the Oxford School have at length gone over to Rome. Shame on them that they did not do so long since! Their attempt to remain

in the Church of England while they held opinions such as they have published, only proves that fanaticism and vulgar honesty can seldom shake hands and live together. I pity their delusion, I despise their sophistry, and I hate their dishonesty.' Clark, *Sedgwick*, vol. II, p. 93.

6. Camb. Univ. Papers, C. I (Statutes), July, 1856.
7. Peterhouse, Clare, Caius, Trinity Hall, and Corpus Christi were founded between 1257 and 1351; King's, Queens', St Catharine's, Jesus, Christ's, and St John's between 1441 and 1511; Trinity was the creation of Henry VIII; Emmanuel (1584) and Sidney Sussex (1596) were largely Puritan in influence. See George Peacock, *Observations on the Statutes*, pp. 28, 34. Also see Albert Mansbridge, *The Older Universities*, p. XVI.
8. The clearest nineteenth-century description of the Elizabethan statutes and their impact on the modern university is provided by Peacock's book, esp. pp. 1–74.
9. See J. Blagborne, *The Revenues of the National Universities considered, with a view to their being open to Dissenters*, London, 1835. Blagborne argued that the state had the right to distribute these 'national' resources anyway it liked; if the 'confiscation' of Catholic property had been legal so would be the admitting of dissenters to the benefits thereof.
10. Lewis Campbell's book describing the opening of the universities was named precisely *On the Nationalization of the Old English Universities* (London, 1901). George Dyer, in *Academic Unity*, London, 1827, argued from historical evidence that the universities were 'national', that they had originally been non-sectarian, and that they should be open to all Englishmen. R. M. Beverley's letter . . . *on the Present Corrupt State of the University of Cambridge* was designed – after exposing the corruption at Cambridge – to threaten the University with public seizure of its assets if it did not willingly adapt itself to the needs of the country. See pp. 45–47.
11. Hansard, third series, vol. XXII, col. 3, March 11, 1834.
12. *Ibid.*, vol. XXII, col. 570, March 24, 1834.
13. George Peacock, who was an ardent advocate of reform and a careful student of the legal/historical structure of the University, warned against underestimating the power and the binding nature of the various ancient academical oaths: 'a careful examination of the oaths which [the] statutes exact, and which continue to be taken, and of the formulae which continue to be used, in different academical proceedings, will sufficiently show that they not only recognize the authority of the statutes, but require from those who take or use them an extent of obedience, which can only be lightly regarded when it is imperfectly understood'. The conclusion Peacock drew was that Parliamentary interference was necessary – and desirable – in order to reform the ancient statutes. See Peacock, *Observations on the Statutes*, p. 75. G. Ainslie's *An Historical Account of the Oaths and Subscriptions required in the University of Cambridge*, Cambridge, 1833, made much the same point. Thomas Turton, later the Bishop of Ely (*Thoughts on the Admission of Persons without Regard to their Religious Opinions to Certain Degrees in the Universities of England*, Cambridge, 1834) and Thomas Thorp (in an 1834 sermon entitled 'On Obsolete Rules' – Camb. Univ. Papers, Cam. C. 834. 35) argued that an observance of the traditional arrangements was necessary from both legal and practical standpoints.
14. W. J. Conybeare, *Remarks on a Pamphlet entitled 'Church Privileges as Bearing on Certain Statutes'*, Cambridge, 1841, pp. 14 and 20.
15. Campbell, *Nationalization*, p. 40.

16. 'The Cambridge Controversy', *Quarterly Review*, vol. LII, no. 104, November, 1834, pp. 480–481.
17. Christopher Wordsworth, *On the Admission of Dissenters to Graduate in the University of Cambridge; a Letter to the Rt. Hon. Viscount Althorp, M.P.*, Cambridge, 1834.
18. Quoted, with approval, in the *Quarterly Review*, 'The Cambridge Controversy', p. 467.
19. See Hansard, vol. XXII, cols. 589–592, March 24, 1834.
20. This may seem to have been an unreasonable fear, since the clerical livings and pastoral positions involved were Anglican and thus hardly available or desirable to dissenters. But long practice had made the progression from wranglership to fellowship to living seem inevitable and the contemporary arguments made frequent reference to the problem of the 'emoluments'. See Goulbourn's speech in Parliament, March 24, 1834, cited above. George Pryme the next day in the House 'denied . . . that university advantages were exclusively intended for the Church of England. With regard to the claims to emolument, they were the result of the foundation of particular colleges, and were or might be limited to the will of the founders, or by the statutes of the college.' Col. 624, March 25. But the Duke of Gloucester, col. 981, April 21, specifically warned that admitting dissenters to degrees 'amounted to giving them the right to a place in the Senate – to giving them votes as to all alterations of the laws of the University – as to all the offices there – and as to the disposal of the general patronage of the University'. Connop Thirlwall directly accused the conservative faction of being actuated by this motive; was it not their real fear 'lest any of the endowments, provided for the most part by the munificence of our Roman Catholic ancestors, of the *dark ages*, and now exclusively enjoyed by members of the Church of England, should ever be shared by Dissenters, for instance, by persons of the same creed with the founders?' Quoted at p. 74 of Thirlwall, *Connop Thirlwall*.
21. 'The Cambridge Controversy', *Quarterly Review*, p. 482.
22. Hansard, vol. XXII, col. 623, March 25, 1834.
23. See 'The Cambridge Controversy', *Quarterly Review*, p. 474.
24. *Ibid.*, p. 476. Also see Winstanley, *Early Vic. Camb.*, p. 91.
25. Thomas Turton, the Regius Professor of Divinity, was particularly worried about the dissension and turmoil which would result from opening the Universities. In an idealized vision he wrote of Cambridge: 'Amongst the younger students of the University as at present constituted, every thing wears the aspect of tranquillity. They have nothing to unsettle their minds. They are – taking them as a body – assiduously pursuing their studies, and qualifying themselves for the stations for which they are designed.' *Thoughts*, pp. 21–22. This halcyon existence would be shattered by the arrival of nonconformists.
26. Adam Sedgwick, in a letter to Bishop Blomfield, April 27, 1834, quoted in Clark, *Sedgwick*, vol. I, pp. 422–423. See also Samuel Lee, *Some Remarks on the Dean of Peterborough's Tract 'Admission to Degrees'*, Cambridge, 1834; Lee was Regius Professor of Hebrew. George Biddle Airy, soon to be made Astronomer Royal, also took the side of moderate reform; see *Autobiography*, p. 102.
27. Connop Thirlwall, *A Letter to the Rev. Thomas Turton, D.D. on the Admission of Dissenters to Academical Degrees*, Cambridge, 1834, pp. 6, 17, 21. For voicing these opinions so publicly Thirlwall was severely criticized by the conservative faction, especially by Christopher Wordsworth, the Master of Trinity,

who dismissed Thirlwall from his position as assistant tutor. But other equally realistic assessments of University religion were not hard to find. The previous year F. R. Hall, a fellow of St John's, had written of the neglect of theological instruction: 'The Margaret Professor of Divinity has held the office twenty-six years during which time he has delivered and published *twenty-three lectures*, forming a moderately sized 8vo. volume. His stipend is £1000 per annum . . . The Norrisian Professor delivers yearly the same course of lectures, and *without any examination*, gives a Testimonial to every student, or B.A., who has attended twenty-five of them; though nothing is more notorious than that his lecture-room is anything but a place of Study, many indulging themselves in lounging upon the seats or reading the news-papers, or a novel.' *A Letter Respectfully Addressed to the Heads of Houses and the Senior Fellows in the University of Cambridge on the Defective State of Theological Instruction*, privately circulated, Cambridge, 1833. Debate in the House of Commons could be even more scathing; see Lord Palmerston's remarks on Mar. 26, 1834, Hansard, vol. XXII, col. 701. 'It had again been contended, that the relaxation of the rule might do away with compulsory attendance of the undergraduates at the religious services of the church. Now, he would ask, if there would really be any great harm in such a change? Was it either essential or expedient, that young men should rush from their beds every morning to prayers, unwashed, unshaved, and half dressed; or, in the even-ing, from their wine to chapel, and from chapel, back again to their wine?'

28. See Thirlwall, *Connop Thirlwall*, pp. 76–81.
29. See J. E. Smith, *Considerations Respecting Cambridge, More Particularly Relating to its Botanical Professorship*, London, 1818, and *A Defence of the Church and Universities of England*, London, 1819; and J. H. Monk, *A Vindication of the University of Cambridge from the Reflections of Sir James Edward Smith*, London, 1818, and *Appendix to a Vindication* . . ., Cambridge, 1819.
30. George Dyer, *Academic Unity*, London, 1827.
31. See Winstanley, *Early Vic. Camb.*, pp. 152, 154, 160–166.
32. As Airy wrote in his diary; *Autobiography*, p. 102.
33. Clark, *Sedgwick*, vol. I, p. 419. Among the signers were the masters of Caius and Corpus Christi, nine professors including Sedgwick, Babbage, Airy, and several college tutors.
34. Hansard, vols. XXII, XXIII, XXIV, XXV.
35. *Ibid.*, vol. XXII, col. 902.
36. *Ibid.*, vol. XXV, cols. 886–888, Aug. 1, 1834.
37. See 'Christopher Wordsworth, Master of Trinity', Chapter V, Winstanley, *Early Vic. Camb.*, pp. 59–88.
38. Maurice was a strangely complex man. Raised as a Unitarian, his religious scruples prevented his professing himself a member of the Church of England at graduation; he therefore entered Trinity Hall, the law college, and left the University 'by passing through the examinations and the Act required for a student in civil law'. Maurice, *Life of Maurice*, vol. I, p. 177. Very shortly after leaving Cambridge Maurice became convinced of the truth of orthodox Christianity and entered the Anglican Church, and then – at the urging of his friend Sterling – decided to enroll at Oxford. In his own words (in a letter to his son, included in his *Life*, vol. I, pp. 173–184): 'In Cambridge it was demanded of every person taking a degree that he should declare himself a *bona fide* member of the Church of England. That, when I left Cambridge, I had declined to do. At Oxford every student at matriculation was required to sign the Thirty-nine Articles. This, when I entered the

University, I had deliberately done. Some reformers . . . argued that the Cambridge plan was a great advance on the Oxford, and might be reasonably substituted for it . . . Reviewing my own experience with the two Universities . . . I came to this conclusion: That the Cambridge demand was much more distinctly and formally exclusive than the Oxford, in as much as it involved a direct renunciation of Nonconformity; that the subscription to Articles on entering Oxford was not intended as a test, but as a declaration of the terms on which the University proposed to teach its pupils, upon which terms they must agree to learn; that it is fairer to express than to conceal these; that they are not terms which are to bind down the student to certain conclusions beyond which he cannot advance, but are helps to him in pursuing his studies . . . [Writing this analysis in 1870 Maurice went on to say] the Liberals were clearly right in saying that the Articles did not mean to those who signed them at the Universities or on taking orders what I supposed them to mean, and I was wrong. They were right in saying that subscription did mean to most the renunciation of the right to think, and, since none could renounce that right, it involved dishonesty. All this I have been compelled by the evidence of the facts sorrowfully to confess.' Pp. 180–181, 183. Despite the subtlety of his ideas, it is clear that at no time did Maurice favour regulations which would be restrictive of thought or religious freedom.

39. See the letter from Whewell to G. B. Airy, Trinity College MSS, o.15.47[5], 1842: 'I have passed through the Senate a grace for dissenting, but our dissent will affect only the station, not the main line.'
40. Hansard, vol. No. LXIX, col. 855, May 25, 1843.
41. See the correspondence between James D. Forbes (of the University of Edinburgh) and Whewell in which they express pleasure at the removal of religious tests at the Scottish universities; Trinity College MSS, Add. Ms. a. 204[67], May 27, 1845. Also see Clark, *Sedgwick*, vol. 1, pp. 418–419: 'For the moment he [Sedgwick] and his friends were unsuccessful, and thirty-seven years elapsed before tests were completely swept away. In the interval, between 1834 and 1871 whenever an occasion presented itself, Sedgwick shewed unflagging interest in the cause, and one of the last occasions on which he spoke in public was a meeting at St. John's College Lodge, to assist the movement which resulted in the Test Act of 1871.'
42. The clearest expression of the philosophy behind the moderate reformers' program can be found in Sedgwick's 1834 letter to Bishop Blomfield, already extensively quoted from; see Clark, *Sedgwick*, vol. 1, pp. 421, 425. 'Dissenters may have some foolish expectations from the operation of the intended Bill, but we cannot help this.'
43. See Campbell, *Nationalization*, pp. 129 ff.
44. The best survey of the Cambridge of this period (1860 forward) is provided in Sheldon Rothblatt, *The Revolution of the Dons*, London, 1968.
45. This struggle was not an easy one; Henry Sidgwick, for example, felt it inconsistent with his religious principles to retain his fellowship at Trinity and resigned it in 1869. This did much to rally reform opinion as Sidgwick, an eminent scholar, the Knightbridge Professor of Moral Philosophy, and one of the founders of Newnham College for Women, was very highly respected. And the triumph was not absolute even then. The headships of some colleges remained the preserve of the clergy, for example. But in the main from a legal standpoint Oxford and Cambridge became essentially secular institutions. A clear narrative of events surrounding the passage of this Bill

can be found in Campbell, *Nationalization*, pp. 152–175, Chapter VIII, 'University Tests Act of 1871'.

46. Clark, *Sedgwick*, vol. II, p. 451.
47. See Sedgwick's letter to Bishop Blomfield quoted in Clark, *Sedgwick*, vol. I, pp. 421–425.
48. Quoted in Campbell, *Nationalization*, p. 212.
49. Winstanley, *Early Vic. Camb.*, p. 84.
50. See Cockburn, *Strictures on Clerical Education*, who asserted that the University was granting theological certificates to students 'devoid of ecclesiastical information' (p. 34); or *A Letter to the Right Rev. John, Lord Bishop of Bristol*, London, 1822, by 'Philograntus' (a pseudonym for J. H. Monk), a plea for establishing serious examinations in theology and classics in addition to mathematics.
51. See Hall, *A Letter*, for a forceful but not exaggerated depiction of the absenteeism and ineffectiveness of the theological professors. For a more extreme appraisal, see Beverley, *A Letter*, p. 28.
52. Hester Jenkins and D. Caradog Jones, through a statistical study of Venn's *Alumni Cantabrigiensis* have shown that between 1850 and 1900 two-thirds of them did so. 'Social Class of Cambridge University Alumni of the Eighteenth and Nineteenth Centuries', *British Journal of Sociology*, 1950, vol. I, pp. 93 ff.
53. Winstanley, *Early Vic. Camb.*, pp. 65–66.
54. *Ibid.*, p. 292. Richard Watson was the Regius Professor of Divinity from 1771–1816. 'He stated that he "knew as much of divinity as could reasonably be expected of a man whose course of studies had been directed to, and whose time had been fully occupied in, other pursuits," but the Regius chair had "long been the secret object" of his ambition, and, "by hard travelling and some adroitness" he obtained the King's mandate and was created D.D. in time for the election. He left Cambridge in 1787.' See J. A. Venn, *Alumni Cantabrigiensis*, Cambridge, 1954, pt 2, vol. VI, p. 374.
55. 'The scandal had, indeed, formerly [before 1800] been greater, but it was still sufficiently widespread to disgrace the University. For nearly a hundred years no lectures had been delivered by the Lady Margaret Professors of Divinity, who did not blush to draw the comfortable stipend of one thousand pounds a year.' Winstanley, *Early Vic. Camb.*, p. 155.
56. *Ibid.*, p. 168.
57. For a clear treatment of the establishment of the classical tripos see *ibid.*, pp. 65–71. Also Camb. Univ. Papers, D.C. 1350, May, 1822.
58. See Beverley, *A Letter*, pp. 21–28; and Hall, *A Letter*.
59. Peacock, *Observations on the Statutes*, p. 168.
60. James Hildyard, *The Obligation of the University to provide for the Professional Education of its Members designed for Holy Orders*, Cambridge, 1841.
61. Charles Perry, *Clerical Education Considered with an Especial Reference to the Universities*, London, 1841.
62. See 'Rusticus', *Remarks on Clerical Education: Addressed to the Rev. Charles Perry and the Rev. James Hildyard*, London, 1841. 'Rusticus' argued that provincialism could be avoided if several dioceses banded together to set up the new institutions, that having such an experience would build a seriousness and an *esprit de corps* among the clergy, and that narrowness would be prevented by the requiring of the previous B.A. Similar schemes were proposed in 1847 (C. E. Walkey, *The Church and the Universities and their Present Relation towards one another with Regard to the Priesthood of the Church of England and Ireland*, Exeter, 1847) and in 1853 (C. Hebert, *Theological Colleges and the Universities*,

London, 1853), and several bishops had indeed set up separate institutions for the training of clergy (see Perry, *Clerical Education*).

63. See Perry, *Clerical Education*.

64. See Winstanley, *Early Vic. Camb.*, pp. 168–174, for a treatment of the early reforms of the theological program.

65. See Trinity College MSS, Add. Ms. a. 53¹, May 11, 1843. Winstanley incorrectly dates this report as 1842. *Early Vic. Camb.*, p. 174.

66. Winstanley, *Early Vic. Camb.*, p. 174. Whewell wrote an open letter to the bishops in 1843 asking their support for the new examination, 'trusting . . . that you will agree with me in the wish to promote the study of Theology in this University'. Trinity College MSS, Add. Ms. a. 53⁵, Oct. 28, 1843.

67. See Camb. Univ. Papers, Cam. a. 500. 5¹²³, Oct. 16, 1848, p. 3.

68. The Cambridge Camden Society, a group interested in restoring church architecture according to High Church and/or romantic principles, was certainly not a trivial organization. But its existence in Cambridge was brief; 'after a few years and one complex and ramifying row it left Cambridge for London, changed its name, and subsided into comparative obscurity'. P. 119, Elliot Rose, 'The Stone Table in the Round Church and the Crisis of the Cambridge Camden Society', *Victorian Studies*, vol. x, no. 2, Dec. 1966. See also James F. White, *The Cambridge Movement*, Cambridge, 1962.

69. See Winstanley, *Early Vic. Camb.*, pp. 18–25. The University tolerated this project only rather grudgingly.

70. See Winstanley, *Early Vic. Camb.*, p. 183. In 1841 Philip Freeman, a young fellow at Peterhouse, argued that excessive attendance by undergraduates at churches in the city of Cambridge was detrimental to University discipline. *Church Principles as bearing upon Certain Statutes of the University of Cambridge*, Cambridge, 1841.

71. See for example J. R. Crowfoot, 'The New Honours Triposes', *Cambridge Advertiser*, Mar. 7, 1849, Trinity College MSS, Add. Ms. a. 63⁸⁵, in which he argues that mathematics has kept Cambridge free of the theological 'unsoundness' which afflicted Germany and from unhealthy flights of fanciful imagination.

72. Frances Brookfield, *The Cambridge Apostles*, New York, 1906, p. 3. A much more thorough treatment of this group is presented in Allen, *The Cambridge Apostles*.

73. Quoted at p. 14, Brookfield, *Cambridge Apostles*.

74. Thirlwall, *Connop Thirlwall*, p. 57.

75. *Ibid.*, p. 56. Other modern scholars agree with this assessment; see Sanders, *Coleridge and the Broad Church Movement*, esp. pp. 183, 186, 205.

76. A fellow of Trinity and after 1848 Vicar of Exminster, Devon, and a university liberal, he wrote a pamphlet about college statutes, noted above. See Venn, *Alumni Cantabrigiensis*, pt 2, vol. II, p. 113.

77. 'Church Parties', *Edinburgh Review*, vol. xcviii, no. 200, Oct., 1853, pp. 330–335. The article is unsigned but Sanders, *Coleridge*, p. 7, credits it to Conybeare. Sanders regards this article as basic in defining the term 'Broad Church' and even thinks that the general use of the label dates from the publication of this essay.

78. 'Contemptuous of the outworn subjects and authorities of Cambridge, they [Hare and Thirlwall] showed the "Apostles" a better system. While most of the students were memorizing Aristotle, Plato, Euclid, Newton, and Paley, the "Apostles" were discussing modern authors of meaning and value. They performed their assigned duties faithfully, but devoted their spare time to

German and English metaphysics and poetry.' Thirlwall, *Connop Thirlwall*, pp. 57–58. For Maurice's attitude to the ancient philosophers see his 1850 letter to F. J. A. Hort, just then graduating from Cambridge, later a fellow of Trinity and Lady Margaret Professor of Divinity: 'I have never taken up any dialogue of Plato without getting more from it than from any book not in the Bible. I do not think it signifies much where you begin. The attempts to systematise his writings seem to me in general unfortunate; his own beautiful and wonderful method is contained in each one, and any one thoroughly studied is the initiation to the rest . . . I have always contended that Plato is quite as practical as Aristotle; nay, that if he is rightly studied as he would have us study him, in connection with the life and purposes of Socrates, he is more practical. But I am sure Aristotle has excellences of a very kind which Plato has not . . . I would advise you to study the "Politics" as well as the Nichomachean Ethics; and not to forget the Rhetoric . . . The "Politics", though it may be difficult always to trace the course of the thought, seems to me a book of the highest value; I am most thankful for what it taught me. It should be combined with the study of the Republic by any one who is meditating on ecclesiastical or civil polity.' Maurice, *Life of Maurice*, vol. II, pp. 37–39.

79. T. Wemyss Reid, *The Life, Letters, and Friendships of Richard Monckton Milnes, First Lord Houghton*, New York, 1891, vol. I, p. 115.

80. Maurice, *Life of Maurice*, vol. I, p. 420. 'Niebuhr's History received thoughtful approval except from the ultraorthodox and fanatical. Through the championship of Arnold and Hare, it became a revered text at both Oxford and Cambridge, in translation, to be sure, for neither University had gone the length of teaching German . . . "Niebuhr-madness" became general. The most important result in England, however, was that Niebuhr's courageous destruction of long-cherished myths smoothed the path for independent investigations in all ancient history.' Thirlwall, *Connop Thirlwall*, pp. 47–48.

81. Sanders, *Coleridge*, p. 188.

82. In the opinion of Milnes' good friend Aubrey de Vere, quoted in vol. I, p. 116 of Reid, *Milnes*.

83. Sanders, *Coleridge*, p. 248 on Maurice; Thirlwall, *Connop Thirlwall*, p. 49 on Thirlwall.

84. Thirlwall, *Connop Thirlwall*, p. 30.

85. Thirlwall's biographer characterizes Schleiermacher's approach thus: '[He had] a logical theory of the inspiration and authority of the Bible . . . presenting the Synoptic Gospels as history rather than as direct revelation. He instructed the student of Scripture to train himself in languages and in the historical method, the better to work on the canon, which he considered incomplete. Disregarding orthodox interpretations of the life of Jesus, he evolved the figure of a man whose soul, perfected by God, could perform miraculous cures. Denying categorically the divinity of Christ, an act of exceptional bravery in those days, he presented Him as not so much a personality as an expression of Christian faith, the archetypal, sinless man. But scattered sayings of Jesus had to be reconciled to his central scheme or ignored. Such a reconciliation Schleiermacher attempted in his *Critical Essay on the Gospel of St. Luke*.' Thirlwall, *Connop Thirlwall*. For a clear survey of Schleiermacher's theology see Karl Barth, *Protestant Thought: from Rousseau to Ritschl*, New York, 1959, Chapter VIII.

86. See Otto Pfleiderer, *The Development of Theology in Germany since Kant and its Progress in Great Britain since 1825*, London 1909, pp. 209–210. 'Historical

instinct was not Schleiermacher's strong point, and his preference for the Fourth Gospel [as being the first written] did not rest upon historical grounds but upon his theological postulates and his sympathy as one of the Romanticists, with the Johannine idea of Christ.'

87. The sermons were published as *Discourses on the State of the Protestant Religion in Germany*, Cambridge, 1824; they were intended to 'forewarn and forearm the Church of England against the rationalistic criticism of the continent . . .' *D.N.B.*, vol. xvii, p. 240.

88. 'The Bishop of St. David very injudiciously translated, about twenty years ago, Schleiermacher's book on St. Luke . . . In consequence of the rumour that Thirlwall would be made archbishop, all the most revolting passages in this treatise . . . have been carefully hunted out and paraded in the newspapers as exhibiting the deep-seated rationalism and blasphemous temper of a man whom an English bishop had delighted to honour.' Maurice, *Life of Maurice*, vol. i, p. 454.

89. See Thirlwall, *Connop Thirlwall*, p. 34.

90. Similarly, George Grote and Thirlwall were each able to write important 'scientific' histories of Greece by drawing on the spirit of the new criticism which the Apostles and their friends had imported from the Continent. On Grote, see Venn, *Alumni Cantabrigiensis*, pt 2, vol. iii, p. 164.

91. Consider Kant, Herder, Hegel, Goethe, Schleiermacher. Clearly a treatment of the basis of this German romanticism is beyond the scope of this book; for a very useful treatment – both of the German ideas and of corresponding English thought – see M. H. Abrams, *The Mirror and the Lamp*, New York, 1953.

92. Milnes was probably characteristic of the group, 'at that time much devoted to German literature, and in sympathy with German philosophy – at least so far as it stands opposed to that of Locke and his followers. He was ardent in his admiration for both the Schlegels, for Tieck, for Heine and Schiller . . .' Reid, *Milnes*, vol. i, p. 116.

93. Reid, *Milnes*, vol. i, pp. 73–74.

94. Maurice, *Life of Maurice*, vol. i, p. 176; see also p. 317.

95. 'Among English authors, Hare interpreted the poetry of Wordsworth and Shelley and the prose of Coleridge and championed their doctrines against the Philistines, or *Stumpfs*, as they were called.' Thirlwall, *Connop Thirlwall*, p. 9. When, in a debate on the relative merits of Wordsworth and Byron, Milnes managed to muster only twenty-three votes, Hare remarked that 'the number was too large, for there were not twenty-three men in the room worthy to be Wordsworthians'. Reid, *Milnes*, vol. i, p. 73.

96. The terms come from Walter Cannon's article 'Scientists and Broad Churchmen', p. 65.

97. Whewell visited Wordsworth several times; see Douglas, *Life of Whewell*, pp. 237, 267. Sedgwick also was a frequent guest in the Lake District; see Clark, *Sedgwick*, vol. i, pp. 247, 431, vol. ii, p. 122. Although somewhat critical of the more extreme bits of romanticism in the poet's work ('he is not half as Wordsworthian as his admirers, and I am more and more puzzled that a man of his acuteness and good sense should write poems with white rabbits and waggon drivers for their heroes', Douglas, p. 67), Whewell thought highly enough of Wordsworth to compose a sonnet in his honor in 1838; see *ibid.*, p. 33.

98. See Thirlwall, *Connop Thirlwall*, p. 27.

99. The best treatment of Coleridge's influence on this group and through them

on the Broad Church Movement is provided in the Sanders book already cited (Note 75). It is a series of connected studies of Coleridge, Thomas Arnold, J. C. Hare, Thomas Carlyle, and F. D. Maurice. See also Thirlwall, *Connop Thirlwall*, p. 189: 'Coleridge's ideal . . . was a Christian Church working hand in hand with a well-ordered State, which would interrelate religion with all the higher activities of the outer world – art, literature, philosophy, science, and history. Religion was designed, he taught, "to improve the nature and faculties of man, in order to the right governing of our actions, to the securing of peace and progress, external and internal, of individuals and of communities, and lastly, of rendering us capable of a more perfect state".'

100. Letter from Hare to Whewell, Oct., 1834, Trinity College MSS, Add. Ms. a. 206[166].

101. Hare to Whewell, Oct. 25, 1838, Trinity College MSS, Add. MS. a. 206[173]. This is a very interesting letter, giving insight into the contemporary intelligentsia's response to Mill. Hare goes on: 'It must be six or seven years since Wordsworth told me how much he had been struck by him, and that he was one of the most remarkable young men of the age . . . [His works are] most masterly in execution, shewing a logical power and a metaphysical subtlety very rare in England, united with a high tone of moral feeling. Having long been an intimate friend of Sterling's he tried when the London Review was set up, to get him as a contributor. But at that time there was much of his father's leaven poisoning the review, and I [*sic*] refused. During his father's life, I believe, Mill was withheld by a most praiseworthy feeling from declaring how completely he differed from the Benthamites: but on his father's death, he got the Review entirely in his own hands and resolved to make it as far as he could a Review for principles, and for the best of literature . . . [Hare feels that Mill has succeeded and has found new, worthy contributors] while the Benthamites are reviling him as a Coleridgean Tory. It does not seem to me that one ought to look with suspicion on a man who comes over in this way from the enemy's camp, openly, and by a change of which one may trace the progress. Converts have ever been the most powerful of champions . . .'

102. Maurice, *Life of Maurice*, vol. I, p. 178: '[Coleridge's] book on the "Idea of the State" . . . impressed me very much. I accepted to a great degree the principle of it, though not all the conclusions. With the Benthamites, therefore, I was still at war.'

103. *Ibid.*, vol. I, pp. 251–252, on developing differences from Coleridge's thought, and p. 510 for Maurice's attitude towards Coleridge as a critic.

104. He approved of the Declaration of Independence, 'a document in which the old Protestant feeling, that each man is a distinct being possessing distinct privileges and rights, is curiously blended with a vague notion of general fellowship, which was beginning to gain currency in Europe, and which was rather a reaction against Protestantism than the natural result of it'. Quoted from *Kingdom of Christ*, p. 176 in Sanders, *Coleridge*, p. 248, note no. 30.

105. Letter from Sir Thomas Acland, quoted in Maurice, *Life of Maurice*, vol. II, p. 451.

106. See Brookfield, *Cambridge Apostles*, p. 299 and Sanders, *Coleridge*, p. 136, on Sterling; Milnes wrote that Coleridge's 'Church and State' 'has given me the only idea I ever had of the English constitution'. Reid, *Milnes*, vol. I, p. 88. Thirlwall's biographer regards his subject and the poet as definitely part of the same unified philosophical group; see pp. 188–190, 196.

107. Consider the University's rejection of Paleyan thought in favor of a more organic social view, described in Chapter 4. For Whewell on Coleridge see Douglas, *Life of Whewell*, pp. 28, 31, 32, 94.

108. Maberley, *Melancholy and Awful Death*, p. 34 (1833). Some sample questions from the Voluntary Theological Examination of 1843: 'What internal evidence is there for the date of the First Epistle of Clemens? What evidence for the genuineness of our copies of it? How do you account for one or two quotations made from it by ancient writers, not being now found in it?' Or 'Compare the doctrine of the XVIth Article with the Collect for Ash Wednesday, and with the Prayer after the Absolution in the Office for the Visitation of the Sick. Establish it by Holy Scripture. Who was Novatian and of what erroneous tenet was he the author? What texts were urged in support of that tenet at the time of the Reformation, and how are those texts explained in the Homily on Repentance? At the Hampton Court Conference what was proposed to add to those words of this Article "we may depart from grace given"?' Or 'Shew that Christ was "clearly void" of sin and that no *man* is void of sin.'

109. Whewell was somewhat dubious about the scheme to begin with, thinking the phrase 'Philosophy of Christianity' too technical and the possibility of getting the University to establish a prize in such a speculative field rather remote (see Oct. 27, 1834, letter to Hare, quoted in Todhunter, *Wm Whewell*, vol. II, p. 197). In February of 1835 Whewell wrote to Hare: 'I do not know whether your hopes were very confident that the Heads would embrace our proposition about a Coleridge Essay: but, if so, it would appear they were delusive . . . I hear both from him [the Vice-Chancellor] and from our Master that the objection is not to any accidental and extraneous part of the scheme but to the name of Coleridge. With our governors, it seems, the vagaries of his earlier times are better known than the Christian philosophy, which he has impressed upon so many in his riper years. I am sorry for this, for I think the Essay might, with good management and good fortune, have been of beneficial influence here; but I do not see what further can be done in the present state of things.' *Ibid.*, vol. II, pp. 202–203.

110. Hare made several unsuccessful efforts during the forties to have Maurice appointed to some responsible theological post at the University (see letters from Hare to Whewell, Trinity College MSS, Add. Ms. a. 77[132, 133, 135, 136].) On Oct. 21, 1843, Hare wrote: 'I think there is hardly any position, except a theological chair in one of our universities (which he has no chance of obtaining), where he would do so much good: and it is quite a scandal, that, after having done what he has done, he should be wearing out his life almost in indigence . . .' Later Maurice was accused of heterodoxy by the *Quarterly Review* and had to retire from his post at the University of London; it was not until 1866 that he returned to Cambridge, as the Knightbridge Professor of Moral Philosophy. See Venn, *Alumni Cantabrigiensis*, pt 2, vol. IV, p. 368.

111. See Thirlwall, *Connop Thirlwall*, p. 226. They were Rowland Williams and Charles Wycliffe Goodwin.

112. John Robert Seeley; see Venn, *Alumni*, pt. 2, vol. V, p. 458.

113. See Douglas, *Life of Whewell*, pp. 99, 108–109; Todhunter, *Wm Whewell*, vol. I, p. 284.

114. Letter from Hare to Whewell, Oct. 25, 1838, Trinity College MSS, Add. Ms. a. 206[173].

6. THE CHALLENGE OF DARWIN

1. Walter F. Cannon, in 'The Basis of Darwin's Achievement: a Revaluation', *Victorian Studies*, vol. v, no. 2, Dec., 1961, pp. 109 ff., argues that Darwin 'stole' the universe of the natural theologians from them. That is, working with many of the fundamental premises of the natural theologians – nature as purposive, for example – Darwin put forth a doctrine which at the same time absorbed and annihilated their position.

2. W. L. Alexander, 'Theology', *Encyclopaedia Britannica*, 8th edition, Edinburgh, 1860, vol. xxi, p. 181. The eighth edition, being the last one compiled before the *Origin* appeared, is generally regarded as a good source for common opinion, pre-Darwin.

3. For a clear evaluation of the Bridgewater series, as well as for the charge quoted here, see Gillispie, *Genesis and Geology*, pp. 209–216.

4. Gillispie takes essentially such a sneering position – *Genesis*, pp. 209–216. But see p. 39: 'His [Paley's] explanation of the course of nature has been stood on its head so completely by the acceptance of evolutionary theories that it now seems almost a caricature rather than a sample of a framework of opinion, but this is partly because no one else had succeeded in making the explanation as clear and explicit as it was in Paley.'

5. Todhunter quoted complimentary letters from Davies Gilbert, Malthus, H. J. Rose, and J. Blanco White – *Wm Whewell*, vol. i, pp. 73–74.

6. See for example articles in the *Quarterly Review*, vol. i, no. 99, Oct., 1833, pp. 1 ff., and in the *Edinburgh Review*, vol. lviii, no. 118, Jan., 1834, pp. 422 ff.

7. Sedgwick, *A Discourse on the Studies of the University*, p. 17.

8. See Herschel's *Preliminary Discourse on the Study of Natural Philosophy*, esp. pt. 1, Chapter 1. Babbage wrote *The Ninth Bridgewater Treatise* (London, 1838) the object of which was to show through a discussion of scientific phenomena 'that the power and knowledge of the great Creator of matter and of mind are unlimited', p. ix. Babbage's Treatise was not part of the series commissioned by the will but was written at his own initiative to combat what he perceived as a lack of enthusiasm in Whewell's essay.

9. Maurice, *Life of Maurice*, vol. i, p. 284.

10. See Herschel, *Preliminary Discourse*, pp. 37, 101: 'This use of the word *law*, however, our readers will of course perceive has relation to us as understanding, rather than to the materials of which the universe consists as obeying, certain rules.' 'We may therefore regard a law of nature either, 1st, as a general proposition, announcing, in abstract terms, a whole group of particular facts relating to the behaviour of natural agents in proposed circumstances; or 2ndly, as a proposition announcing that a whole class of individuals agreeing in one character agree also in another.' Contrast this view of law-as-descriptive with the view of law-as-prescriptive characteristic of the contemporary German *naturphilosophie*. This latter position was Kantian and Platonic and quite distinct from natural theology – see Merz, *History of Scientific Thought*, vol. i, pp. 178, 207, vol. ii, p. 315.

11. Alexander Pope's *Essay on Man* sums up this attitude.

All nature is but art, unknown to thee;
All chance, direction, which thou canst not see;
All discord, harmony not understood;
All partial evil, universal good . . .

12. See Paley, *Natural Theology*, Chapter xxvi, 'On the Goodness of the Deity'. Also see above, Chapter iv. The *Encyclopaedia Britannica* article on 'Paley'

(written by Henry Rogers, 8th edition, vol. XVII, p. 205) praised him for coping squarely and effectively with the problem of evil.

13. On the static quality of natural theology see Cannon, 'Darwin's Achievement', p. 125.

14. Paley specifically invoked Malthusian principles of superfecundity in his analysis, *Natural Theology*, pp. 67 ff. See Arthur O. Lovejoy, *The Great Chain of Being*, Cambridge, Mass., 1957, esp. Chapter VI, 'The Chain of Being in Eighteenth-Century Thought, and Man's Place and Role in Nature', pp. 183–207. I am indebted for much of the preceding analysis to Dr Robert Young, King's College, Cambridge.

15. Alexander, 'Theology', *Ency. Brit.*, vol. XXI, p. 188. Also see Whewell's warning about the limitations of natural theology in his Bridgewater Treatise, *Astronomy and General Physics considered with Reference to Natural Theology*, pp. 12–13.

16. 'Crombie's Natural Theology', *Quarterly Review*, vol. LI, no. 101, Mar., 1834, p. 216.

17. Alexander, 'Theology', pp. 187–188. It is interesting to consider why arguments appear convincing to certain eras and not to others; St Anselm's marvelous twelfth-century ontological proof was dismissed in the Britannica article as 'this piece of scholastic subtlety'. It is easy to find other examples of thinkers who found Paleyan arguments effective. J. J. Blunt, later Lady Margaret Professor of Divinity, wrote an 1828 article in the *Quarterly Review* (vol. XXXVIII, no. 76, pp. 304–335) on the 'Works and Character of Paley'. 'We think it next to impossible for a candid unbeliever to read the Evidences of Paley, in their proper order, unshaken. His Natural Theology will open the hearts, if any thing can. It is philosophy in its highest and noblest sense; scientific, without the jargon of science; profound but so clear that its depth is disguised.' P. 312.

18. For a narrative survey of these geological schools see Gillispie, *Genesis*, throughout, or Francis C. Faber, 'Fossils and the Idea of a Process of Time in Natural History', in *Forerunners of Darwin, 1745–1859*, ed. Bentley Glass, Owsei Tempkin, William L. Straus, Baltimore, 1959, pp. 222 ff.

19. From Hutton's *Theory of the Earth*, 1795, quoted in Gillispie, *Genesis*, p. 46.

20. For example, H. Cole, a Cambridge graduate and parish priest, in 1834 wrote a pamphlet entitled *Popular Geology Subversive of Divine Revelation* (London, 1834), in which he tried to prove that when Moses wrote 'days' he meant days, not epochs. William Cockburn, Dean of York, opposed even those geologists like Buckland who tried to preserve the connection between the geological and the Biblical versions of the creation story; see Clark, *Sedgwick*, vol. II., pp. 76–77.

21. See Clark, *Sedgwick*, vol. I, pp. 153–165. Sedgwick's opponent, obviously disgruntled, wrote: 'Sedgwick is put up by a large College, merely as a *man of talent*, who *can* soon fit himself for his office. For myself, I feel a conviction that few persons in the University have followed up the Science more seriously than I have.' Sedgwick himself remarked: 'I had but one rival, Gorham of Queens', and he had not the slightest chance against me, for I knew absolutely nothing of geology, whereas he knew a great deal but it was all wrong!' *Ibid.*, vol. I, pp. 157, 160–161.

22. By 1828 he was President of the Geological Society of London; see paper by him, Nov. 6, 1829, *Proceedings of the Geological Society*, vol. I, p. 274.

23. Douglas, *Life of Whewell*, p. 122.

24. See Todhunter, *Wm Whewell*, vol. I, pp. 33, 37, 41. Whewell's most dramatic

efforts involved two unsuccessful attempts at determining the density of the earth by observing the behavior of pendulums at some depth underground. These measurements were conducted with G. B. Airy at the bottom of a coal mine in Dolcoath – *ibid.*, vol. I, pp. 37–40; Airy, *Autobiography*, pp. 66–68, 83–84.

25. See Clark, *Sedgwick*, vol. I, pp. 283–297, 529–539; vol. II, pp. 200–206, 306–310, 502–563.

26. *Ibid.*, vol. I, p. 285, quoting from letter to editor, *Annals of Philosophy*, Mar. 11, 1825.

27. On Sedgwick's attitude to and gradual rejection of Wernerianism see Clark, *Sedgwick*, vol. I, p. 284–5. 'His earlier papers, and some of his admissions in conversation or in lecture, show that, like many of his predecessors, he had once been a mineralogist, and a staunch Wernerian. In his first paper, for instance, several pages are devoted to an enumeration of the mineral constituents of the Cornish rocks; but this does not appear in any subsequent treatise, and as for Werner, we find him dismissed with a jest: "For a long while I was troubled with water on the brain, but light and heat have completely dissipated it" . . . This utterance might be understood to imply an allegiance to the rival views of Hutton; but such was by no means the case. Throughout his geological life Sedgwick – thanks no doubt to his mathematical training – was no theorist. He held firmly to inductive observation.' See also p. 357.

28. See Gillispie, *Genesis*, p. 96, for an assessment of general geological opinion ca. 1820.

29. A. Sedgwick, Presidential Address, Feb. 18, 1831, *Proceedings of the Geological Society of London*, vol. I, p. 313.

30. On the catastrophists, including those mentioned here, see Gillispie, *Genesis*, pp. 98–120.

31. Quoted in Clark, *Sedgwick*, vol. I, pp. 295–6. Sedgwick's geological work is full of similar phrases, even when he is not explicitly enunciating the catastrophist hypothesis; see for example, his paper delivered to the Geological Society, Nov. 6, 1829 (*Proc. Geol. Soc. London*, vol. I, pp. 152–155): 'In the basins which have been examined, there is an entire break between the secondary and tertiary groups. But the great mechanical agents which in these localities have elevated and ground down the secondary rocks, before the commencement of the tertiary, may not have acted universally . . .'

32. Sedgwick, Presidential Address, pp. 304–306. See also p. 311: 'We must . . . conclude that there have been in the history of the earth long periods of comparative repose, during which the sedimentary deposits went on in regular continuity, and comparatively short periods of violence and revolution, during which that continuity was broken. And if we admit that the higher regions of the globe have been raised from the sea by any modification of volcanic force, we must also admit that there have been several successive periods of extraordinary volcanic energy.'

33. Quoted in Todhunter, *Wm Whewell*, vol. I, p. 51.

34. Presidential Address, p. 305.

35. Gillispie says of the *Vestiges*: 'Authorship was not certainly known until the 12th edition in 1884, when Alexander Ireland, who acted as go-between in arranging for the initial publication, disclosed the author's identity with a view to doing justice to his memory.' *Genesis*, p. 286.

36. Robert Chambers, *Vestiges of the Natural History of Creation*, 5th edition, London, 1846, pp. 161–2.

37. *Ibid.*, p. 163.

38. Clark, *Sedgwick*, vol. II, p. 83. Whewell wrote a letter to J. D. Forbes in April of 1845 saying that Sedgwick was composing the Edinburgh article: 'He is in a most *threshing* humour on this matter.' Trinity College MSS, O. 15. 4759.

39. Quoted in Clark, *Sedgwick,* vol. II, p. 88.

40. See the review of Sedgwick's *Discourse* which the *British Quarterly Review* published in 1850; though generally extremely hostile to Sedgwick's style and basic ideas, the review said of his treatment of the *Vestiges*: 'This we must say, that, as an array of hostile *facts*, there has been no such answer as the one given in this *Discourse*, though the same looseness of argument, upon which we have already commented, follows the Professor even here . . . The sections on spontaneous generation, transmutation of species, foetal transformation, and on the organic phenomena of geology, are enriched from the opulence of a well-stored mind.' Vol. XII, 1850, p. 380.

41. Sedgwick, 'Natural History of Creation', *Edinburgh Review*, vol. LXXXII, no. 165, July, 1845, p. 27. Sedgwick contrasted the ignorance displayed in the *Vestiges* with his own scientific work: 'We are not describing nature at second hand, and as far as we know, we speak of her works in the words of simple truth; and, we repeat, that she will not regulate her labours by an imaginative system or conform to such roles as we lay down for her.' p. 33.

42. *Ibid.*, p. 8.

43. *Ibid.*, pp. 20 ff. where Sedgwick says that the nebular hypothesis, though attractive, is 'At present, utterly unfit to form the basis of any system of nature such as our author presumes to erect upon it.'

44. Chambers had claimed that occasionally oat seeds produced rye and that insects had been 'generated' in a laboratory through the use of electricity. *Ibid.*, pp. 68, 72.

45. 'As all our exact knowledge of the "celestial mechanics" is derived from our previous exact knowledge of the laws of matter studied on earth; so all our exact knowledge of the organic laws of the old world can only be learnt from a study of the organic phenomena of living nature. With such phenomena we must begin or we have no philosophical starting point.' *Ibid.*, p. 50.

46. *Ibid.*, pp. 84–85.

47. *Ibid.*, p. 32. See also p. 52: 'We next come to the *muschelkalk* . . . It has a very remarkable fauna, and we have seen many good collections derived from it. And what are the organic types? We do not find so much as one single species with which we are familiar in the palaeozoic series. All the older families and orders have disappeared; and even the saurians differ in their order from those of the preceding epoch. It is not too much to say that nature has destroyed all her moulds of workmanship, and begun a new work on a different plan. Yet is there no break or interruption in the regular sequence of the deposits. We accept these facts of nature as we find them. The physical conditions of the earth were changed, and creative wisdom called into new being organic structures to suit the change. With this we are content; and we defy any man living, whatever may be his knowledge, to prove that in these steps of the great ascending series, "the stages of advance were very small" – "only a new stage in the process of gestation, an event simply natural" – "a development from species to species – phenomena of a simple and modest character!" (p. 231 [in the *Vestiges*]) Assertions more opposed to the works of ancient nature were never before recorded in the written language of a gratuitous hypothesis.'

48. *Ibid.*, p. 3.

49. Chambers, *Vestiges*, pp. 342–345.
50. *Ibid.*, p. 349.
51. *Ibid.*, p. 345.
52. Sedgwick, 'Natural History of Creation', p. 14.
53. 'Catastrophist and uniformitarian, astronomer and biologist, joined in repudiation. Even to quote a sentence or so from each of the leading figures would require pages – they all spoke out: Herschel, Whewell, Forbes, Owen, Prichard, Huxley, Lyell, Sedgwick, Murchison, Buckland, Agassiz, Miller, and others.' Gillispie, *Genesis*, p. 162.
54. Trinity College MSS, Add. Ms. a. 206[68], Aug. 16, 1847.
55. Todhunter, *Wm Whewell*, vol. I, p. 155.
56. See letter from Frederic Myers (Whewell's brother-in-law) quoted in Douglas, *Life of Whewell*, pp. 316–317. J. D. Forbes wrote to Whewell on April 8, 1845: 'I have also re-read with pleasure the "Indications of the Creator" intended as an antidote I presume to that very dangerous book: *Vestiges of Creation.*' Trinity College MSS, Add. Ms. a. 204[15].
57. Douglas, *Life of Whewell*, pp. 318–319. Quoting from 1845 letter to Myers.
58. William Whewell, *Of the Plurality of Worlds*, London, 1854, p. 198. See also pp. 118, 163 ff. Whewell says that while it is possible to imagine forces-still-in-operation changing the face of the earth (i.e. uniformitarian geology) there is no evidence that there are species-creating forces still operating.
59. *Ibid.*, pp. 180–181.
60. *Ibid.*, p. 265.
61. 'How far previous periods of animal existence were a necessary preparation of the earth, as the habitation of man, or a gradual progression towards the existence of man, we need not now inquire. But this we may say; that man, now that he is here, forms a climax to all that has preceded; a term incomparably exceeding in value all the previous parts of the series; a complex and ornate capital to the subjacent column; a personage of vastly greater dignity and importance than all the preceding line of procession.' P. 199. 'The assumption that there is anything of the nature of a regular law or order of progress from nebulae to conscious life . . . is in the highest degree precarious and unsupported.' p. 263.
62. *Ibid.*, p. 194.
63. 'If the earth, as the habitation of man, is a speck in the midst of an infinity of space, the earth, as the habitation of man, is also a speck at the end of an infinity of time.' p. 191.
64. Dr Robert Young, King's College, Cambridge. Actually Whewell's essay seems to have been more convincing religiously than scientifically. His correspondence preserves a series of grateful letters from scientific laymen who claimed that the *Plurality* had strengthened their faith. But Sir John Herschel and Adam Sedgwick reserved judgment on the basic issue, while agreeing that the book was delightful literarily. See Trinity College MSS, Add. Ms. I. 216[90–99]. For Herschel's response ('I find myself obliged to admit that I should not have thought there was so much to be said on the non-plurality side of the question.') see Add. Ms. a. 207[90]. Sedgwick wrote to Herschel, 'I was amused by it, but not convinced. But how can a man be convinced who has a bad cold?' Clark, *Sedgwick*, vol. II, p. 269.
65. Whewell, *History of the Inductive Sciences*, 3rd edition, London, 1857, vol. III, pp. 514–515.
66. On Lyell's opposition to a concept of 'geological development' (opposition which Cannon believes grew out of Lyell's determination to keep his theory

free from 'the alien Christian tendency which had marred the whole history of geology prior to the work of James Hutton') see Cannon, 'Darwin's Achievement', pp. 116–118.

67. Whewell, *Inductive Sciences*, vol. III, p. 156.
68. *Ibid.*, p. 478.
69. *Ibid.*, p. 477.
70. *Ibid.*, p. 479. Whewell cited Lyell, Prichard, Lawrence, Cuvier, and de-Blainville as agreeing with this analysis. He quoted deBlainville: 'Against this hypothesis, which, up to the present time, I regard as purely gratuitous, and likely to turn geologists out of the sound and excellent road in which they now are, I willingly raise my voice, with the absolute conviction of being in the right.' P. 482.
71. *Ibid.*, pp. 484–489.
72. From a vantage point of fifty years later Lewis Campbell characterized the intellectual strains of this period largely in terms of the writings of these various Cambridge scholars: 'The progress of scientific discovery could not fail to have a modifying and disturbing influence on religious thought. In spite of Bridgewater Treatises and other well-meant attempts at reconcilement, the obvious discrepancies between the new and old, between knowledge and tradition, caused uneasiness that could not be ignored. Whewell's *History of the Inductive Sciences* produced a great impression, both from its ability and the position and authority of the writer. It began to be felt that in the present day the miraculous element, so far from being a support to Christianity, was rather a stumbling block. The uniformity of nature was a necessary postulate of physical science, and some men already perceived that the Reign of Law extended also to the moral world. Not to anticipate too far it may suffice here to quote from Julius Hare, who asks, in his *Life of Sterling*, "whether in the pure ore of the gospel, the physically marvellous be not a separable alloy," and adds, "The great problem of the age is to reconcile faith with knowledge, philosophy with religion"; and this from Adam Sedgwick, the venerable Professor of Geology, "We are justified in saying that in the moral, as well as the physical world, God seems to govern by general laws . . . and it is our bounden duty to study those laws and as far as we can, to turn them to account." ' Campbell, *Nationalization*, pp. 65–66.
73. Clark, *Sedgwick*, vol. II, pp. 356–357. Sedgwick closed: 'I have written in a hurry, and in a spirit of brotherly love. Therefore forgive any sentence you happen to dislike; and believe me, spite of our disagreement on some points of the deepest moral interest, your true-hearted old friend, A. Sedgwick', *ibid.*, pp. 358–359.
74. 'It repudiates all reasoning from final causes; and seems to shut the door upon any view (however feeble) of the God of Nature as manifested in His works. From first to last it is a dish of rank materialism cleverly cooked and served up.' To Miss Gerard, Clark, *Sedgwick*, vol. II, p. 360. And again: 'I think that Darwin (whether he *intends* it or not, or knows it or not) is a teacher of that which savours of rankest materialism, and of an utter rejection of the highest moral evidence, and the highest moral truth.' *Ibid.*, p. 361, to Professor Owen.
75. *Ibid.*, vol. II, p. 362.
76. *Ibid.*, vol. II, p. 411, in a letter to the missionary Livingstone.
77. Trinity College MSS, O. 15. 97[83], July 24, 1860. Forbes agreed with Whewell and contemplated writing a geological essay to answer Huxley and Darwin. See Add. Ms. a. 204[133].

78. Two letters to Lyell, Nov. 23, 1859, and Dec. 12, 1859, Darwin, *Life and Letters*, vol. ii, pp. 26 and 37.
79. *Ibid.*, pp. 120, 114. Also see Henslow's letter to J. D. Hooker, quoted in Nora Barlow, *Darwin and Henslow, the Growth of an Idea*, Berkeley, 1967, pp. 205–206.
80. Darwin, *Life and Letters*, vol. ii, p. 120. He went on: 'I believe that Hopkins is so much opposed because his course of study has never led him to reflect much on such subjects as geographical distribution, classification, homologies, etc., so that he does not feel it a relief to have some kind of explanation.'
81. See, for example, the assessment of Sedgwick in David L. Hull's *Darwin and his Critics*, Cambridge, Mass., 1973, pp. 166–170. Walter Cannon ('Darwin's Achievement') sums up modern criticism: 'It is interesting how often Lyell's and Darwin's scientific opponents are castigated as being credulous, prejudiced, or simply "unscientific" by modern critics who do not point out how excellent and lasting the scientific work of many of these men has proved to be. It would not be hard to construct a case, for example, to show that Sedgwick was the best geologist who has ever lived . . . They were as "objective" and "empirical" in their research as were Lyell and Darwin.' P. 132.
82. A perusal of the Victorian biographies of any of these Cambridge figures should convince the reader of the seriousness of their scientific work. Also impressive is the evidence contained in their unpublished correspondence, of which only a sample survey can be presented.

   a) J. D. Forbes to William Whewell – a series of letters between 1831 and 1860 in which the scholars discussed the relationship between heat and light (Feb. 2, 1831), theories of glacier formation (Mar. 5, 1845), the philosophy of science (Feb. 20, 1842), Euclidean geometry (Feb. 17, 1846), and evolutionary theory (July 14, 1860.) In a letter dated Feb. 23, 1851, Forbes introduced to Whewell young James Clerk Maxwell, who would become the first Cavendish Professor of Physics. (See Trinity College MSS, Add. Ms. a. 204[26, 47, 63, 71, 97, 133].)

   b) James Henslow to Whewell – letters between 1836 and 1857, all containing personal references but also dealing with the species question (Aug. 16, 1847, Add. Ms. a. 206[72].) Whewell was regarded as an expert at coining useful scientific terms, using his classical education to formulate precise descriptive language.

   c) Many letters from George Peacock to Whewell about mathematics and the organization of the University (e.g. Mar. 10, 1842, Add. Ms. a. 210[108] and May 28, 29, 1854, Add. Ms. c. 90[38–39]) and about using Cambridge as the headquarters for the British Association (undated, Add. Ms. a. 210[114–115]).

   d) Many personal letters between Sedgwick and Whewell; see particularly those in which Sedgwick asks Whewell's advice about arrangements for the new Woodwardian Museum of Geology (undated, Add. Ms. a. 65[43]).

   e) Whewell wrote letters in reply to all of these people, many of them printed in Todhunter's biography. But also see MSS letters to Airy, Herschel, DeMorgan, and John Lubbock on a whole range of serious mathematical and scientific topics – Trinity College MSS, O. 15.47[1, 2, 3, 5, 10, 23, 29, 125, 138, 235]. Also O.15.46 *passim*.

83. See again Walter Cannon's 'Scientists and Broad Churchmen', p. 65.
84. The correspondence between Lyell and Sedgwick and Lyell and Whewell is voluminous; see biographies of the two latter figures. Also see Trinity College MSS, Add. Ms. a. 208[124–128], a series of friendly letters in which Lyell tried to explain his uniformity principle to Whewell. Such correspondence obviously had impact – some of Lyell's phrases appear in Whewell's

History of the Inductive Sciences. Although Darwin was of a different generation he too was in contact with Sedgwick and Whewell – see biographies. Also see Trinity College MSS, Add. Ms. c. 88[6], a thank-you note from Darwin to Whewell for a wedding present. About Whewell's *History*, Darwin wrote: 'I will run the risk of appearing exceedingly presumptuous by telling you how much I enjoyed it – to see so clearly the steps by which all the great scientific discoveries have been come to is a capital lesson to everyone, even to the humblest follower of science and I hope I have profited by it.'

85. 'The violence of the attack was simply Sedgwick's customary method of arguing; he had been raised in a less genteel atmosphere for debating than was current in 1860 – he never learned to adapt to the new Victorian set of manners... Sedgwick was simply too vigorous, physically and argumentatively, for Darwin to stomach. At the age of 85 he took his sometime student on a museum tour of Cambridge that left Darwin exhausted for days.' Cannon, 'Darwin's Achievement', p. 133.

86. 'Does not our author see that he binds the Divinity (on his dismal material scheme) in chains of fatalism as firmly as the Homeric gods were bound in the imagination of the old blind poet?' Sedgwick, 'Natural History of Creation', *Edinburgh Review*, p. 63.

87. Chambers, *Vestiges*, see esp. pp. 28, 161, 173, 204. These are all extended treatments of the God-in-nature theme, but the *Vestiges* is full of many more references besides.

88. See Gillispie, *Genesis*, p. 77.

89. *Ibid.*, pp. 133 ff.

90. Henslow, in a letter to J. D. Hooker, May 10, 1860, describing the meeting of the Cambridge Philosophical Society. Quoted in Nora Barlow, *Darwin and Henslow*, p. 205. Darwin's personal religious views, which evolved gradually from orthodoxy to a mellow, undogmatic agnosticism, are clearly described in his *Life and Letters*, vol. I, pp. 274–286. 'The theory of Evolution is quite compatible with the belief in a God; but... you must remember that different persons have different definitions of what they mean by God... Science has nothing to do with Christ, except in so far as the habit of scientific research makes a man cautious in admitting evidence. For myself, I do not believe that there has ever been any revelation. As for a future life, every man must judge for himself between conflicting vague possibilities... The old argument from design in Nature, as given by Paley, which formerly seemed to be so conclusive, fails, now that the law of natural selection has been discovered.'

91. See Hull, *Darwin and his Critics*; Hull's work is mainly an anthology designed to provide the student with evidence with which to assess this question, but he appears to me to asking in a sense 'what deluded these older scholars?' E.g., 'One would expect men like John Herschel, William Whewell, and John Stuart Mill, who had carefully investigated the nature of science as such, to be better able to evaluate a new and novel theory than ordinary scientists and philosophers. Such was not the case. All three men rejected the tenets of evolutionary theory either entirely or in part.' P. viii.

92. Gillispie, *Genesis*, pp. 208–209.

93. *Ibid.*, p. 226.

94. Cannon, 'Darwin's Achievement', p. 129.

95. Herschel, *Preliminary Discourse*, pp. 7–14.

96. Henslow, *Questions on the Subject Matter of Sixteen Lectures in Botany Required for*

a Pass Examination, Cambridge, 1851, p. vi. Henslow's sense of the unity of truth and of the efficacy of scientific study for general mental training is well discussed in David Layton's *Science for the People*, London, 1973.

97. Sedgwick, 'Natural History of Creation', p. 85.
98. Whewell, *Inductive Sciences*, vol. III, p. 487.
99. Babbage, *Ninth Bridgewater Treatise*, esp. Chapter VIII, pp. 92–107.
100. *Ibid.*, pp. 174–175, quoting as the conclusion to and the summary of his thesis from a sermon by the Archbishop of Dublin. Babbage also formulated this same idea in his own words throughout the book; see, for example, pp. vi–vii, 28. Even Darwin paid at least lip-service to this world-view: in thanking Sedgwick for his reply to the *Origin* he wrote 'I cannot think a false theory would explain so many classes of facts, as the theory seems to be to do. But *magna est veritas*, and, thank God, *praevalebit.*' Clark, *Sedgwick*, vol. II, p. 359.
101. Whewell, *Plurality*, p. 323.
102. Clark, *Sedgwick*, pp. 358–359, letter dated Dec. 24, 1859.
103. Maurice's son wrote of him: 'Every discovery made by Mr. Darwin and Mr. Huxley was a discovery of truth which had been true in itself ages before it was discovered. It could not therefore be altered by any knowledge of it by men. He believed the thing itself to be, when discovered, just in so far as it was true, a revelation to man by God whether the discoverer accepted it in that sense or not. Therefore as the thing had been at first fixed and unchangeable from all time by the fiat of God, it seemed to him that every discovery of science was as much the result of an investigation of "a word once given" as any investigation of a sentence in the Bible. On the other hand the whole progress of the history of the modern world and of the ancient seemed to him just as much the history of a progressive revelation as the history of the discoveries of science.' *Life of Maurice*, vol. II, pp. 452–453.
104. Sedgwick, Presidential Address, p. 305.
105. Sedgwick, 'Natural History of Creation', *Edinburgh Review*, 1845, p. 7.
106. Gillispie recognizes and describes this dialectic process in the unfolding geological crises, but he does not stress the role of the Cambridge circle in it – see *Genesis*, pp. 220–221.
107. Reprinted from *Transactions of the Cambridge Philosophical Society*, May 19, 1851, vol. IX, pp. 139–47, in R. E. Butts, *William Whewell's Theory of Scientific Method*, Pittsburgh, 1968, pp. 251–262.
108. *Ibid.*, p. 252.
109. Clark, *Sedgwick*, vol. II, p. 357.
110. See Hull's *Darwin and His Critics*, p. 6, and Cannon, 'Darwin's Achievement', p. 125.
111. Whewell, 'Of the Transformation of Hypotheses in the History of Science', quoted in Butts at p. 251.
112. Trinity College MSS, O.15.97[83], July 24, 1860.

7. THE DISINTEGRATION OF AN IDEAL

1. Mill, 'Civilization', *London and Westminster Review*, 1836, reprinted in *Dissertations and Discussions*, London, 1859, vol. I, pp. 160 ff.; and *Inaugural Address: delivered to the University of St. Andrews*, London, 1867. Huxley, 'A Liberal Education and Where to Find It', *Lay Sermons, Addresses, and Reviews*, London, 1880 (first published in *MacMillan's Magazine*, 1868); Newman, *On the*

Scope and Nature of University Education, London, 1965 (first published 1852); Pusey, *Collegiate and Professorial Teaching and Discipline*, Oxford, 1854; Pattison, *Suggestions on Academical Organization*, Edinburgh, 1868.

2. Whewell, *Principles of English University Education*, 1837, and *Of a Liberal Education in General, with Particular Reference to the Leading Studies of the University of Cambridge*, 1845.

3. Whewell, *Principles*, pp. 40–42.

4. Sedgwick, *Discourse*, p. 9. Of the third field: 'Under this head are included ethics and metaphysics, moral and political philosophy, and some other kindred subjects of great complexity, hardly touched on in our academic system, and to be followed out in the more mature labours of after life. Our duty here is to secure a good foundation on which to build . . .'

5. Leslie Stephen, man of letters, editor of *Cornhill*, founder of the *Dictionary of National Biography*, and father of Virginia Woolf, attended Cambridge right at the end of the period under consideration. In 1854 he was elected a fellow of his college (Trinity Hall) and during his residence at the University was a great favorite with the young 'rowing men' who went out in the poll. His biographer says: 'It was he and not Charles Kingsley who should be regarded as the founder of muscular Christianity.' His own life epitomized the intellectual crisis that overcame Cambridge in this period; under the influence of Darwinian thought he gradually lost his faith, resigned his fellowship and left Cambridge in 1864. He loved the University and was sympathetic to the earlier reformers and to the ones who would follow him; and, although his writings fall somewhat outside the period treated, he seems to me to be a perceptive and valuable source of information. See Noel G. Annan, *Leslie Stephen: His Thought and Character in Relation to his Time*, London, 1951.

6. Winstanley, *Early Vic. Camb.*, p. 65, note 2.

7. Stephen, *Sketches from Cambridge*, London, 1865, p. 9. This book was published anonymously by 'a don'. Or see p. 20 on non-intellectual, athletic students: 'Their sphere of thought is somewhat limited; but they are very good fellows, and are excellent raw material for country parsons, or for any other profession where much thinking power is not required.'

8. Stephen, *Sketches*, p. 47.

9. Stephen, *The Poll Degree from a Third Point of View*, Cambridge, 1863, p. 18.

10. *Sketches*, p. 45. For confirmation of the accuracy of Stephen's various assessments see Winstanley, *Early Vic. Camb.*, pp. 65, 151, 154, 159. An interesting perspective on the question of competition is provided in Charles Astor Bristed's *Five Years in an English University*. An American, unused to the British system, Bristed could not simply relax once he realized he could not get honours and continued to struggle to do his best even while accepting the fact that he would go out in the poll. His English contemporaries regarded this behavior as positively aberrant; see vol. II, pp. 11 ff.

11. See Winstanley, *Early Vic. Camb.*, pp. 154, 167–168, 218–220. Winstanley cites anonymous pamphlets advocating such an examination in 1836 and 1845. See also J. J. Smith, *Letter to the Vice-Chancellor*, Cambridge, 1846, and *A Letter to the Vice-Chancellor on the late rejection by the Caput of a Grace Respecting an Examination Previous to Entrance*, Cambridge, 1847. Also see an 1853 anonymous flysheet advocating the establishment of an entrance exam; Camb. Univ. Papers, D 21, April, 1853.

12. The examination was established by Grace of the Senate, March 13, 1822. 'The Subjects of Examination shall be one of the four Gospels or the Acts of the Apostles in the original Greek, Paley's Evidences of Christianity, one of

the Greek and one of the Latin Classics.' Camb. Univ. Papers, Cam. a. 500. 5²⁸.

13. Winstanley, *Early Vic. Camb.*, p. 167, quotes an anonymous 1845 pamphlet to this effect.

14. J. H. Monk, *A Letter to the Right Reverend John, Lord Bishop of Bristol*, p. 42.

15. To include a paper on Old Testament History; see 'Report of Syndicate Appointed to . . . Provide a More Efficient System of Theological Instruction . . .,' May 11, 1842, Camb. Univ. Papers, DC 5300.

16. Winstanley, *Early Vic. Camb.*, pp. 216 and 282; also Camb. Univ. Papers, D 21, Feb. 21, 1853.

17. Camb. Univ. Papers, DC 1350, May 24, 1822.

18. Camb. Univ. Papers, HC1, Mar. 27, 1828; HC1, Dec. 12, 1836; DC 5300, Feb. 25, 1843.

19. Camb. Univ. Papers, DC 5300, Nov. 19, 1845.

20. Quoted in Winstanley, *Early Vic. Camb.*, p. 260.

21. Stephen, *The Poll Degree from a Third Point of View*, p. 14.

22. In 1821 when attempting to establish the classical tripos Christopher Wordsworth had tried to require it of all but the top ten wranglers, but this effort had failed and the classics honours examination established the next year was voluntary. Camb. Univ. Papers, Cam. a. 500.5²⁴, DC 1350, May 24, 1822. Between 1842 and 1855 mathematics honours students were required to attend the regular degree examination in Paley's Moral Philosophy, the New Testament and Ecclesiastical History. This was part of the program to encourage the theological studies of the University, but as honours candidates' names were to be published in alphabetical order only – that is, their showing would not affect their place in the wrangler list – this requirement could be all but ignored. It was abolished in 1855. Trinity College MSS, Add. Ms. a. 53¹; Camb. Univ. Papers, DC 5300, Mar. 14, 1855.

23. '. . . the balance between the two lines of study . . . is commonly so utterly deranged in our Classical Schools. In those, the student, if he have tolerable talent and industry, acquires a knowledge of Greek and Latin Literature, which enables him to pursue it with ease and pleasure, while of Mathematics, he generally acquires only enough to learn to dislike the study, without deriving from his acquirements any help to his future progress.' Whewell, *Of a Liberal Education*, p. 214.

24. See *Early Vic. Camb.*, p. 216.

25. See *Of a Liberal Education*, pp. 210–212. When the classical tripos was established, 'That the Mathematical student should be acquainted with Classics was not . . . provided by any University regulation; being assumed, as I conceive, to be sufficiently secured by the general course of School and College education . . . The Previous Examination was, I believe, assented to by many members of the Senate, on the ground that it would secure a certain degree of attention to Classical Studies in the first year and a half of the residence of pupils at the University . . . [It has served this essentially remedial purpose] but it has given a great check to all good schemes of College Education and to all larger and more progressive plans of University Education . . . ' He goes on to suggest that the Previous be made into an entrance examination and that college instruction 'may, by a proper selection of Classical Subjects, as well as of Mathematical (to which the Progressive Sciences ought also to be added,) be made to carry on a system of Education, which, at the end of three years and a half, shall leave all students with their

minds more cultivated, more expanded, and more instructed, than they were when they entered upon their residence'. Of the ineffectiveness of thus depending on college instruction, more later.

26. Sedgwick could see that it might 'well admit of question, when we consider the shortness of life and the multitude of things demanding our efforts and pressing on our attention, whether the study of the dead languages ought to form a prominent part of academic discipline'. *Discourse*, p. 30. He answered the question affirmatively of course, if only to allow the student to study 'the oracles of God, and . . . read the book wherein man's moral destinies are written . . .' (p. 31); but he urged that classical study should not become too drily critical. (See pp. 32–34.)

27. See Chapter 2, for a survey of the places won in the tripos by the students who later became the reforming dons; Sedgwick, e.g., was fifth wrangler, Whewell, second.

28. Camb. Univ. Papers, DC 1350, May 24, 1822.

29. A very few prizes – the Chancellor's Medal, the Craven Scholarship – in classics had existed since before the beginning of the century and it was towards the winning of these that college classics instruction, especially at Trinity, was directed. Such a small number of awards, however, would obviously not serve as an adequate stimulus to scholarship among more than a few. On Trinity's encouragement of classical scholarship, see A. H. Wratislaw, *Observations on the Cambridge System*, Cambridge, 1850. Wratislaw asserted that Whewell had overestimated the classical training of Cambridge freshmen because he was at Trinity, where the student body came more exclusively from public schools than at the other colleges. He also objected to Whewell's equating mathematics with 'reasoning power', classics merely with 'language'. On university classics instruction, see Camb. Univ. Papers, DC 5300, Feb. 25, 1843.

30. '. . . he who forgets that language is but the sign and vehicle of thought, and while studying the word, knows little of the sentiment – who learns the measure, the garb, and fashion of ancient song, without looking to its living soul or feeling its inspiration – is not one jot better than a traveller in classic land, who sees its crumbling temples, and numbers with arithmetical precision, their steps and pillars, but thinks not of their beauty, their design, or the living sculptures on their walls – or who counts the stones in the Appian Way instead of gazing on the monuments of the "eternal city"'. *Discourse*, p. 32.

31. Camb. Univ. Papers, Cam. a. 500.5^{132}, May 30, 1849.

32. Bristed, *Five Years*, pp. 15 ff., p. 123. Bristed's testimony is strengthened because he was able to compare the training he received at Cambridge to the program at Yale. On the other hand his book is throughout almost excessively sympathetic and uncritical.

33. The establishment of these triposes will be discussed in more detail later. See Camb. Univ. Papers, Cam. a. 500.5^{123}, Oct. 16, 1848.

34. By this time the poll degree was also divided into classes. See Camb. Univ. Papers, Cam. a. 500.5^{132}, May 30, 1849.

35. Camb. Univ. Papers, D21, Mar. 21, 1854.

36. I think it is also an influential concept. Though it is clearly beyond the scope of this book to trace the idea out beyond Cambridge, I strongly suspect that it could be shown that the arts-and-sciences concept of many of America's colleges and universities is derived from roots similar to those leading to this Cambridge ideal, and that the 'distribution requirements' imposed on

modern undergraduates may well be based on a rationale Whewell could have understood.

37. 'Cambridge University', *Fraser's*, vol. XLI, p. 617, 1850, pp. 618–623.

38. Sir William Hamilton, 'On the Study of Mathematics as an Exercise of the Mind', first published in the *Edinburgh Review*, 1835, reprinted in *Discussion on Philosophy and Literature, Education and University Reform*, London, 1852, pp. 257–328.

39. See Wratislaw, *Observations on the Cambridge System*, pp. 5–9, in response to Whewell's claims for mathematics: 'Now what is meant by the faculty of Reason and the faculty of Language? Is it the power of forming and contemplating Conceptions in the mind and of expressing and enunciating them when formed? Few will be found to claim the former for Mathematics, at any rate the Conceptions, which that study exclusively assists in forming, would be comprised in the briefest and most meagre of categories. . . . But, "a knowledge of Mathematics is requisite in order to familiarize students with exact *Reasoning*;" that is, with exact and consecutive Reasoning upon already formed or furnished Conceptions. No one will be prepared to deny the utility of Mathematics in this respect, though surely few, who have pursued both subjects, can have failed to perceive, that there are many most important and practical processes of Reasoning, wherein the Classical student is perpetually exercised, to which there is little analogy to be found in the exercises of the Mathematician, none at all in those of a very large proportion of the candidates for Mathematical Honours at Cambridge, in whose minds the only faculties cultivated are the Attention and the Memory. And surely it is not the having got up the productions of another's Reason, but the power and habit of using his own, that renders a man a valuable and useful member of society. Yet it is notorious, that very high distinctions on the Mathematical Tripos are attained by the merest powers of Acquisition, Retention, and Disgorgement . . . the mere Mathematician has been through the merest course of intellectual drilling.'

40. 'University Education', *Fraser's*, vol. XXVII, no. 458, 1868, p. 147. Also see Stephen, *Sketches from Cambridge*, pp. 32–33. 'Now, apologizing beforehand to philosophers, nothing can be less generally useful than cricket, except mathematics . . . Knowledge, [the mathematics enthusiast] thinks, is knowledge; the more remote it is from all concrete things the better; the special merit of mathematics is that you can sit in your own room and spin it like a spider out of your own inside without ever even looking out the window.'

41. Whewell, *Principles*, p. 35.

42. A book called *Essays on Liberal Education*, edited by F. W. Farrar and published in London in 1867, provides a nice compendium of university thought on classics in the second half of the century. Farrar was a fellow of Trinity, a classicist of note, and later the headmaster of Marlborough and the dean of Canterbury. The essays made two main points: exclusive dependence on the ancient languages was foolishly narrow, especially at a time when a wide variety of other disciplines was available for the training of young minds. And, even assuming the classics to be important, they were at present by and large badly taught, with too much emphasis on imitation and too little on understanding. Other contributors to the book included Henry Sidgwick (fellow of Trinity, 'Senior Classic' – the classical tripos equivalent of senior wrangler – and Professor of Moral Philosophy), E. E. Bowen (fellow of Trinity, assistant Master at Harrow), Monckton Milnes, Lord Houghton (honorary fellow of Trinity), J. R. Seeley (fellow of Caius and Christ's,

Professor of Modern History), W. Johnson (fellow of King's, tutor at Eton) and J. M. Wilson (fellow of St John's). Sidgwick argued for the serious study of the English language, Farrar advocated abandoning Greek and Latin verse composition; several writers stressed the significance of history, philology and modern languages.

43. The requirement of Greek at matriculation was dropped in 1917, Latin not until the middle of the twentieth century. Albert Mansbridge's *The Older Universities of England: Oxford and Cambridge*, written in 1923, gives a good sense of the tenacity of the conservative viewpoint; see pp. 173–174.

44. In 1854 a series of curricular reforms were presented to the Senate which would have established several possible 'major fields' and drastically reduced the time spent on the subjects of the traditional liberal education. In explaining why he was going to vote against the changes F. J. A. Hort, a fellow of Trinity and later professor of theology, wrote: 'The principle of permitting the exclusive pursuit of any one study for a great part of the academical course is false and mischievous, because the primary function of the University is neither the encouragement of the Sciences (including Mathematics, the Literae humaniores, and Theology), nor the bestowal of rewards and distinctions, but education . . . Certain parts of Classical and Mathematical study (especially in combination) afford the best known means and tests of education. A Degree in Arts is simply a certificate of a certain amount of education, or at least of elementary education and elementary information combined. No one should be allowed to graduate in Arts unless he has proved by the recognized tests that he possesses the required amount, however great may be his proficiency in any single study. Any one who, through want of ability or industry, is unable to acquire *both* kinds of proficiency during his undergraduate course, does not deserve Honours at all. The University degrades itself if it sacrifices its authority as a teacher to the "inclinations" and vanities of its learners.' Camb. Univ. Papers, D 21, May 3, 1854. Hort was obviously not alone in his sentiments – major sections of the proposals were defeated decisively (see Winstanley, *Early Vic. Camb.*, p. 281).

45. See Whewell, *Principles*, pp. 5–17.

46. *Ibid.*, p. 55.

47. 'Teachers often prefer [the examination] system, because it relieves them from the constantly repeated effort and anxiety which accompanies direct instruction, – at least, when bestowed on unwilling, or unintelligent pupils. If all solicitude about the student's daily attendance, his daily progress, his transient difficulties, his fluctuating diligence, can be rendered superfluous, by examining, at last, what has been the general result of his study, they are naturally glad to escape so easily a burden so oppressive.' *Principles*, p. 59.

48. Peter Primrose, *Hints on Examinations*, Cambridge, 1822, Camb. Univ. Papers, Cam. c. 822.16: 'Perhaps I am singular in my mode of thinking and of feeling, but I confess I cannot consider without uneasiness that almost incessant examination, for one purpose or another, to which we subject the most promising of our students . . . there is something like cruelty in keeping their minds forever hurried with preparation for contest, and harassed with anxiety for its result . . . I [also doubt] whether such a plan of proceeding be entirely calculated to secure some of the most valuable purposes of Academical Education. – Knowledge acquired under such circumstances will infallibly be at command when it is called for; but will it, also be very sound and permanent? [The new examination should be at least voluntary] if it

were only for the sake of those young men whose minds may be so unaccountably constituted as to believe that there is some value in knowledge independently of its display.' Pp. 9–11.

49. Trinity College MSS, Add. Ms. a. 77^{134}, Dec. 3, 1841. Hare said that Maurice shared his feelings: 'When I asked Maurice what he thought might be done for the improvement of theological education at Cambridge, he answered, "a divinity tripos (wch is the usual retort when any improvement is to take place) wd surely be an abomination"'. In 1843 Hare wrote complaining of 'those two terrible evils in our system, the practice of private tuition, and the use of emulation as the one great spur to the acquirement of knowledge . . . we shall continue to sink, unless we get rid of our system of drilling for parade and of our morbid stimulants, – adopt a system which will call forth a living power and train our students to walk without leading strings'. Add. Ms. a. 206^{180}.

50. See DeMorgan, *DeMorgan*, pp. 100, 169 ff., 305–306.

51. See *Principles*, p. 58.

52. Charles Perry suggested that students in the new theological examination be classified 'according as the individual has acquitted himself with credit, or as merely approved. I should object to a more particular classification of the candidates, as I think all undue emulation should be excluded.' *Clerical Education*, p. 25. A flysheet by J. J. Smith from 1845 exemplifies the complexities this sort of debate could wander into. Re: bracketing the lower students of the mathematics tripos: 'Now the distribution of the candidates into a *small fixed* number of divisions, for instance into *four* classes, might be advocated on the ground of putting an end to extravagant emulation, and a false ambition; but I think it may be fairly objected, that it would establish distinctions too *broad* to be *true*, and so still give food for the same excessive emulation in some; while in others it would discourage commendable efforts to obtain a proper knowledge of the subjects of examination.' Camb. Univ. Papers, DC 5300, Nov. 18, 1845. J. W. Blakesley objected to too precise ranking: 'By this change we did our best to substitute the love of Excelling for the love of Excellence as a motive to exertion, and we are now reaping the fruits of our acts.' *Where Does the Evil Lie?*, London, 1845, p. 30.

53. William Hopkins, *Remarks on Certain Proposed Regulations respecting the Studies of the University*, Cambridge, 1841. W. Linwood about the same time put forward the same argument with respect to Oxford – what were needed were more distinctions and more prizes; *Remarks on the Present State of Classical Scholarship and Distinctions in the University of Oxford*, Oxford, 1845.

54. 'Athletic Sports and University Studies', *Fraser's*, Dec. 1870, vol. II, no. 12, p. 704. H. Brandreth, tutor at Trinity, wrote a pamphlet in 1868 complaining about the over-emphasis on university examinations; *On Modern Education*, London, 1868, Camb. Univ. Papers, Cam. c. 868. 16.

55. Graffiti in the Cambridge University Library in May of 1970 included, 'Alas, alas! The dread tripox fever is once again abroad in the land.'

56. William Hopkins, the famous mathematics coach of the middle part of the century, was the best example of an excellent private tutor. He 'had among his pupils nearly 200 wranglers, of whom 17 were senior and 44 in one of the first three places: these included Stokes, Kelvin, Tait, Fawcett, Clerk Maxwell, Routh, and Todhunter'. Venn, *Alumni Cantabrigiensis*, pt 2, vol. iii, p. 439. In an 1845 pamphlet J. W. Blakesley pointed out that the degree of Master of Arts was precisely a license to teach, so that there was nothing illegal about the practice of private tuition. *Where Does the Evil Lie?*

57. James Hildyard, *The University System of Private Tuition Examined*, London, 1844.

58. At the end of a proposal to forbid private tuition during the regular school year Hildyard wrote: 'Lastly, if it be insisted that the richer classes have a title to some extra consideration, as giving weight themselves to the University at large; it may be replied, that even the present proposition does not exclude them from any advantage to be derived by additional assistance during the vacations, when the poorer scholars would be left to their own resources.' *Ibid.*, p. 25.

59. One of the purposes of the mathematics tripos reforms of 1843 and 1846 was to make the subject matter of the examination 'more steady and better known', thus diminishing the significance of a clairvoyant private tutor. Camb. Univ. Papers, DC 5300, April 8, 1843.

60. See Whewell, *Of a Liberal Education*, p. 138. It should perhaps be noted, however, that it was the official 'public' tutor in each case who advised Babbage and Airy not to waste time studying questions outside the scope of the tripos: 'After a few days, I went to my public tutor Hudson, to ask explanation of one of my mathematical difficulties. He listened to my question, said it would not be asked in the Senate House, and was of no sort of consequence, and advised me to get up the earlier subjects of the university studies.' Babbage, *Passages from the Life of a Philosopher*, in Philip and Emily Morrison's *Charles Babbage and his Calculating Engines*, p. 23. See also Airy, *Autobiography*, p. 25. And with names like Maxwell, Stokes and Todhunter to his credit the private tutor Hopkins must have been doing something more than mere 'cramming'.

61. As Bristed noted, 'Private tuition is nowhere alluded to in the University or college statutes; it is entirely a personal and individual matter; yet it is, after the examinations, the great feature of the university instruction, and the public lectures have come to be entirely subordinate to it.' 'There is little likelihood that the practice will be abolished or essentially modified unless the whole system of the University and college examinations should undergo a fundamental change. The present staff of college lecturers could not, except in some few of the smallest colleges, supply the demand for instruction.' *Five Years*, vol. III, pp. 93–94, 112.

62. J. R. Crowfoot recommended this – which he would have regarded as the reestablishment of traditional practice – in 1845. *College Tuition Considered in a Letter to a Friend*, Camb. Univ. Papers, Cam. c. 845.26, pp. 11–12.

63. James Hildyard made this suggestion in his *Further Considerations of the University System of Education in a Letter to the Rev. The Vice-Chancellor of the University of Cambridge*, London, 1845. Blakesley, *Where Does the Evil Lie?*, suggested that official lines of communication between public and private tutors could at least be established, with coaches reporting on the pupils' progress on a weekly basis, for example. William Hopkins, not surprisingly, also thought that private tutors should be brought into the system and paid by the University. They would supplement, not supplant, college tuition. *Remarks on the Mathematical Teaching of the University of Cambridge*, Cambridge, 1854.

64. Crowfoot favored this plan – see untitled open letter dated Mar. 6, 1847, Trinity College MSS, Add. Ms. a. 64[23]. He also wanted the University itself to establish hostels, supervised by resident M.A.s, where student expenses could be kept within reasonable limits – *Remarks with Reference to Building a University Hostel*, Cambridge, 1849. M. Wilkinson, a fellow of Clare and

headmaster of Marlborough, argued, on the contrary, that it would be better to lower student expenses generally and to provide more scholarships than to open halls and thereby create 'a new division (where already too many fictitious divisions exist) in society at large'. *Expenses of Undergraduates*, London, 1845, p. 4.

65. In an undated MS draft entitled 'System of Education at Cambridge University' Whewell wrote: 'The relation of the student to his *public tutor* is one of the most important and most peculiar features of the Cambridge system. According to the usage of the University the tutor occupies the combined situations of teacher or professor, of superintendent of the young man's conduct, controler [*sic*] of his expenses, and of his guardian and protector in case of need . . . There is I believe at present found in no other such body a *discipline* like that of the two English universities, that is to say a code of rules respecting the student's daily habits: regulating his attendance not only in the lecture room, but at morning and evening prayer, and in the dinner halls . . . and providing also a person most closely connected with the student (the tutor) who is expected to influence the pupil's studies and conduct by his personal intercourse and advice. This class of persons – the tutors of the different colleges – (who are to be distinguished altogether from the *private tutors*) are by their position and office highly important parts of the Cambridge system.' Trinity College MSS, Add. Ms. a. 78[59].

66. Reliance on the central University and diminishing the power of the colleges was the remedy most quickly suggested by critics outside Cambridge; the political manifestations of this sentiment were the investigative and reforming Royal Commissions appointed in the 1850s. The Commissions spent most of their energies on reorganizing university government; see Commission Reports cited above. This governmental reform is discussed very thoroughly in Winstanley. It should be noted, however, that the reforming dons here treated were also active in strengthening the resources of the University – they were members of syndicates to build museums and libraries, they served as professors themselves, and they were active scholars in the advanced disciplines. Sedgwick, Peacock, and Herschel were even members of the Royal Commissions. Whewell wrote to Forbes in 1855 that he felt his work in this line was finally complete: 'I have now got our Professorial scheme into a condition which I hope has some coherence and stability, so that I may devolve the management of it into other hands . . .' Trinity College MSS, O.15.47.75.

67. Collegiate resistance to a university entrance examination, for example, was particularly vehement. See Winstanley, *Early Vic. Camb.*, pp. 154, 167–168, 218–220, 260, 338.

68. See Crowfoot, *Remarks on Some Questions of Economy and Finance Affecting the University of Cambridge*, Cambridge, 1848.

69. Words Whewell used to mean 'not yet fixed as received truths' or 'ideas still in the process of development'. He felt that such subjects – if pursued without the stabilizing influence of the liberal disciplines – would make a student flighty and unsteady, for he would not have the mental habits and discipline with which to make sound judgments, nor would he be in a position to evaluate modern thought, not being thoroughly familiar with thought which had gone before. See *Of a Liberal Education*, p. 21–22; *Principles*, pp. 6–7.

70. Camb. Univ. Papers, Cam. a. 500.5[123], Oct. 16, 1848. 'The necessary means' at that point included professors of laws, physics, moral philosophy, chemistry,

anatomy, modern history, botany, geology, natural and experimental philosophy, laws of England, medicine, mineralogy, and political economy.

71. See Hamilton articles in *Edinburgh Review* (1831, 1835, 1836), Lyell's *Travels in North America*, and Mill's 'Civilization'. From Mill: 'The only studies really encouraged are classics and mathematics; neither of them a useless study, though the last, as an exclusive instrument for fashioning the mental powers, greatly overrated . . . The mere shell and husk of the syllogistic logic at the one University, the wretchedest smattering of Locke and Paley at the other, are all of moral or psychological science that is taught at either. As a means of educating the many, the Universities are absolutely null. The youth of England are not educated.' P. 199 (reprinted in *Dissertations and Discussions*).

72. See *Of a Liberal Education*, p. 126.

73. C. R. Kennedy, a fellow of Trinity, wrote a pamphlet in 1837 arguing that while 'there is no doubt that literature is the only medium through which liberal education can be communicated', modern literature could serve nearly as well as the classics and would in many ways be more valuable. Henslow, as noted above, welcomed the scientific flourishing which he noted at Cambridge in the forties; *Classical Education Reformed*, London, 1837.

74. Trinity College MSS, Add. Ms. a. 77^{134}, Dec. 3, 1841.

75. Camb. Univ. Papers, Cam. a. 500.5^{123}, Oct. 16, 1848. Lists of professorial lectures and examination schedules began appearing in the university records around 1850. See Camb. Univ. Papers, HC1; Cam. a. 500.1^{30}.

76. Stephen, 'University Organisation', *Fraser's*, 1868, p. 137.

77. 'Studies Syndicate' (a pamphlet), Cambridge, 1854.

78. Camb. Univ. Papers, Cam. a. 500.5^{123}, Oct. 16, 1848.

79. Camb. Univ. Papers, DC 5300, Oct. 31, 1848.

80. See J. B. Mayor, untitled open letter, Dec. 1859; J. Grote, 'To the Members of the Senate', Feb. 20, 1860; W. G. Clark, untitled open letter, Feb. 22, 1860.

81. Clark was a fellow and classical tutor at Trinity, and later a lecturer on English literature. Camb. Univ. Papers, DC 5650, Feb. 22, 1860.

82. 'And, as for works of profound research on any subject . . . why, a third-rate, poverty-stricken German university turns out more produce of that kind in one year than our vast and wealthy foundations elaborate in ten.' Of men like Darwin, Mill, Lyell, Faraday: 'Our universities not only do not offer them positions in which it should be their highest duty to do, thoroughly, that which they are most capable of doing; but as far as possible, university training shuts out of the minds of those among them, who are subjected to it, the prospect that there is anything in the world for which they are specially fitted.' Huxley, 'A Liberal Education and Where to Find It', pp. 48–49.

83. For the opinions of various professors on the need for support to research see *Report of H. M. Commissioners . . . on the University and Colleges of Cambridge*, 1852, pp. 73–137. J. A. Jeremie, Regius Professor of Divinity, for example, felt it was 'impossible to give a complete and systematic course in theology unless the period of residence . . . be extended at least one year.' P. 77. W. H. Mill, Regius Professor of Hebrew, would have liked the University to support cognate disciplines like Arabic and other Semitic languages. G. G. Stokes, Lucasian Professor of Mathematics, complained of the inadequate laboratory facilities for doing demonstrations or experiments in the physical sciences. Whewell, in his capacity as Professor of Moral Philosophy, asked for more lecture rooms and suggested establishing professorships in international law, zoology, and comparative philology; p. 102.

84. Camb. Univ. Papers, D 21, Mar. 21, 1854.

85. After 1855 the Previous was a four-day affair, covering the four Gospels and the Acts in Greek, the Evidences of Christianity, Old Testament History, Euclid, and arithmetic and algebra. For potential honours candidates there were also the 'Additional Subjects, which were exclusively mathematical', designed to fill the gap left by disconnecting the classical tripos from the mathematical one. See Camb. Univ. Papers, D 21, Mar. 21, 1854; also Winstanley, *Later Victorian Cambridge*, Cambridge, 1947, p. 144. See *ibid.*, pp. 151–152, 163–181 for later improvements in the preliminary examination (or the 'Little go', as it came to be called by the end of the century).

86. The *Fraser's* review of Whewell's *Of a Liberal Education* cited above made just this point – that classics and mathematics were undoubtedly the basis of a good education but that they should be attended to at school. Whewell himself saw a natural educational sequence – the 'liberal' core should come first and be followed by the 'progressive' disciplines. 'A man who really participates in the progress of the sciences, must do so by following their course when the time of education is past. The Progressive Studies are to be begun towards the end of a Liberal Education.' *Of a Liberal Education*, p. 22. Also see Thomas Bisset (an alumnus of Peterhouse), *Suggestions on University Reform*, London, 1850. He recommended that liberal education be made the business of schools: 'So much more relatively difficult is knowledge of attainment when the proper period of acquiring it is allowed to pass away unimproved; the mental faculty has lost its suppleness from long disuse, and becomes hard and rigid as a bone.'

87. See Farrar, *Essays on a Liberal Education.*

88. J. R. Seeley pointed out that the Old Universities molded the whole of English education, both by determining subject matter and by training the teachers who would go out to staff the schools. 'Liberal Education in Universities,' *Lectures and Essays*, London, 1870. And the same scholars who recommended 'modernizing' the Cambridge curriculum in the second half of the century advised the schools to update their programs, teaching English and French instead of Greek. See Henry Sidgwick, 'The theory of Classical Education', in *Essays on Liberal Education*, ed. F. W. Farrar, pp. 81–145. Also see above, note 42. Later, when the Greek requirement was abandoned at Cambridge, Greek instruction in the schools declined immediately.

89. See Hildyard, *Further Consideration*, and Crowfoot, *College Tuition Considered*, cited above. Confidence in the collegiate system was very wide-spread; a well-argued defense of the colleges was presented in Edward Pusey's *Collegiate and Tutorial Teaching and Discipline*, 1854.

90. Whewell, *Remarks on the Proposed Changes in the College Statutes*, Cambridge, 1857 (privately circulated), pp. 2–3. Whewell wrote many other pamphlets and flysheets in defense of the collegiate system – see Trinity College MSS, Add. Ms. a. 64⁶, Jan. 18, 1858; Add. Ms. a. 64⁷, June 23, 1858.

91. See his letters to Whewell, Jan. 1, 1842, Trinity College MSS, Add. Ms. a. 213³⁹ and Jan. 5, 1854, Add. Ms. a. 213⁹⁰. In the latter he suggested going back to the form of instruction he regarded as traditional: 'my belief is that a sufficient number of good and sufficient men could be had for a *double fellowship*. Among these, all the students should be divided, in selected classes of men who could march together. As there would be nothing to do but teach, (for with the domestic duties of tutor, these college professors would have nothing to do), I am pretty sure the immediate compensation would

get better men for this work, than you get now, and all rivalry of an unfavourable kind would be done away with. I should expect, with the good classes, to do away nearly with the monstrous and expensive evil of private tutors; but those who required private tutors might be arranged in a very few squads (by the college professors) and assigned to two or three private teachers, to whom a moderate and regulated compensation might be made by their pupils. This scheme would surely take in everybody who was worth having, and I should refuse to take, or should give notice to quit to, those who could not be included.' This whole letter is valuable and interesting as a conservative statement of what the college might be able to accomplish.

92. G. B. Airy, *On the Draft of Proposed New Statutes for Trinity College, Cambridge*, Cambridge, 1859.

93. Tradition, inaccurate as it turned out, but nevertheless venerated, had it that King's had been granted this privileged status in the 'Composition' of 1456; see Winstanley, *Early Vic. Camb.*, p. 237.

94. Camb. Univ. Papers, Cam. a. 500.5[132], May 30, 1849.

95. See Winstanley, *Early Vic. Camb.*, p. 237. On the debate preceding this decision, see Crowfoot, *The Interpretation of the Composition between the University and King's College*, Cambridge, 1846. He argued that the privilege was no privilege at all since it kept King's students from being eligible for honours degrees. Also Edward Thring, *A Few Remarks on the Present System of Degrees at King's College, Cambridge*, Cambridge, 1846.

96. Trinity College MSS, O. 15.47.75.

97. Lewis Campbell and William Garnett, *The Life of James Clerk Maxwell*, London, 1884.

98. Students were forbidden to race or bet on racing (May 11, 1803; May 16, 1825; Oct. 28, 1825; May 9, 1846), to fire pistols within the town of Cambridge (May 9, 1825), to shoot pigeons (Dec. 1, 1842), to go 'abroad' without proper academic dress (Oct. 10, 1825), or to give false names to University proctors (May 3, 1823). All these regulations are recorded in Camb. Univ. Papers, Cam. a. 500.5.

99. For two such cases see Camb. Univ. Papers, Cam. a. 500.5, Feb. 18, 1822; Mar. 12, 1824. In 1819 Edward Litchfield and John Litchfield, fruiterers, were discommuned for having been 'convicted of assisting in carrying into effect a Marriage between an Undergraduate and a Servant-maid of the said John Litchfield'. Nov. 29, 1819.

100. Whewell did not become Master until 1841.

101. Trinity College MSS, Add. Ms. a. 64[26].

102. Airy, *On the Draft of Proposed New Statutes*, p. 7.

103. *Ibid.*, p. 17.

104. 'Book of the Memorabilia [of Socrates] is named on account of its containing the very important argument for the existence of a Supreme Creator, and other points touching some of the common faults of young men.' Trinity College MSS, Add. Ms. a. 64[62], a letter to Whewell dated Mar. 18, 1847. Potts was a graduate of Trinity and a private tutor living in Cambridge.

105. Sheepshanks to Whewell, Jan. 5, 1854, Trinity College MSS, Add. Ms. a. 213[30]. 'I think it is a fault in our schools and universities to draw a very tight rule, and then wink at exceptions; just as it is the fault of almost all parents to spoil their children by severity or indulgence, and to expect the college to cure all that. I would send the cubs home, and tell the parents, that they had mistaken my calling, which was not that of a moral orthopodist, but to make the most of unspoiled subjects.'

106. In Mill's words: 'The proper function of an University in national education is tolerably well understood. At least there is a tolerably general agreement about what an University is not. It is not a place of professional education. . . . Men are men before they are lawyers, or physicians, or merchants, or manufacturers; and if you make them capable and sensible men, they will make themselves capable and sensible lawyers or physicians. What professional men should carry away with them from an University, is not professional knowledge, but that which should direct the use of their professional knowledge, and bring the light of general culture to illuminate the technicalities of a special pursuit . . . Education makes a man a more intelligent shoemaker, if that be his occupation, but not by teaching him how to make shoes; it does so by the mental exercise it gives, and the habits it impresses.' *Inaugural Address*, 1867, pp. 6–7.

107. Mill, 'Civilization', *Dissertations and Discussions*, vol. 1, p. 202–205.

108. Newman, *On the Scope and Nature of University Education*, 'Theology a Branch of Knowledge', Discourse I, pp. 1–29; and MacGrath, *Newman's University – Idea and Reality*, London, 1951, pp. 133–135.

109. Huxley, *A Liberal Education and Where to Find It*, p. 73.

110. All of these undoubtedly positive, creative developments are dealt with in Rothblatt, *Revolution of the Dons*.

BIBLIOGRAPHY

MANUSCRIPTS AND UNIVERSITY PAPERS:

TRINITY COLLEGE MANUSCRIPTS

Whewell Collections: large numbers of letters between William Whewell and

G. B. Airy	J. F. W. Herschel	George Pryme
Thomas Chalmers	James Heywood	J. F. Rose
W. J. Clark	John Lubbock	Adam Sedgwick
Charles Darwin	Charles Lyell	Richard Sheepshanks
Augustus DeMorgan	Francis Martin	James Stephen
J. D. Forbes	F. D. Maurice	Alfred Tennyson
George Grote	J. S. Mill	Connop Thirlwall
John Grote	R. R. Milnes	Thomas Thorp
William Hamilton	J. H. Monk	Richard Trench
Julius Hare	George Peacock	Thomas Turton
Thomas Hedley	Robert Peel	Christopher Wordsworth
J. S. Henslow	Robert Potts	William Wordsworth

Also, a few miscellaneous Whewell MSS – a journal between 1841 and 1861, drafts of several papers later published, several memoranda circulated within Trinity College.

Houghton Collection: Smaller but still sizeable collection of correspondence between Richard Monckton Milnes, Lord Houghton, and Julius Hare, John Kemble, F. D. Maurice, A. P. Stanley, and Connop Thirlwall.

CAMBRIDGE UNIVERSITY LIBRARY COLLECTION

University Pamphlets: collections of flysheets, committee reports, committee assignments, open letters, etc. 1819–1858.

Cambridge University Papers: papers related to various Studies Syndicates – General, Classics, Mathematics, Moral and Natural Sciences, Degrees, 1822–1860.

CAMBRIDGE UNIVERSITY ARCHIVES

University Grace Books: records of official university acts, regulations, Senate decisions, etc. 1823–1859.

Bibliography

PAMPHLETS, SERMONS, LETTERS, ETC.,
PRINTED BUT CIRCULATED MAINLY IN CAMBRIDGE:

Ainslie, G., *An Historical Account of the Oaths and Subscriptions required in the University of Cambridge*, Cambridge, 1833

Airy, G. B., *On the Draft of Proposed New Statutes for Trinity College, Cambridge*, Cambridge, 1859.

Bisset, Thomas, *Suggestions on University Reform*, London, 1850.

Blagburne, J., *The Revenues of the National Universities considered, with a view to their being open to Dissenters*, London, 1835.

Blakesley, J. W., *Seminaries of Sound Learning and Religious Education*, Cambridge, 1839.

Where does the Evil Lie?, Cambridge, 1845.

Brandreth, H., *On Modern Education*, London, 1868.

Cockburn, W., *Strictures on Clerical Education at the University of Cambridge*, London, 1809.

Cole, H., *Popular Geology Subversive of Divine Revelation*, London, 1834.

Conybeare, W. J., *Remarks on a Pamphlet entitled 'Church Privileges as Bearing on Certain Statutes'*, Cambridge, 1841.

Copleston, Edward, *A Reply to the Calumnies of the 'Edinburgh Review' against Oxford, containing an account of the Studies pursued at the University*, Oxford, 1810.

A Second Reply to the 'Edinburgh Review' by the Author of a Reply to Calumnies of that Review Against Oxford, Oxford, 1810.

Cowling, J., *Regrets of a Cantab*, London, 1825.

Crowfoot, J. R., *College Tuition Considered in a Letter to a Friend*, Cambridge, 1845.

The Interpretation of the Composition between the University and King's College, Cambridge, 1846.

'The New Honours Triposes', *Cambridge Advertiser*, Mar. 7, 1849.

Remarks with Reference to Building a University Hostel, Cambridge, 1849.

Remarks on Some Questions of Economy and Finance Affecting the University of Cambridge, Cambridge, 1848.

Dalby, W., *The Real Question at Issue between the Opponents and Supporters of a Bill now before the House of Commons*, London, 1834.

'Eubulus', *Thoughts on the Present System of Academic Education*, London, 1822.

Eyres, C., *Observations on University Reform*, Cambridge, 1849.

Freeman, Philip, *Church Principles as bearing upon Certain Statutes of the University of Cambridge*, Cambridge, 1841.

Hall, F. R., *A Letter Respectfully Addressed to the Heads of Houses and the Senior Fellows in the University of Cambridge on the Defective State of Theological Instruction*, Cambridge, 1833.

Harper, F. W., *On some of the Changes Proposed in the Course of Study Pursued within the University*, Cambridge, 1848.

Hebert, C., *Theological Colleges and the Universities*, London, 1853.

Henslow, J. S., *Questions on the Subject Matter of Sixteen Lectures in Botany Required for a Pass Examination*, Cambridge, 1851.

Hildyard, James, *Further Consideration of the University System of Education in a Letter to the Rev. The Vice-Chancellor of the University of Cambridge*, London, 1845.

Bibliography

The Obligation of the University to provide for the Professional Education of its Members designed for Holy Orders, Cambridge, 1841.

The University System of Private Tuition Examined, London, 1844.

Hopkins, W., *Remarks on certain Proposed Regulations respecting the Studies of the University*, Cambridge, 1841.

Remarks on the Mathematical Teaching of the University of Cambridge, Cambridge, 1854.

Kennedy, C. R. *Classical Education Reformed*, London, 1837.

Lawson, M., *Strictures on the Rev. F. H. Maberley's Account of 'The Awful and Melancholy Death of Lawrence Dundas, Esq.'*, London, 1818.

Lee, S., *Some Remarks on the Dean of Peterborough's Tract 'Admission to Degrees'*, Cambridge, 1834.

Linwood, W., *Remarks on the Present State of Classical Scholarship and Distinctions in the University of Oxford*, Oxford, 1845.

Maberley, F. H., *The Melancholy and Awful Death of Lawrence Dundas, Esquire with an Address to the Younger Members of the University, on the Evil Nature, Tendency, and Effects of Drunkenness and Fornication, followed by an Appeal to the University on the Laxity of its Discipline and Licentiousness*, London, 1818.

Maurice, F. D., *Subscription no Bondage*, Oxford, 1835.

Mayor, J. B., Untitled open letter re: Moral Science Tripos, Cambridge, 1859.

Monk, J. H., *Appendix to a Vindication of the University of Cambridge, from the Reflections of Sir James Edward Smith*, Cambridge, 1819.

A Letter to the Right Rev. John, Lord Bishop of Bristol (published as 'Philograntus'), London, 1822.

A Vindication of the University of Cambridge from the Reflections of Sir James Edward Smith, London, 1818.

Mowbray, M., *Autobiography of a Cantab.*, Cambridge, 1842.

Perry, Charles, *Clerical Education Considered with an Especial Reference to the Universities*, London, 1841.

Primrose, P., *Hints on Examinations*, Cambridge, 1822.

Pryme, George, *Ode to Trinity College*, London, 1812.

Pycroft, J., *The Collegian's Guide, or Recollections of College Days*, London, 1845.

'Rusticus', *Remarks on Clerical Education: Addressed to the Rev. Charles Perry and the Rev. James Hildyard*, London, 1841.

Sedgwick, Adam, 'Four Letters to the Editors of the *Leeds Mercury*', Cambridge, 1836.

Smith, James E., *Considerations Respecting Cambridge, More Particularly Relating to its Botanical Professorship*, London, 1818.

Smith, J. J., *Letter to the Vice-Chancellor*, Cambridge, 1846.

A Letter to the Vice-Chancellor on the late rejection by the Caput of a Grace Respecting an Examination Previous to Entrance, Cambridge, 1847.

Stephen, Leslie, *The Poll Degree from a Third point of View*, Cambridge, 1863.

Thirlwall, Connop, *Circular to Fellows of Trinity College*, Cambridge, 1834.

A Letter to the Rev. Thomas Turton, D.D. on the Admission of Dissenters to Academical Degrees, Cambridge, 1834.

Thorp, T., *On Obsolete Rules*, Cambridge, 1834.

Bibliography

'Thrasybulus', *Letter to Lord Holland on the Regulation of Undergraduate Expense and Moral Improvement*, Oxford, 1837.

Thring, E., *A Few Remarks on the Present System of Degrees at King's College, Cambridge*, Cambridge, 1846.

Thurtell, A., Untitled open letter re: quality of mathematical education, Cambridge, 1845.

Turton, T., *Thoughts on the Admission of Persons without regard to their Religious Opinions to Certain Degrees in the Universities of England*, Cambridge, 1834.

Wainewright, L., *The Literary and Scientific Pursuits which are encouraged and enforced at the University of Cambridge*, London, 1815.

Walkey, C. E., *The Church and the Universities and their Present Relation towards one another with Regard to the Priesthood of the Church of England and Ireland*, Exeter, 1847.

Whewell, Wm., *Remarks on Proposed Changes in the College Statutes*, Cambridge, 1857.

Wilkinson, M., *Expenses of Undergraduates*, London, 1845.

Wordsworth, Christopher, *On the Admission of Dissenters to Graduate in the University of Cambridge; a letter to the Rt. Hon. Viscount Althorp, M.P.*, Cambridge, 1834.

Wratislaw, A. H., *Observations on the Cambridge System*, Cambridge, 1850.

Wright, J. M. F., *Alma Mater, or Seven Years at the University of Cambridge*, London, 1827.

PUBLISHED PRIMARY SOURCES:

Alexander, W. L., 'Theology', *Encyclopaedia Britannica*, 8th edition, Edinburgh, 1860, vol. XXI, p. 178.

Anonymous, 'The Bridgewater Treatises', *Edinburgh Review*, 1834, vol. LVIII, no. 118, p. 422.

'The Bridgewater Treatises', *Quarterly Review*, 1833, vol. I, no. 99.

'The Cambridge Controversy', *Quarterly Review*, 1834, vol. LII, p. 466.

'Cambridge University', *Fraser's*, 1850, vol. XLI, p. 617.

'Crombie's *Natural Theology*', *Quarterly Review*, 1834, vol. LI, no. 101, p. 216.

'Sedgwick on the Studies of Cambridge University', *British Quarterly Review*, 1850, vol. XII, no. 24, p. 360.

'University Education', *Fraser's*, 1868, vol. XXVII, no. 458, p. 147.

Babbage, Charles, *The Ninth Bridgewater Treatise*, London, 1838.

Reflections on the Decline of Science in England and on Some of Its Causes, London, 1830.

Beverley, R. M., *A Letter to His Royal Highness the Duke of Gloucester on the Present Corrupt State of the University of Cambridge*, 3rd edition, London, 1833.

Blunt, J. J., 'Works and Character of Paley', *Quarterly Review*, 1822, vol. XXXVIII, no. 76, p. 304.

Bonney, T. G., *A Chapter in the Life History of an Old University*, Cambridge, 1882.

Bristed, Charles Astor, *Five Years in an English University*, New York, 1852.

Campbell, Lewis, *On the Nationalization of the Old English Universities*, London, 1901.

Chambers, Robert, *Vestiges of the Natural History of Creation*, 5th edition, London, 1846.

Conybeare, W. J., 'Church Parties', *Edinburgh Review*, 1853, vol. XCVIII, no. 200, p. 273.

Bibliography

Cooper, Charles Henry, *Memorials of Cambridge*, Cambridge, 1861, vols. I and II.

Digby, Kenelm, *The Broad Stone of Honour*, London, 1822.

Dyer, G., *Academic Unity*, London, 1827.

Farrar, F. W., ed., *Essays on a Liberal Education*, London, 1867.

Grote, John, *Examination of the Utilitarian Philosophy*, London, 1870.

 A Treatise on the Moral Ideals, Cambridge, 1876.

Hamilton, William, 'Article VI', *Edinburgh Review*, 1831, vol. LIII, no. 106, p. 384.

 'Article VII', *Edinburgh Review*, 1836, vol. LXII, no. 126, p. 409.

 'Article IX', *Edinburgh Review*, 1831, vol. LIV, no. 108, p. 478.

 Discussions on Philosophy and Literature, Education and University Reform, London, 1852.

Hansard and Sons, eds., *Parliamentary Debates*, 3rd series.

Herschel, John F. W., *A Preliminary Discourse on the Study of Natural Philosophy*, London, 1830; facsimile edition, New York, 1966

 Essays from the Edinburgh and Quarterly Reviews, London, 1857.

 A Treatise on Astronomy (Cabinet Cyclopedia), London, 1833.

Heywood, James, *Academic Reform and University Representation*, London, 1860.

Huber, Victor Aime, *English Universities*, London, 1843, vol. II.

Huxley, T. H., 'A Liberal Education and Where to Find it', *Lay Sermons, Addresses and Reviews*, London, 1880.

Kingsley, Charles, *Alton Locke*, London, 1850.

Lyell, Charles, 'The State of the Universities', *Quarterly Review*, 1827, vol. XXXIV, no. 72, p. 216.

 Travels in North America in the Years 1841–42; with Geological Observations on the United States, Canada, and Nova Scotia, New York, 1845.

Mill, John Stuart, 'Article I – Civilization', *London and Westminster Review*, 1836, vol. XXV, no. 1.

 Dissertations and Discussions, London, 1859.

 Inaugural Address (delivered Feb. 1, 1867, University of St. Andrews), London, 1867.

Newman, John Henry, *On the Scope and the Nature of University Education*, London, 1965.

Paley, William, *Natural Theology*, Frederick Ferre, ed., New York, 1963.

 Principles of Moral and Political Philosophy, Boston, 1825.

 A View of the Evidences of Christianity, 5th edition, London, 1791.

Pattison, Mark, *Suggestions on Academical Organization*, Edinburgh, 1868.

Peacock, George, *Observations on the Statutes of the University of Cambridge*, London, 1841.

 Treatise on Algebra, London, 1830.

Pusey, Edward B., *Collegiate and Professorial Teaching and Discipline*, Oxford, 1854.

Report of H.M. Commissioners Appointed to Inquire into the State, Discipline, Studies and Revenues of the University and Colleges of Cambridge, 1852, State Papers, vol. XLIV.

Rogers, Henry, 'Paley', *Encyclopaedia Britannica*, 8th edition, Edinburgh, 1860, vol. XVII, p. 205.

Rose, Hugh James, *Discourses on the State of the Protestant Religion in Germany*, Cambridge, 1824.

Sedgwick, Adam, *A Discourse on the Studies of the University*, Cambridge 1833; facsimile 1st edition, eds. Eric Ashby, Mary Anderson, New York, 1969; 5th edition, Cambridge, 1850.

'Natural History of Creation', *Edinburgh Review*, 1845, vol. LXXXII, no. 165, p. 27.

Presidential Address and other papers, *Proceedings of the Geological Society of London*, 1834, vol. I, pp. 274, 313, 152.

Seeley, J. R., *Liberal Education*, London, 1870.

Lectures and Essays, London, 1870.

Smith, Sydney, 'Article I', *Edinburgh Review*, 1808, vol. XI, no. 22, p. 249.

'Article X', *Edinburgh Review*, 1809, vol. XIV, no. 28, p. 429.

'Article III', *Edinburgh Review*, 1809, vol. XV, no. 29, p. 40.

Southey, Robert, (published pseudonymously), *Letters from England by Don Manuel Alvarez Espirella*, London, 1808.

Stephen, Leslie, 'Athletic Sports and University Studies', *Fraser's*, 1870, vol. II, no. 12, p. 691.

'Senior Wranglers', *Cornhill Magazine*, 1882, vol. XLV, p. 225.

Sketches from Cambridge by a Don, London, 1865.

'Some Early Impressions', *National Review*, 1903, vol. XLII, nos. 247, 248, pp. 130, 208.

'Thoughts of an Outsider', *Cornhill Magazine*, 1873, vol. XXVII, p. 281.

Sylvester, J. J., 'Presidential Address', *Report of the British Association*, London, 1870.

Temple, F., et al., *Essays and Reviews*, London, 1860.

Whewell, William, *Astronomy and General Physics considered with Reference to Natural Theology* (Bridgewater Treatise), London, 1834.

Elements of Morality, Including Polity, New York, 1845.

A History of the Inductive Sciences, London, 1837, 3rd edition, 1857.

Lectures on the History of Moral Philosophy in England, Cambridge, 1852.

Of a Liberal Education in General, with Particular Reference to the Leading Studies of the University of Cambridge, London, 1845.

Of the Plurality of Worlds, London, 1854.

The Philosophy of the Inductive Sciences, London, 1840.

On the Principles of English University Education, London, 1837.

Thoughts on the Study of Mathematics as a Part of a Liberal Education, Cambridge, 1835.

SECONDARY SOURCES:

Abrams, M. H., *The Mirror and the Lamp*, New York, 1953.

Albee, Ernest, *A History of English Utilitarianism*, London, 1957.

Allen, Peter, *The Cambridge Apostles, the Early Years*, Cambridge, 1978.

Annan, N. G., 'The Intellectual Aristocracy', *Studies in Social History*, J. H. Plumb, ed., London, 1955.

Ball, Walter William Rouse, *A Short Account of the History of Mathematics*, London, 1940.

Barlow, Nora, *Darwin and Henslow, the Growth of an Idea*, Berkeley, 1967.

Barth, Karl, *Protestant Thought: from Rousseau to Ritschl*, New York, 1959.

Bibby, Cyril, 'Thomas Huxley and University Development', *Victorian Studies*, 1958, vol. II, no. 2, p. 97.

Bibliography

Boyer, Carl B., *A History of Mathematics*, New York, 1968.

Brookfield, Frances, M., *The Cambridge Apostles*, New York, 1906.

Butts, Robert E., 'Professor Marcucci on Whewell's Idealism', *Philosophy of Science*, 1967, vol. XXXIV, no. 2, p. 175.

William Whewell's Theory of Scientific Method, Pittsburgh, 1968.

Cannon, Walter, 'The Basis of Darwin's Achievement: a Revaluation', *Victorian Studies*, 1961, vol. V, no. 2, p. 109.

'Impact of Uniformitarianism', *Proceedings of the American Philosophical Society*, 1961, vol. CV, p. 301.

'Problem of Miracles in the 1830's', *Victorian Studies*, 1960, vol. IV, no. 1, p. 532.

'Scientists and Broad Churchmen: An Early Intellectual Network', *Journal of British Studies*, 1964, vol. IV, no. 1, p. 65.

Faber, Francis C., 'Fossils and the Idea of a Process of Time in Natural History', *Forerunners of Darwin, 1745–1859*, ed., Bentley Glass, Owsei Tempkin, William L. Straus, Baltimore, 1959.

Gillispie, Charles C., *Genesis and Geology*, Cambridge, Mass., 1951.

Hull, David L., *Darwin and his Critics*, Cambridge, Mass, 1973.

Jenkins, Hester and D. Caradog Jones, 'Social-Class of Cambridge University Alumni of the Eighteenth and Nineteenth Centuries', *British Journal of Sociology*, 1950, vol. I, p. 93.

Kitson Clark, G., *The Making of Victorian England*, Cambridge, Mass., 1962.

Layton, David, *Science for the People*, London, 1973.

LeMahieu, D. L., *The Mind of William Paley*, Lincoln, Nebraska, 1976.

Lovejoy, Arthur O., *The Great Chain of Being*, Cambridge, Mass., 1957.

MacGrath, F., *Newman's University – Idea and Reality*, London, 1951.

Mansbridge, Albert, *The Older Universities of England: Oxford and Cambridge*, Boston, 1923.

Merz, J. T., *A History of European Scientific Thought in the Nineteenth Century*, London, 1904, vol. I.

Pfleiderer, Otto, *The Development of Theology in Germany since Kant and its Progress in Great Britain since 1825*, London, 1909.

Powell, John P., 'Some Nineteenth Century Views on the University Curriculum', *History of Education Quarterly*, 1956, vol. V, no. 2, p. 97.

Robson, Robert, 'Trinity College in the Age of Peel', *Ideas and Institutions of Victorian England*, R. Robson, ed., London, 1967.

Rose, Elliot, 'The Stone Table in the Round Church and the Crisis of the Cambridge Camden Society', *Victorian Studies*, 1966, vol. X, no. 2, p. 145.

Rothblatt, Sheldon, *The Revolution of the Dons; Cambridge and Society in Victorian England*, London, 1968.

Sanders, Charles R., *Coleridge and the Broad Church Movement*, Durham, N.C., 1942.

Schneider, Ben Ross, Jr., *Wordsworth's Cambridge Education*, Cambridge, 1957.

Venn, John A., *Alumni Cantabrigiensis: a Biographical List of All Known Students, Graduates, and Holders of Office at Cambridge from Earliest Times to 1900*, Cambridge, 1954.

White, James F., *The Cambridge Movement*, Cambridge, 1962.

Winstanley, D. A., *Early Victorian Cambridge*, Cambridge, 1955.
Later Victorian Cambridge, Cambridge, 1947.
Young, Robert, unpublished lectures, Cambridge University, 1969–1970.

BIOGRAPHIES:

Airy, George Biddle, *Autobiography*, Wilfred Airy, ed., Cambridge, 1896.
Annan, Noel, *Leslie Stephen: His Thought and Character in Relation to his Time*, London, 1951.
Anonymous, 'Charles Babbage', *Smithsonian Institution Annual Report*, 1873, p. 163.
Brose, Olive J., *Frederick Denison Maurice, Rebellious Conformist*, Athens, Ohio, 1971.
Campbell, J. D., *Samuel Taylor Coleridge*, London, 1894.
Campbell, Lewis and William Garnett, *The Life of James Clerk Maxwell*, London, 1884.
Carus, William and Robert Carter, eds., *Memoirs of the Rev. Charles Simeon, M.A.*, New York, 1847.
Clark, John W. and T. McKinney Hughes, *Life and Letters of Adam Sedgwick*, Cambridge, 1890.
Darwin, Francis, ed., *The Life and Letters of Charles Darwin*, London, 1911.
More Letters of Charles Darwin, London, 1903.
DeMorgan, S. E., *A Memoir of Augustus DeMorgan*, London, 1882.
Dodge, N. S., 'Memoir of Sir John Frederick William Herschel', *Smithsonian Institution Annual Report*, 1871, p. 109.
Douglas, Janet Stair, *Life and Selections from the Correspondence of William Whewell, D.D.*, London, 1881.
Faber, Geoffrey Cust, *Jowett, a Portrait with Background*, London, 1957.
Gibbon, Edward, *Memoirs of My Life*, ed. Georges H. Bonnard, New York, 1969.
Holroyd, M., *Memorials of the Life of George Elwes Corrie*, Cambridge, 1890.
MacDonald, Lauchlin D., *John Grote: A Critical Estimate of his Writings*, The Hague, 1966.
MacFarlane, Alexander, *Lectures on Ten British Physicists*, 'J. F. W. Herschel', 'George Biddle Airy', New York, 1919.
Lectures on Ten British Mathematicians, 'George Peacock', 'Augustus DeMorgan', New York, 1916.
Maitland, Frederic William, *Life and Letters of Leslie Stephen*, London, 1906.
Maurice, Frederick Denison, *The Life of F. D. Maurice*, London, 1884, vols. I and II.
Morrison, Philip and Emily, eds., *Charles Babbage and his Calculating Engines*, New York, 1961.
Moseley, Maboth, *Irascible Genius*, London, 1964 (Babbage).
Moule, H. C. G., *Charles Simeon*, London, Inter-Varsity Fellowship, 1965.
Rae, John, *Life of Adam Smith*, London, 1895.
Reid, T. Wemyss, *The Life, Letters and Friendships of Richard Monckton Milnes, the First Lord Houghton*, New York, 1891.
Robson, Robert, 'William Whewell, F. R. S., Academic Life', *Notes and Records of the Royal Society of London*, 1964, vol. XIX, p. 168.

Romilly, Joseph, *Romilly's Cambridge Diary 1832–42*, ed., J. P. T. Bury, Cambridge, 1967.

Smyth, Charles, *Simeon and Church Order*, Cambridge, 1940.

Sparrow, John H. A., *Mark Pattison and the Idea of a University*, London, 1967.

Stanley, A. P. (published anonymously), 'Archdeacon Hare's Last Charge', *Quarterly Review*, 1855, vol. xcvii, no. 183, p. 1.

The Life and Correspondence of Thomas Arnold, 5th edition, London, 1845.

Stephen, Leslie, *Life of Henry Fawcett*, London, 1885.

Thirlwall, John Connop, Jr., *Connop Thirlwall*, London, 1936.

Todhunter, Isaac, *William Whewell, D.D.*, London, 1876.

INDEX

Index

Leibniz, G. W., 29
Linnean Society, 76
literary criticism, as applied to Bible, 86
Locke, John, 4, 87; *Essay on Human Understanding*, in Cambridge curriculum, 57, 60–1, 116
Lyell, Charles, 13, 22, 47, 95, 97–100, 103–4, 106–7, 111; *Principles of Geology*, 97; *Travels in North America*, 40

Maberley, F. H., 11, 14, 88; *Melancholy and Awful Death of Lawrence Dundas, Esq., The*, 10
MacFarlane, A., 37
mathematical honours, 117–18
Mathematical Studies, Board of, 47
mathematics, 28–51, 80; algebra, 37–9; applied, 30–2; calculus, 29–30, 35–7, 48–50; continental, 29–30; examination reform, 47–9; geometry, emphasis on, 34–6; popular, 32–4; relationship to classical honours, 49; theoretical, 32, 37–9
Maurice, Frederick, 14–15, 17, 64, 68, 84–9, 111, 122, 139–40, 155, 171; on natural theology, 93; *Subscription No Bondage*, 77
Maxwell, James Clerk, 26, 30, 131
Melbourne, Lord, 25
Merz, J. T., *History of European Scientific Thought in the Nineteenth Century*, 30
Methodists, 8
Mill, John Stuart, 15, 37–8, 69, 87, 113, 133, 152, 161; critic of Whewell, 66; on utilitarianism, 62
Milnes, Richard Monckton, 64, 84, 86; influence of Niebuhr on, 85
moderate reformers, 17–27
Monk, James Henry, 19, 115, 118
moral philosophy in Cambridge curriculum, 60–9
moral science tripos, 127–9
Munro, C. J., 38
Murchison, J., 97
Muscular Christianity, 134

natural science, 90–112
natural science tripos, 127–9
natural theology, 92–5; Paley on, 53–6
Neptunist/Vulcanist controversy, 95–7, 107
Newman, J. H., 71, 113, 133, 138
Newton, Isaac, 3, 28–9, 31, 53, 94, 118
Niebuhr, B. G., *History of Rome*, Thirlwall's translation, 24, 64, 85
Norrisian Professorship, theological instruction, 81
Norwich, Sedgwick's canonry, 19, 25–6

ordinary degree, 52, 82, 114–17, 126–7
Origin of Species, The, 90, 106
Oxford, 5, 8, 10, 13, 15, 70–1, 77; curriculum, 3
Oxford Movement, 14, 25, 83

Paley, William, 3–4, 52–69, 87, 89, 91, 164; *Evidences of Christianity, The*, 53, 68, 116; in Cambridge curriculum, 57–8, 68; on moral philosophy, 116; on natural theology, 53–6; on teleology, 54–5; *Principles of Moral and Political Philosophy*, 53, 56–7; Sedgwick on, 58–63; Whewell on, 64–8
Parliament, 70, 72; bill for dissenters, 77; criticism of Cambridge, 14; petition to on behalf of dissenters, 76
Pattison, Mark, Lincoln College, Oxford, 14, 113
Peacock, George, 20–1, 23–6, 28–9, 32, 39, 81; *Observations on the Statutes of the University of Cambridge*, 21; on algebra, 37; *Treatise on Algebra*, 37
Peel, Sir Robert, 27
Penny Cyclopaedia, 33
Perry, Charles, 81–2
Peterhouse, 18
Philosophical Society of Cambridge, 34
Platonism, 85
Playfair, John, 107
Potts, Robert, 133
previous examination, 115–16, 129
private tuition, 123–4
professoriate, 125–7, 134
Pryme, George, 19; on dissenters, 74
Pusey, Edward, 113, 138

Quarterly Review, 74, 79, 94
Queen's College, 83

radicals at Cambridge, 17–18
Radnor, Lord, 17
Reform Bill of 1832, 76
Regius Professorships, Divinity, Hebrew, 80
Renan, Ernest, *Vie de Jesu*, 86
Rice, Thomas Spring, 72
romanticism, 86–8
Romilly, Joseph, 20
Rose, Hugh, 86
Rothblatt, Sheldon, *Revolution of the Dons, The*, 129
Royal Academy, 76
Royal Commission, 14, 17, 20–1, 78, 116–17
Royal Institution, 5
Royal Society, 5
Rugby School, 13, 130